デザインから
デザインまで
廣村正彰

From Design
To Design
Masaaki Hiromura

contents

Foreword ——— 004

1 | Question the Ordinary ——— 006

2 | Consciousness in the Unconscious ——— 022

3 | Making the Invisible Visible ——— 044

4 | That Ish Feeling ——— 064

5 | Inviting Decorum ——— 088

6 | Awakened Memories ——— 106

A glimpse into the mind of Masaaki HIROMURA ——— 128

7 | Speed of Design ——— 148

8 | Weaving Information ——— 168

9 | Lurking in the Shadows ——— 186

10 | Giving Form to Desire ——— 202

11 | Creating Creation ——— 212

12 | Settled in Harmony ——— 230

Data of Works ——— 244

Profile ——— 254

目次

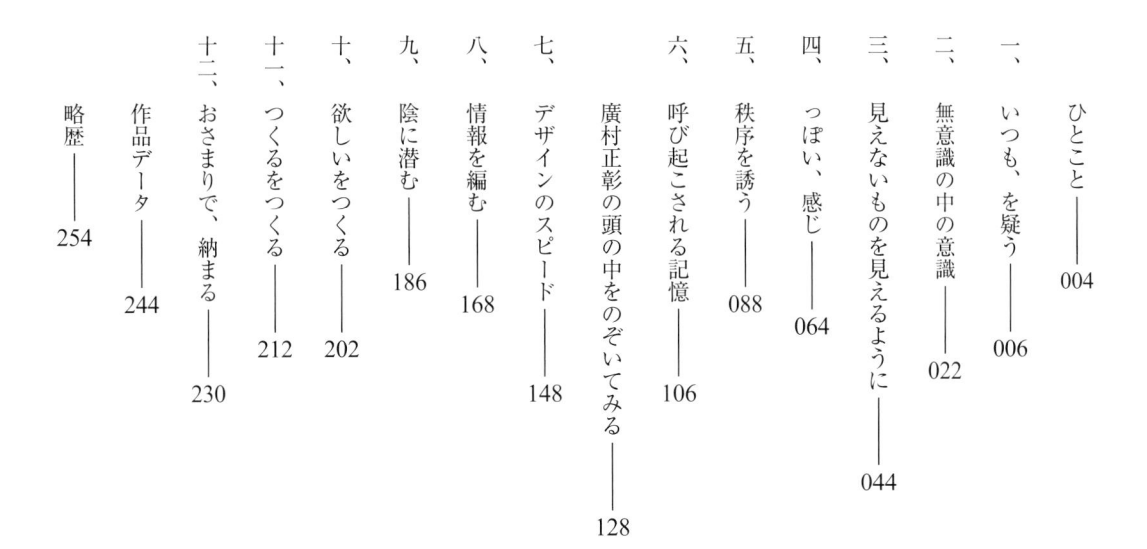

ひとこと —— 004

一、いつも、を疑う —— 006

二、無意識の中の意識 —— 022

三、見えないものを見えるように —— 044

四、っぽい、感じ —— 064

五、秩序を誘う —— 088

六、呼び起こされる記憶 —— 106

七、廣村正彰の頭の中をのぞいてみる —— 128

八、デザインのスピード —— 148

九、情報を編む —— 168

十、陰に潜む —— 186

十一、欲しいをつくる —— 202

十二、つくるをつくる —— 212

十三、おさまりで、納まる —— 230

作品データ —— 244

略歴 —— 254

Foreword

In early 2015 I held an exhibition in Anjo, a city in Aichi Prefecture. This city was my home until the spring following my 19th birthday. Growing up in a rural area, my family made a living off of agriculture, as did everyone else around us. Up until the fall of my third year in high school I really had no clue what design was. I didn't know what a designer's job consisted of or what kind of areas even existed within the world of design. But I remember being excited by the word, 'Design.' It was a word brimming with possibilities—a new future. "That's it! I'll become a designer!" That's what I told my 18-year-old self that fall.
And then by coincidence—some decades after beginning my design studies—I received an invitation to exhibit from the Anjo City Hall. I titled the exhibition 'From Design To Design.' Even though it was an exhibition of my own personal work, I chose the title to represent my desire to share with visitors the design process and the thought that goes into a design. At the time, the editing for this book had also just begun, so I decided to use the same title for the book. Deep down inside there is a part of me that hasn't changed a bit from my days back then in Anjo when running for the track and field club and listening to music were my passions. A part of me that still has no clue what design is. In fact, it feels like it has only grown more difficult to understand. And so it is full of that uncertainty that I share with you what lies within these pages.

ひとこと

二〇一五年のはじめ、愛知県安城市で展覧会を開催しました。

安城は十九歳の春まで暮らしていた私の故郷です。私の家は農家で、周辺もみな農業で生活をしている農村地域です。

高校三年の秋までデザインのことなどよく分からず、デザイナーがどんな仕事なのか、デザインにはどのような領域があるのかも知りませんでした。しかし、デザインという言葉に新しい未来を感じワクワクした気持ちを覚えています。

そうだ、デザイナーになろう！と十八の秋に突然思い立ち、デザインの勉強をはじめてから何十年も経ち、偶然にも安城市役所から展覧会のお誘いを受けました。

タイトルは「デザインからデザインまで」、個人的な仕事の展示ですが、デザインのプロセス、思考の流れが理解されることを願いこのタイトルを付けました。

ちょうどこの本の編集に取りかかっていたこともあり、同じタイトルにしました。

陸上部で走ることと、音楽を聴くことが楽しみだった安城の頃から精神的には何も変わらず、いまだにデザインがよくわからない自分がいます。むしろどんどん難しくなっているように感じています。

そんな不確実な気持ちも含め、この本に書いてみました。

1 | Question the Ordinary

Design begins with questioning.

In this modern world where we are surrounded by design, is there really any point in creating new designs or are we just generating excess trash? Do these new designs add value, or are they actually detrimental in the end? When determining whether or not a design is necessary one must consider the negatives. Rather than simply jumping into creation, potential downsides should be considered to determine whether a design is truly necessary.

Just what is good design? Form, usability, and how it fits into the surroundings must be accounted for. It should offer a fresh, new experience and bring joy and enrichment to one's life. We grow attached to the designs we're familiar with. We find comfort in the ordinary because it requires no deep thought, no questioning. It's the ordinary, after all.

Stability is essential to the ordinary. The same form. Same color. Letters. Placement. It is this sameness that allows us to trust that we will have the same experience as before. But design begins with questioning. Is the ordinary really the best way? And even if it once was, is it still now? A time will come when we must try a different something, even if it means breaking out of our comfort zone.

It is design that draws this new something out from within the ordinary that has become so comfortably familiar. The birth of new design is the birth of a new future.

一、いつも、を疑う

デザインは疑うことからはじめる。

社会にデザインが溢れている現在、本当にデザインする意味があるのか、新たなゴミをつくることになるのでは？と疑い、本当にそのデザインは生まれる価値があるのか、結果的に悪い影響を及ぼすのでは？などと疑う。創造性とは逆にネガティブな要素を検証することでデザインする必然性を確認する。

良いデザインとはなんだろう。
カタチや使い心地、環境に配慮され誰でも新しい体験ができる。そして生活に楽しみや潤いを提供することだろうか。
しかしデザインは疑うことからはじめる。
いままで慣れ親しんだデザインには愛着がある。安心する「いつも」は、疑うことも深く考えることもない。だって同じだからである。

「いつも」はその、同じということが重要。同じカタチ、同じ色、同じ文字、同じ位置、同じであることで、同じ体験ができると信じられるのである。
「いつも」が本当に最善の選択であるのか、時代の変化に対応できているのか、安全な殻を破ってでも別の「何か」を試す時が来る。
デザインは慣れ親しんだ「いつも」から、新たな「何か」を期待されているのである。
新しいデザインが生まれるということは、新しい未来が生まれることになる。

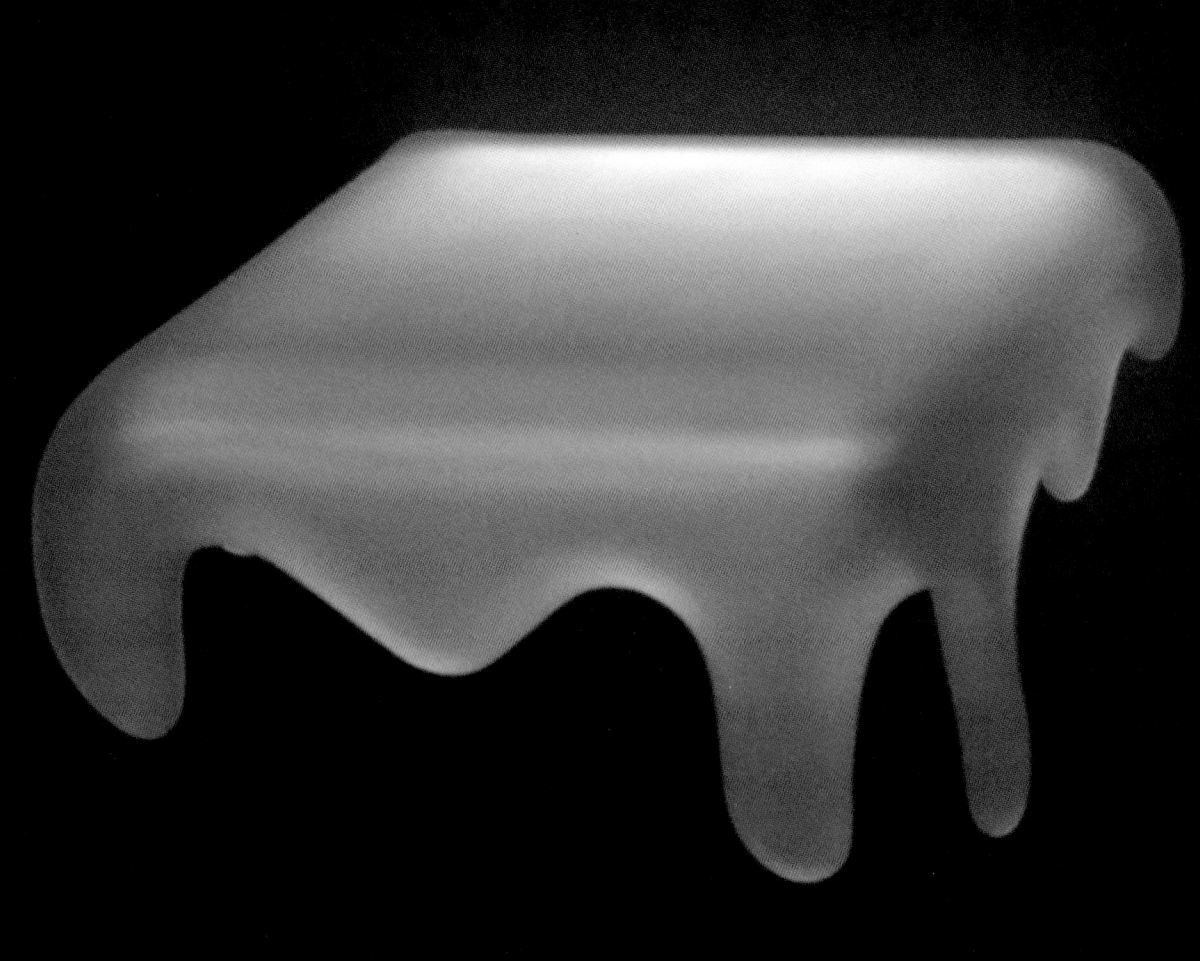

Amorphous

A glass tabletop grows hotter and hotter until it begins to melt. The liquefied glass begins to overflow, oozing over the edges of the surface below, which can no longer contain it. Titled TOKERU, this piece appeared in the 101st Anniversary Works-in-Progress Exhibition for Mihoya Glass. The semi-transparent, melting glass appears soft, but in reality it is cold and hard. If struck, it would shatter. When glass is heated, it becomes soft and molten-like. Such a solid is referred to as amorphous. This physical change is intriguing—it piques our curiosity. A single, beautiful moment in time is captured. This, also, is design.

(101st Anniversary Works-in-Progress for Mihoya Glass, 2009)

アモルファス

テーブルの上のガラスは熱く融けて飽和し、上面では支えきれず隅から垂れはじめている。「三保谷硝子店一〇一年目の試作展」の出品作。タイトルは「TOKERU」。半透明で飴状のガラスはとろん、として見えるが、現実は硬く冷たい。そして叩けば割れる。ガラスの温度が上がり、柔らかく変化することをアモルファス化と呼ぶ。物質は変化する、変化するから面白く、興味がわく。デザインは美しい一瞬をとどめることでもある。

(三保谷硝子店一〇一年目の試作展 二〇〇九年)

The conference room at Mihoya Glass overflows with sample products. One is embedded with fragments of a crushed fluorescent tube, while another holds a rusted metal splinter captive within. There is a piece of glass that was hardened at the exact moment it was shattered. The possibilities offered by glass are surprisingly limitless.
Glass has also improved and brought comfort to our lives. Highly-insulated houses use multi-layered glass panes to reduce energy costs and carbon emissions. Free of endocrine disruptors, glass containers have a reuse rate of over 90% and a recycling rate of over 80%, and they continue to grow lighter. Glass is a great fit for a recycling-conscious world. There is also growing demand for cutting-edge applications such as ultra-thin nano-glass. The future of glass is one rife with creativity.

三保谷硝子店 一〇一年目の試作展

101st Anniversary
Works-in-Progress for
Mihoya Glass

10月27日[火]—11月8日[日]
午前11時—午後7時（最終日は午後5時まで）
アクシスギャラリー 入場料：無料

AXIS GALLERY

　三保谷硝子の会議室はサンプルであふれかえっている。蛍光管を砕いて練り込んだもの、割れた瞬間のガラスを固めたものなど、閉じ込められたもの、金属の破片が錆びたままガラスは想像以上に自由なのだ。
　そしてガラスは明るく快適な暮らしをもたらしてくれた。複層ガラスを用いた高断熱の家はエネルギーの消費を抑え、CO_2を削減する。環境ホルモンとは無縁のガラス容器は九〇％以上のリユース率、リサイクル率は八〇％を超えていて軽量化も進んでいる。循環型社会とガラスの相性はいい。また、最新テクノロジーにおける需要でも薄型のナノガラスが伸びており、ガラスには創造的な未来が開かれている。

Inviting Understanding

In practice, it's hard to judge trustworthiness and safety. This is of particular concern when it comes to something like food, which we put directly into our mouths and bodies. Naruhodo Shohin (Aha! Products) is a store brand belonging to CO-OP Sapporo, a consumer cooperative that serves all of Hokkaido. Using products and materials produced in Hokkaido whenever possible, the brand's goal is to provide consumers with high-quality items that they are happy to choose. This intent is reflected in packaging with large writing that clearly describes the product. By avoiding the use of images and excessive packaging, the design also leads to reduced costs. The simplicity and directness of the packaging elicit an "aha!" feeling of understanding and satisfaction, and the brand has grown to include over 100 different items.
(CO-OP Sapporo, 2012–)

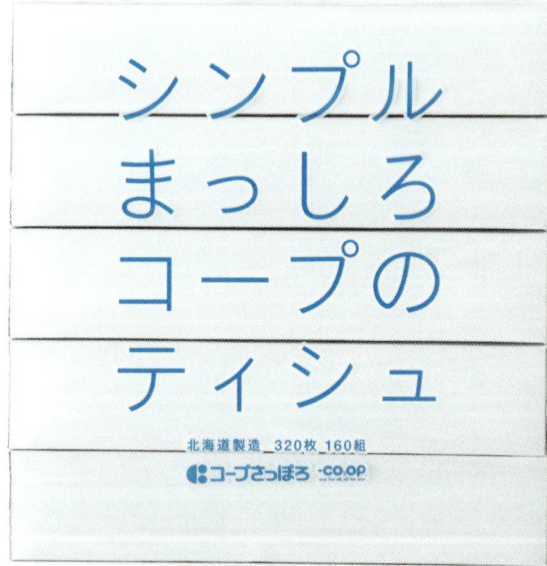

共感の糸口

なにが安心で安全なのかわかりにくい現実。
特に食品などは直接口に入るので心配になる。
北海道全域をカバーする生活協同組合、
コープさっぽろのプライベートブランド「なるほど商品」。
できるだけ北海道産にこだわり、
良質なものを手軽に利用してもらいたい。
その想いを、大きな文字で丁寧に説明したパッケージ。
同時に、費用をおさえるために
写真表現や過剰包装を控えたデザインにしている。
素朴で素直な印象が「なるほど」と納得され、
一〇〇種類以上のアイテムに成長している。
（コープさっぽろ　二〇一二年-）

It can be difficult to succinctly convey what makes a product good. That's exactly why only products where that reason is clear and worth communicating are included in the Aha! Products brand.
Only available in Hokkaido, it's a brand of products that make people proud to live here.

商品の良さを簡潔に表すのは難しい。
だからこそ確固とした理由があり、
伝えたい気持ちがあるモノでなければ
「なるほど商品」と呼ばない。
どこにもない、北海道に暮らすことを自慢できる
商品として育っている。

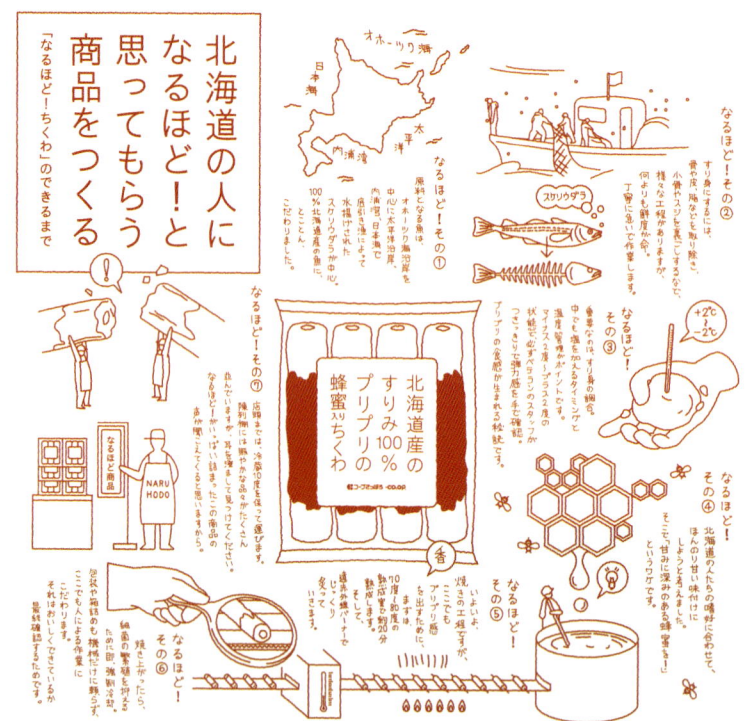

「畑でレストラン」会場風景
Scenes from Meals in the Fields

食料品自給率が二〇〇％の北海道、美味しくて新鮮なものばかりだ。
コープさっぽろが主催する農業賞を受賞した優秀な生産者の農園に、名店のシェフが出張してランチを振る舞う「畑でレストラン」。採れたての野菜を広大な畑の真ん中でいただく。美味しくないわけがない。贅沢というのはこんな時間のことを言うのだと感じる。
食事の前の農園見学や収穫体験、食事の合間には生産者ならではの面白い話が聞ける。
ある日のランチは前菜からデザートまですべてタマネギ料理。無農薬で育てられたタマネギはそのままかじってもうまい。春から秋まで毎週末豊かな北海道をリアルに味わえる企画だ。

With a food self-sufficiency rate of 200%, Hokkaido has no shortage of fresh and delicious foods. CO-OP Sapporo presents outstanding producers with its Agricultural Award, and chefs are dispatched from CO-OP locations to the farms of these producers where they prepare lunch as part of the "Meals in the Fields" program. Fresh vegetables prepared and served in the open fields where they were harvested delight taste buds—practically the definition of indulgence. Participants can tour farms and join in the harvest before meals and producers share unique and interesting stories while partaking. On one occasion every dish—from appetizer to dessert—was prepared from organic onions so delicious they could be eaten raw. The program allows participants to indulge in the flavors of Hokkaido every weekend from spring to fall.

つなぐ
COOP SAPPORO

2015 marked the 50th anniversary of CO-OP Sapporo. As a symbol of its efforts to ensure that the next 50 years in Hokkaido are ones full of joy and pride, the coop decided to renew its visual identity. CO-OP Sapporo's identity had slowly evolved over the years into one of shared understanding, support, and consideration.
This is reflected in the slogan Tsunagu, which means "to connect."
A fresh, verdant green was chosen for the theme's color.

二〇一五年、五〇周年を迎えるコープさっぽろ。これからの五〇年、北海道で生きることを誇りと喜びにすることを目指して新しいVI（ビジュアル・アイデンティティ）をスタートした。ゆっくり何年もかけて変わるVI、「わかちあい、ささえあい、おもいあう」、そんなコープさっぽろの合い言葉は「つなぐ」。若々しいグリーンをテーマカラーにした。

コープさっぽろ江別工場
CO-OP Sapporo Ebetsu Factory

The Little Box of Memories was prepared in commemoration of CO-OP Sapporo's 50th anniversary. A request for stories about employees' experiences working at the company was made leading up to the anniversary. Employees wrote of both joyful and tough times. Some recalled being scolded, while others shared personal reflection. Over 2000 submissions were received and brought together into book form.

0046 「生協がずっと続いて欲しいから言うんだよ」。

2011年9月。野菜の傷みでお客様のところへお伺いし、お叱りを受けました。初老のご婦人は昔からの生協の組合員で、「生協がよくなって欲しいから私は言うんだよ。あなたがた若い人がもっともっとお店を良くしてお客さんにいっぱい来てもらって生協がずっと続いて欲しいから私は言うんだよ」‥と最後は泣きながら笑顔で言ってくれました。
こういう組合員さんのためにも本当に頑張らなくっちゃ！
（石橋祐司　岩見沢東店）

0172 20代、結婚。30代、出産。そして‥‥。

20代、結婚、地域のCOOPさっぽろを利用した。
30代、出産、育児の時、宅配トドックを知った。
そして‥‥40代、私はこのお店で働き共済に出会う。
子供達が共済で守られ、この共済のやさしさにふれ、温もりを実感する。
共済（愛）をみなさんに知ってもらえるよう私は伝えて行きたい‥‥。
（沖村順子　神楽店）

0190 イキがいいね！

売り場で「いらっしゃいませ」と声を出しながら品出しをしていたら、近くにいたお客さんが「同じ魚でもあなたが出したものの方が活きが良く見えるわね」と言って下さった。
照れ臭かったけれどすごく嬉しかった。
（長井夕穂　神楽店）

0521 あなたに、ホレた。

「結婚しているの？」と組合員様「しています」と私。
独身なら娘を嫁にと話された。
理由は、あなたが一番誠実だから安心して娘を嫁にいかせられると思ったとのこと。
自分の行動を見ていてくれている。組合員様がいる。
（金谷広樹　ステイ店）

五〇周年を前に募集した「思い出の小箱」。コープさっぽろの職員が仕事を通じて体験してきたエピソードを集めた。感動したこと、辛かったこと、叱られたこと、反省したこと、二〇〇〇通以上の応募があり、本にまとめた。

サービスとお役所

「お役所仕事」という言葉が流行った時代があった。
公務員が面倒な仕事を他部署などに「たらい回し」することや、細かい規則をたて前に対応を渋る「杓子定規」など、新しい言葉も誕生した。大衆の不満が役所に向いていた時代だ。
しかしいま、役所は行政サービスが最大の仕事で目的になった。
在日アメリカ軍横田基地が市の面積の三分の一を占める東京福生市。当然外国人比率も高い。その福生市の市庁舎建て替えに伴うサイン計画を考えた。他の自治体と比べて転入と転出の手続きが多く、しかも一定の季節（春とか秋）に限らず忙しさのウェーブがやって来る。大体、お役所の仕事はどこかで実施した前例が必要で、絶対安全が条件、クレームが来ないということが目標だったりする。
しかしこの市役所のサインデザインはどの国の人にもわかりやすく、自由で可変的なサービスがテーマだった。
（福生市庁舎 二〇〇八年）

Service and the Municipal Office

There was a time when the phrase "municipal office procedures" in Japanese became synonymous with "red tape." New words were coined to describe the tendency of public officials to hand off unwanted work to other departments, or to make processes more time-consuming by focusing on minor details. It was a time when people were discontent with government offices. But today administrative services are the primary focus of municipal offices and are taken seriously.
The US's Yokota Air Base in Japan occupies one third of the area of Fussa City in Tokyo. It goes without saying that foreigners make up a large part of the city. Remodeling of the city hall offered a chance to redesign the signage within. Notifications of moving in or out are more common here than in other municipalities, and they come in waves not limited to the usual busy seasons of spring and fall. Municipal office procedures usually require precedent and must be fail-safe—avoiding complaints is often the end goal. But the Fussa City Hall adopted a theme of flexible, adaptable service, and the signs were designed to be easily understandable regardless of nationality or language.
(Fussa City Hall, 2008)

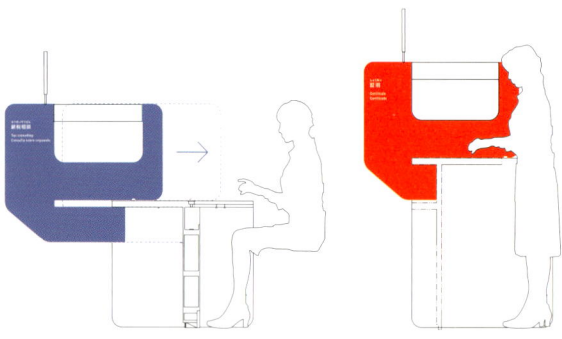

どこの役所でも、一部の手続きカウンターに人が集中し、多くの人が我慢して待っている。新しい福生市役所にはフォーラムと呼ばれる空間に、曲線を描くカウンターがあり、多様な業務に対応する窓口が設置されている。「インデックスパネル」と呼ばれる差し替え可能なパーテーションは、必要に応じてどの場所にも自由に取り付けることができる。プライバシーを確保するパネルは、一目でわかるように業務ごとに色をつけている。

No matter which municipal office you go to, everyone seems to need to visit the same section, resulting in a long line of people waiting (im)patiently. At the new Fussa City Hall, a long counter curves along the edge of the lobby area, which is referred to as the "Forum." This counter is split into multiple service counters that can cater to a variety of business. The placement of these service counters can be modified as needed by moving the freely-adjustable partitions—referred to as "Index Panels"—that separate them. In addition to lending a sense of privacy, these panels are color-coded to signify the types of business handled at each counter.

021

2 | Consciousness in the Unconscious

Slowly stretching out your toes in the morning before getting out of bed, brushing your teeth from the upper left corner of your mouth, or always putting on your right shoe first when leaving the house.

When we inspect the minutiae of our daily lives, it becomes apparent that we often behave in a repetitive manner without being much aware of it. We all find our own patterns and routines that we feel most comfortable with, and repeating them in our everyday actions acts as a kind of stress-relief for our brains. In contrast to this, before taking an exam or giving a speech, we feel a sense of pressure and agitation. We might experience such things as "nerves", "dread", "blanking out", "freezing up", or even "sheer blind panic." Thus acute stress leads to physical changes in us, interfering with our balance of self-control.

Let us then consider not an example of extraordinary stress, but a subtle change to a daily habit. For instance, looking at an everyday morning scene through a mirror, or brushing your teeth with your less dexterous hand, or walking in the opposite direction to your nearest train station. These kinds of small changes to our routines can have a remarkable effect on flaring up our awareness of things. Design is the act of discovering new senses of awareness, within the constant flow of consciousness formed by our daily societal lives. Furthermore, when we are moved by a design that we have never seen before, it is due to the reaction of particles lodged inside the hippocampi in our brains, which play a vital role in forming our memories. For better or worse, we are incapable of liking or disliking any truly unprecedented or "new" experience, because we have no points of reference with which to make such a judgment. If we analyze our emotions, we realize that they are informed by experiences from infancy or when we have a low level of consciousness. Design is the act of forming new hypotheses from disparate pieces of information that mean very little on their own, based on our memories and experiences. Inspecting and scrutinizing our ordinary lives is what propels our art into the future.

二、無意識の中の意識

朝、目が覚めると足の先をゆっくり伸ばしてから起き上がる。

歯ブラシは左上から磨き始め、靴は必ず右足から履く。

自分の生活の軌跡を細かく辿ってみると、強く意識はしていないのに同じ行動パターンをしていることに気がつく。これは日常生活を繰り返す上で、脳のストレスを軽減させているのである。

逆に受験やスピーチの前などプレッシャーを感じると、ドキドキして落ち着かないのも事実。

「あがる」「テンパる」「真っ白になる」「凍りつく」「パニくる」状態になる。

極度のストレスは体に変調をきたし、自制バランスを崩すことになる。

それほど強いストレスではなく、いつもと少し違うことに意識を向けてはどうだろう。

何気ない朝の風景を鏡で見る。

歯ブラシを利き手ではない方で磨いてみる。

駅とは反対方向に歩いてみる。

などちょっとした試みが、思いがけなく無意識を発火させることがある。

デザインは日常と社会という連続する無意識な流れの中に新しい意識を発見すること。

いままで見たこともないデザインに出会った時の感動は、実は記憶の海馬に埋もれる粒子が反応して起きる。

本当の未体験は良くも悪くも、好きも嫌いも無い。そもそも判断する基準が無いからだ。

感動を冷静に分析してみると、幼い頃や意識の浅い体験に理解の因子があることに気がつく。

ひとつでは意味を持たないバラバラの情報を、記憶や経験をもとに新たな仮説を組み立てるのがデザイン。日常を深く見つめることが未来に繋がるのである。

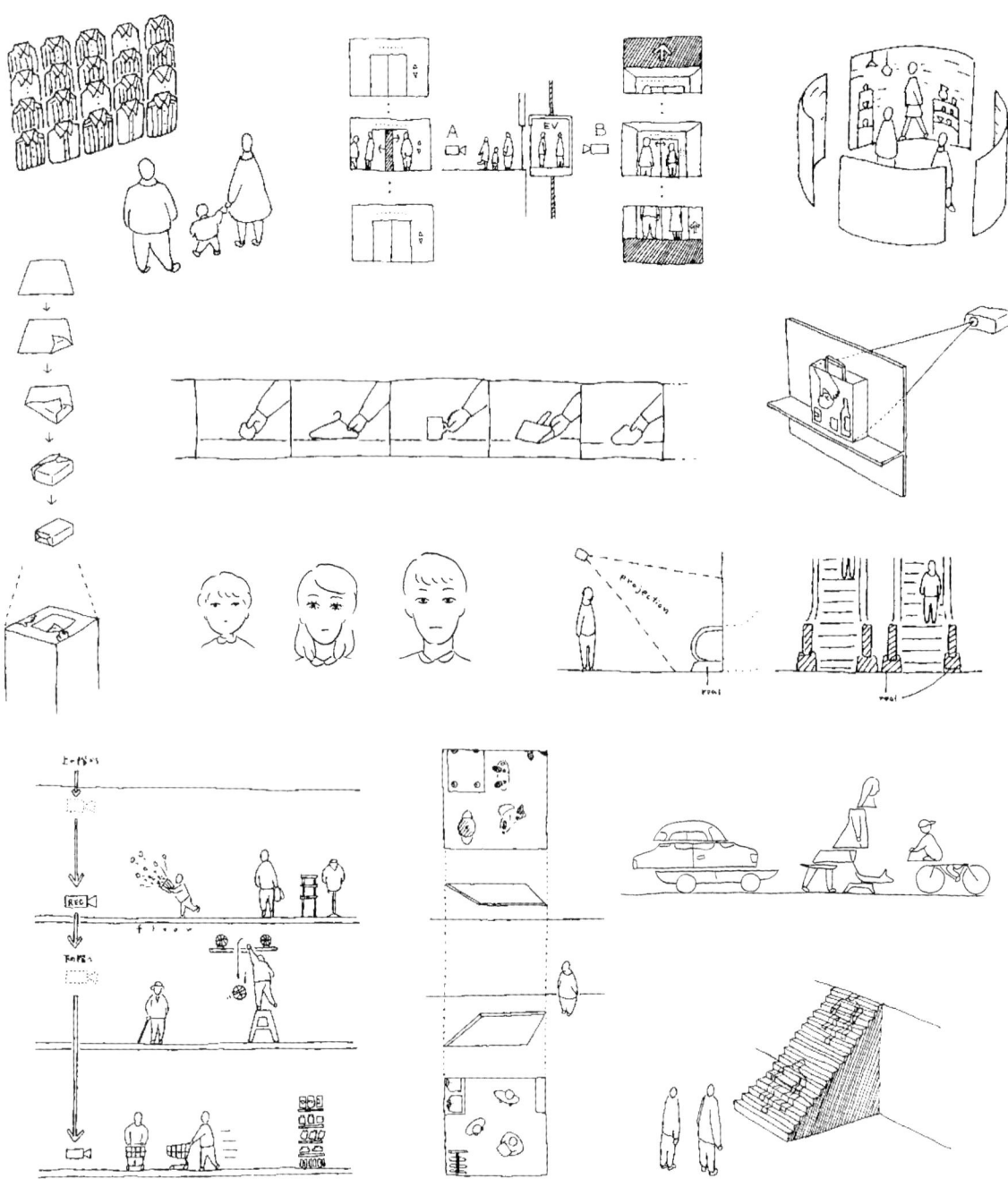

Junglin'

ジュングリン

日常からデザインを発見する展覧会を企画した。
何気ない動きや行為は、本人は意識していないが大きな結果を示唆するサインだったりする。無意識に行う行動にも意味がある。いや、意味のない行動に意味付けすることで新たな価値が生まれることを証明したかったのだ。
順繰り＋ＩＮＧ＝じゅんぐりん。という言葉が浮かんだ。
観て楽しい映像を目指し、スタッフ総動員でテスト撮影をした。
脱いでも脱いでも着ているＴシャツ、家から会社まで毎朝足元だけ撮影する。階段を登る人を階段に投影する、文字を書き続け、その後から消し続ける。
など実現しなかった企画がほとんど。
しかし、くだらないアイデアほど面白かったりする。

Junglin'

I organized an exhibition focusing on abstracting designs from everyday life. The most nonchalant or inadvertent act can often be the most suggestive sign in this regard. There is meaning even in the behavior of which we are unconscious. Or rather, I wanted to show that giving meaning to our meaningless actions can create something new and valuable. I made up this word Junglin'; a play on the Japanese word junguri, meaning "in order" or "by turns", and the English "-ing." My staff and I set out about shooting video footage with the aim of making something fun to watch. A shirt that stays worn no matter how many times you take it off; footage of just someone's feet walking to work every morning; projecting the image of someone walking up a flight of stairs onto the staircase itself; writing a series of words while simultaneously erasing them shortly afterwards. Most of these tests and ideas never amounted to anything. But the silliest ideas are often the most fun.

Color-batons

From one hand to another, colorful products are passed on at a steady and orderly pace. I came up with the title for my exhibition, Junglin', when we were editing this piece of film. This is a visualization of the process that goods go through, from their production, distribution, sale, and into the consumer's home. The constant passing of goods from one body to another, in a society practically overflowing with "stuff", struck me as being rather similar to a relay baton race. We painstakingly searched for things in department stores to get the gradated coloring effect of the products. The sense of detachment and dispassion in the film almost has a meditative effect on the viewer. Yet once in a while, a completely different kind of product is thrown in, like a clock with a ringing alarm, or a rolling ball of yarn. Moments when the brain suddenly gets jolted awake.
(Junglin', 2011)

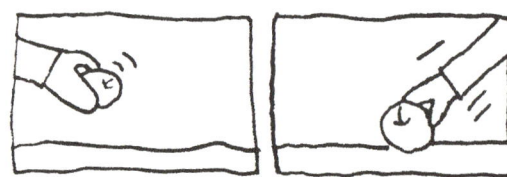

色バトン

手から手に。カラフルな商品が一定のリズムで順番に送られていく。

ジュングリンという展覧会のタイトルはこの映像を編集しているときに思いついた。商品が生産され流通から販売へ、そして家庭に届くまでのプロセスを絵にした。モノで溢れる社会、誰かから誰かに渡る商品。まるでバトンのようだ。

送られる商品の色彩はグラデーションにしようと、百貨店の中をくまなく探して集めた。

淡々と進む映像に少し頭がぼーっとしてくる。しかし途中、ベルが鳴る時計や、転がる毛糸玉など、いつもと違う商品が登場する。

脳が覚醒しハッとする瞬間である。

(Junglin' 二〇一一年)

ラッピング

包装紙で商品を包んでいく。しかし商品と包装紙の内側が暗いために何を包んでいるのか最初はわからない。次第に包まれたカタチが表れると、中に包まれたモノが何なのか想像できるようになってくる。暮らしの中で使われるモノや道具は機能がそのままシルエットになっているのだ。トンカチはTのカタチだし、フライパンは円形に棒がついたカタチになっている。商品はラッピングすることで、色や質感が隠され、カタチのシルエットだけが浮かび上がる。映像を観て子どもたちが大声で中身を言い当てているのが面白い。脳は大量の記憶をストックするために、モノの質感や色を省きアウトラインのエッジだけ残して記憶するのだ。デザインはそのシルエットからユーザビリティを感じることが重要なのである。

(Junglin' 二〇一一年)

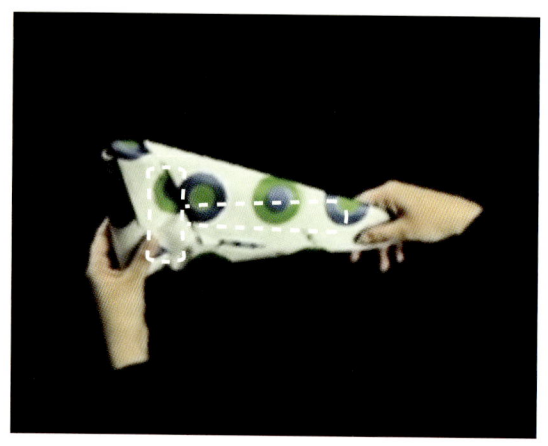

Wrapping

A product is being encased in wrapping paper, although it is not apparent what the product is at first. As the packaging starts to take shape, it gradually becomes apparent what the thing inside is. The functions of the products and tools that we use in our daily lives are themselves silhouettes. A hammer is T-shaped, and a frying pan is a circle with a rod sticking out of it, for example. Wrapping a thing conceals its color and texture, thereby accentuating the silhouette of its shape. It was fun listening to the children watching this film, loudly shouting out and guessing what the contents of each package were. When stockpiling images, our memories tend to override colors and textures of things in favor of their basic outlines. In design, it is important to create a sense of usability from the silhouette of any given product.

(Junglin', 2011)

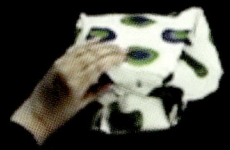

ショッピングバッグ

買い物と都市の関係は深い。自給自足型社会では生産者と消費者は重なっているので買い物比率は低い。都市が形成され産業や流通が発達すると、必然性のないものも欲しくなり、欲望が買い物を加速する。ショッピングは買う者の本質を探るのにも有効である。

買い物をした紙袋の中を透視してみる。五つの紙袋は五人の買い物。レジでバッグに詰める様子を透かして見るとその人の生活スタイルを知ることができる。年齢、性別、趣味、職業などが、そのまま買い物に表れて面白い。またレジの店員が瞬時に商品のサイズと重さを理解して、整然とバッグに詰めていくのも驚きだ。

(Junglin' 二〇一一年)

The Shopping Bag

There is a deep-rooted relationship between shopping and urban life. In self-sufficient societies, producers and consumers overlap, so there is inevitably less purchasing. As industry and distribution develop along with urbanization, we become more prone to buying things we don't really need, and our lust for consumption grows ever more rapidly. A person's shopping is also an effective way of finding out about his or her basic characteristics and personality traits. Here, we have x-rayed five different shopping bags belonging to five different individuals. Peering through the bags that are being filled with goods at the checkout counter gives us an insight into the shoppers' lifestyle habits. It is interesting to see that we can learn a lot about the age, gender, interests, and occupation of a person just by looking at what they buy. Also of note is how the checkout clerk is able to register the size and weight of each item instantaneously, packing them in a systematic and well-ordered manner.

(Junglin', 2011)

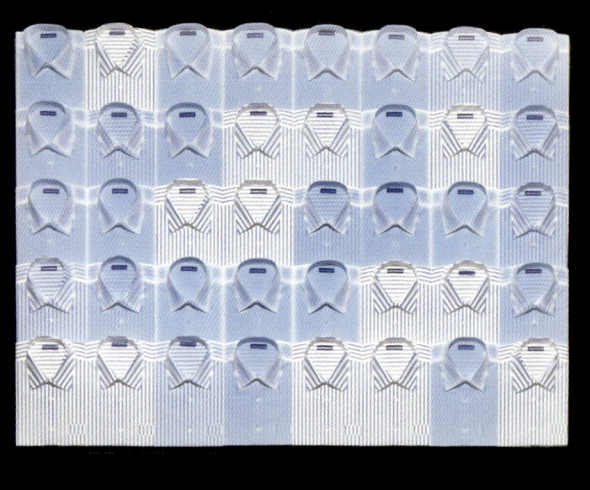
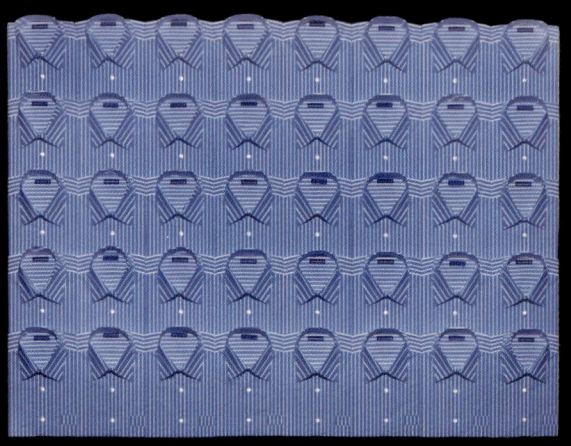

シャツ

元々は、男女共用の下着だったシャツ。十六世紀に服の切れ目から下着を見せることが流行し、アウターとしても着られるようになった。いつしかビジネスマンは一年中ワイシャツを着るようになった。機能が充実して、エリの形から柄まで本当に種類が多い。

紳士服売り場で整然と並んでいるストライプのシャツ。その模様が時間をかけてゆっくり変化する。細いストライプが徐々に太くなっていき、気がついた時はぼんやり滲んでいる。見ているはずなのにいつ変化したのかわからない。瞬間的な変化には脳は敏感だが、ゆっくりした変化は見落としやすい。「気づかない」という現象から、「気づき」とは何かを問う。

(Junglin'、二〇一一年)

The Shirt

The shirt was originally an undergarment for both men and women. In the sixteenth century, it became fashionable to show parts of the shirt from under the collars or sleeves of one's jacket, and from then on it evolved into a piece of outerwear. Eventually, the collared shirt became the standard year-round uniform for every businessman. While being a highly functional piece of clothing, it is also highly versatile in its wide range of collar-shapes and fabric patterns.

Striped shirts displayed in an orderly set of rows and columns in a gentlemen's clothing section. The patterns on the shirts change at a slow pace. Thin stripes gradually become thicker, and before one realizes, they blur into the shirts themselves. The effect is one of not being fully aware whether there has been a change in the image, even though one is watching it the entire time. The brain is sensitive to very sudden changes, but gradual changes can be easy to miss. By highlighting a state of 'unawareness', this piece questions what it really means to be 'aware.'

(Junglin', 2011)

The Door

The interior and exterior of a department store were filmed separately, and the two pieces of footage were then merged.
We normally walk in and out of buildings without being particularly aware or circumspect about their entrances. Yet when aligning these footages filmed at different times, our brains immediately begin to look for patterns in our unconscious actions and behaviors. The human brain works through predictions based on past experience. For example, during every green light, around 3000 people walk across the scramble-intersection in Shibuya. But the reason why they don't bump into each other is that we are able to predict the movements of people walking towards us. Or in reenactment films on TV, the reason why we are able to get emotionally involved despite the fact that the events are portrayed by actors rather than the actual people involved is that our brains can suppose or imagine otherwise. In other words, the brain can make predictions and shift its awareness or consciousness of things, depending on its surrounding circumstances.
(Junglin', 2011)

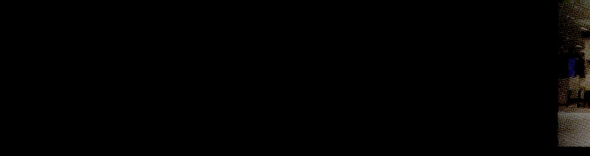

ドア

百貨店の入口の内側と外側を別々に撮影し、二つの映像を合体した。普段入口を凝視することはない。別の時間で撮影された二つの映像を並べることで、無意識に行われている動作や行為に脳は連続した関係を見つけようとする。
人間の脳は体験学習により、予測しながら行動している。渋谷スクランブル交差点には一度に三〇〇〇人以上が流れ込むが、誰もぶつからないのは前から来る人の行動を予測し、避けているからだ。また、テレビのワイドショーでの再現フィルムで、本人とは違う役者でも感情移入ができるのは、脳が本人だと思い込むように仕組まれているからのようだ。脳は大兄こ忘こと券手こ意識を切り替えて予則っている

Book Clock

Three books indicate hours, minutes, and seconds respectively, measuring time as a hand turns a page. Compared with standard clocks, the image of a physical being turning these pages gives us the impression of somehow being in control of time, rather than time being something which moves automatically and irrespective of our will. Time is the same for everyone, and yet subjectively speaking, its speed, quality, and quantity can feel quite different from person to person.
(Junglin' 2, 2014)

西武渋谷店 モヴィーダ館　常設設置
Permanent display, SEIBU SHIBUYA-MOVIDA Bld.

ブッククロック

本が時を刻む。
三冊の本はそれぞれ時間、分、秒にわかれ、ページをめくることで時を刻む時計である。長短針やデジタルの時計と比べると、ページをめくるという行為は、自動的に過ぎる時間ではなく、自身で時を操っているようにも感じる。誰にでも平等な時間だが、人によって早さも質量も違うのが時間だとわかる。
(Junglin' 2　二〇一四年)

037

スライス

都会にたたずみ、しばらく観察していると多くの発見がある。まず時間という概念だ。新旧の建物が入れ替わっているのに気づく。速度は遅いが確かに変化しているのがわかる。その逆で、道行く人々は足早に過ぎるがなかなか記憶に残らない。この時間感覚の差を表してみたいと思った。

渋谷スクランブル交差点。信号待ちをしていた人達がいっせいに動き出すと、体がバラバラに分裂していく。映像を細くスライスし、始動タイミングをずらすことでおこる視覚マジック。動くものと止まっているものの差があらわになる。都市での人間の動きは浮遊する塵のようでそれは飛び交う情報の流れとシンクロしているように見え

(Junglin' 2 二〇一四年)

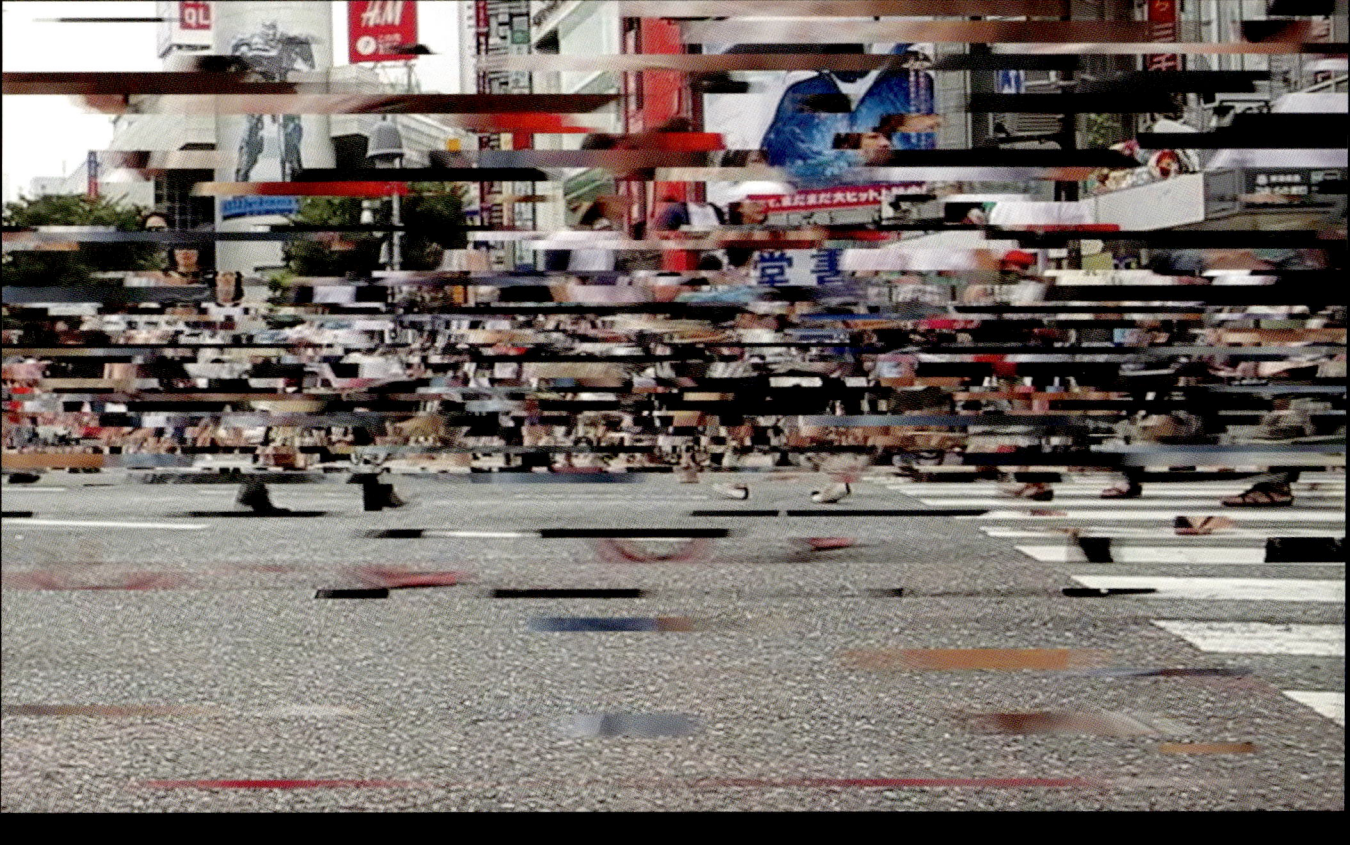

Slice

Observing the cityscape, you start to notice a number of changes, the most noticeable of which revolves around time. You become aware that older buildings are constantly being replaced with new ones. Although the pace of this change is relatively slow, it is clearly visible when viewed from a certain distance. Contrastingly, the people briskly walking through the city are a very rapid and instant form of change, and yet our memories seem to discard them as quickly as they register them. I wanted to capture this difference in the way we sense the passing of time.

Take the Shibuya scramble-intersection, for instance. As soon as the traffic lights turn green, a mass of bodies splinters into all directions. By intricately slicing this video footage and delaying its starting time, a remarkable thing occurs. You become strikingly aware of the contrast between the things that are in motion and those that are stationary. People moving through the city resemble floating particles of dust, which seem to mimic in turn the multitude of advertisements and information darting to and from in this modern and hectic environment.
(Junglin' 2, 2014)

テスト映像
Test movies

Plastic Rails

Assemble the rails, place a toy train on them, and take them apart again; a sequence of actions within a single unit. Putting together a number of these units horizontally and vertically has the potential for varied and vast expanses. And putting together video footage of it, filmed in a very narrow space, can make for a practically endless loop. The idea is rather similar to that of the puzzle game Waterworks. It is a demonstration of how the brain reimagines disjointed pieces of information as a continuum.
(Junglin' 2, 2014)

プラレール
レールを組み立て電車が走り、レールを解体する。一連の流れがひとつのユニット。これを上下左右に組み合わせると壮大な世界ができる。狭い空間で撮影された映像は組み合わせることで無限にループする。「水道管ゲーム」でカードが自由に伸びて行く様子に似ている。脳はバラバラな情報を連動したものとして創造する。
(Junglin' 2 二〇一四年)

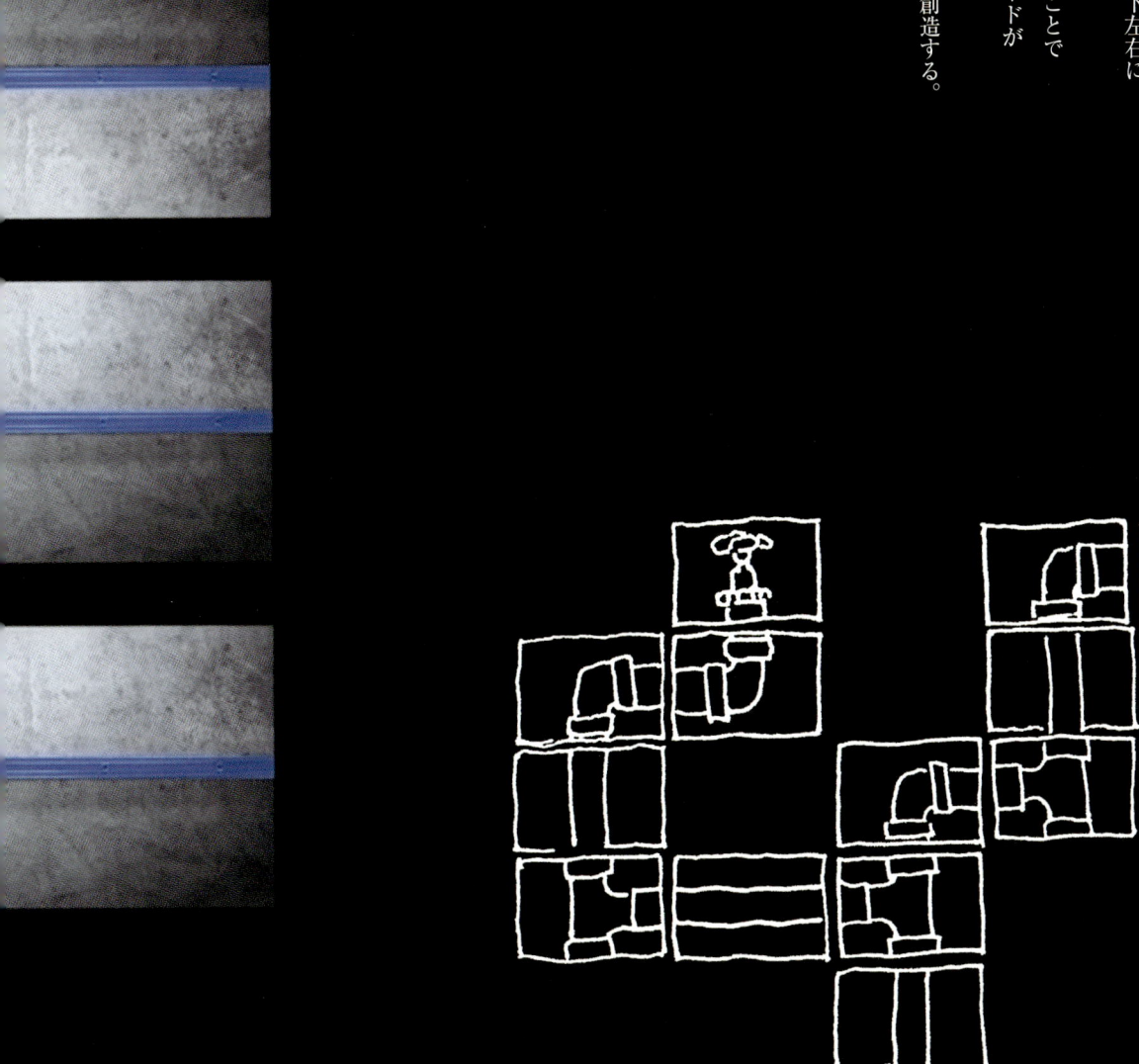

めがね

レンズに眼が投影されている。「まばたき」や「キョロキョロ」したりする。眼だけがあり、顔がない不思議。しかしよく見ると誰の眼なのか想像できる。写真を撮るとき、眼にピントを合わせるのは顔の中心が眼だからだ。三〇秒に一度全員が同時に「まばたき」したり、同じ方向を見る。不思議なことに鑑賞者もつられて同期する。
(Jungin'2 二〇一四年)

Glasses

Images of blinking or restless eyes are projected onto the lenses. There is something rather odd about just seeing the eyes without the face. However, looking at this piece carefully, you begin to get an image of the face to which the eyes might belong. The reason why we adjust the focus to the eyes when taking photographs of people is that the eyes are located in the middle of the face. Every 30 seconds, all eyes blink or dart in one direction at once. And strangely, the eyes of the viewer often end up unwittingly mimicking them.

3 | Making the Invisible Visible

As human beings we process information through our five senses, but over 80 percent of our perception is mediated through vision. Since ancient times, we have affirmed all that is visible and we have had to make an effort to envision all that cannot be seen.

"Time" is intangible, but people in the olden days invented clocks by conceptualizing time based on the movement of the sun or the moon. "Electricity" is also unseen, but its presence is visible in a room illuminated by a light and an operating washing machine. Then, how about "the heart and soul?" Though, we might be so inclined, we are unable to glimpse inside someone else's heart and see their inner thoughts or their worries.

There is a Buddhist saying, "Shikisokuzekuu, kuusokuzeshiki." It is a concept that all form is emptiness and all emptiness is form. "Shiki" means all that is visible, and "Kuu" means all that is invisible. It suggests that "What is visible is in fact invisible, and what is invisible is in fact visible." Therefore it can be concluded to mean "What exists actually does not exist, and what does not exist actually exists." Even if asked to do so, we cannot literally display our heart and soul. If then queried, as to whether we really do possess these intangible things, we can only affirm that we do. Buddhism tells us to embrace all that cannot be seen with our eyes.

Design aims to visualize "reliability" or "reassurance" in some form. Product design seeks to express feeling of the material, texture, and recognition. Architecture creates a space that brings warmth and comfort, where one does not want to leave. Whereas, graphic design serves the eye, which accounts for 80 percent of all human senses. "Reliability" or "reassurance" are sought out from a visual point of view by utilizing colors and typography. Having established the above, are companies designing successful products? It is hard to determine if their products have good design elements. The amount of good design elements that goes into a product is hard to measure. In the end, it is the heart that determines if the design is questionable or successful.

三、見えないものを見えるように

人は五感で情報を認識するが、その中でも視覚が全体の八割以上を占める。昔から見えることを信じ、見えないモノを見えるように努力してきた。

「時間」は目に見えないが、古代の人々は太陽や月の動きを時間という概念の基本にして時計を発明した。「電気」も目に見えないが、部屋を明るくし、洗濯機が動くことで電気の存在が可視化されている。

では「心」はどうだろう。他人の心の中は見たくても見えない。何を考え、何を望んでいるのか、悩み苦しんできた。

仏教に「色即是空 空即是色」という言葉がある。

「色（しき）」は目に見えること、「空（くう）」は見えないことを表し、「見えるものは即ち、見えない。見えないものは即ち見える」ということ、言い換えると「有るけど無い、無いけど有る」ということになる。

「心」を見せて欲しいと言われても見せられない、では心が無いかと問われれば、有ると答える。仏教では目に見えないモノを大切しなさい、と説いている。

デザインは「信頼」や「安心」を見えるカタチにする。

プロダクトデザインは、素材感や手に持った感触、漂う親みやすさなどを表現し、建築空間なら包み込まれるようなぬくもりや、いつまでも居たい心地良さをつくる。グラフィックデザインは八割を占める視覚が中心のデザイン。色彩やタイポグラフィなどを駆使して「信頼」と「安心」を視覚的に訴求する。

しかし依頼される企業や商品は本当に「信頼」されるに足るのか？ デザインを「疑う」か、「認める」かは、「心」が決めるのである。絶対「安心」なのか実際はわからない。デザインが踏み込める深度が限られているのも事実である。

鮮度をカタチに

無添加の液体石鹸は鮮度が命である。
「ミヨシファクトリーソープ」はできたてのフレッシュな石鹸を生鮮食品のように直接ユーザーに届けたいと考え、生まれた商品とシステム。
石鹸が新鮮かどうか一瞬見てもわからない、鮮度が価値であることをカタチにするのがデザイン。
テトラ式の紙パックは牛乳を連想させる。白いパッケージは、装飾を排し、なるべく簡素に。石鹸に製造年月日を表示することなど、誠実という見えないものをカタチにするのが、デザインだと思った。

(ミヨシファクトリーソープ 二〇〇九年)
※現在は販売終了

MIYOSHI FACTORY SOAP

Freshness Visualized

A principle element of natural liquid soap is its freshness.
"MIYOSHI FACTORY SOAP" was conceived based on the idea of delivering freshly made soap, in the same manner that fresh produce is delivered, to consumers. One is unable to tell whether or not soap is fresh by simply looking at it. The design relays that the freshness of the soap is of significant merit. The triangular tetra pack conjures up images of a triangular milk carton. The white packaging is kept as simple as possible, without any design embellishments. Each package has a production date stamp. We believe with such packaging details the integrity of the product can be presented through design.
(MIYOSHI FACTORY SOAP, 2009)
*No longer available

アイコンとピクトグラム

サインデザインではピクトグラムが多用される。絵文字とも呼ばれ、年齢や言語を越えて早く理解されるので空港や駅など公共性の高い施設で使用されている。一方アイコンは、コンピューターの発達に合わせ操作性を高めるために生まれた記号表記。同じ単純化された絵記号だが、成り立ちと使用形式で違った進化をしている。

ピクトグラムは「いつでも」「どこでも」「だれでも」という絶対性を望まれているし、アイコンは次の動作を促し新たな「気づき」を生むことを期待されている。

標準ピクト
Standard pictogram

Icons and Pictograms

Pictograms are commonly used in signage. Also referred to as emoji, they transcend age and language boundaries. As pictograms are quick and easy to comprehend they are used in busy public facilities, such as airports and stations. On the other hand, icons are stylized symbols of objects, which were developed to help ease the navigation of rapidly evolving computing systems.

Though pictograms and icons can be defined as simplified pictorial symbols, their creation, development and usage are markedly different.

Pictograms must be understood by everyone, regardless of time or place, whereas icons innovatively aim to generate "recognition" of the represented object and action.

横須賀美術館アイコン習作
Study of icons for Yokosuka Museum of Art

不規則脈波	測定姿勢ガイド	フィットカフ	カフぴったり巻きチェック	無音測定
体動検知	血圧値レベル表示	ユーザー選択	データ消去	ログイン
月別表示	消費カロリー	朝平均	測定記録	平均値
気温／快適	気温／寒い	アラーム	バックライト	ブザー

オムロン 商品アイコン
Omron product icons

ヒトを想うカタチ。
いつも健康であること、未病を発見することは人類の課題である。体調を手軽にチェックし、良い状態を維持するための機器が続々と開発されている。かつては病院でしか計測できなかった機器も、自宅で使えるようになり、現在はモバイル化が進んでいる。データは分析されカラダの未来を予測する。対話するのはインターフェイス、見えない向こう側からの声は、我々の体調をいちばんよく知っているのである。
（オムロンヘルスケア　二〇〇九年−）

A Contour of Care

Early detection of illness in order to maintain good health is a challenge that faces mankind. New medical devices have rapidly developed, assisting with the analysis of overall health. Initially, only hospitals offered access to such technology. However, now they are often available for home use, even interfacing with personal mobile devices.
This technology can capture data on the user and provide an analysis for future ailments. We can communicate with our bodies through a digital interface.
This new technology provides the interface to listen to our bodies from within, as this is the best way to know our overall health.
(Omron Healthcare, 2009–)

止	おしり	おしりソフト	おしりワイド
ビデ	ワイドビデ	ソフトビデ	乾燥
水勢 弱	水勢 強	位置 左	位置 右
流す 大	流す 小	流す eco 小	便座開閉
便ふた開閉	便ふた 開	便座 開	便座便ふた 閉

Intuitive Symbols

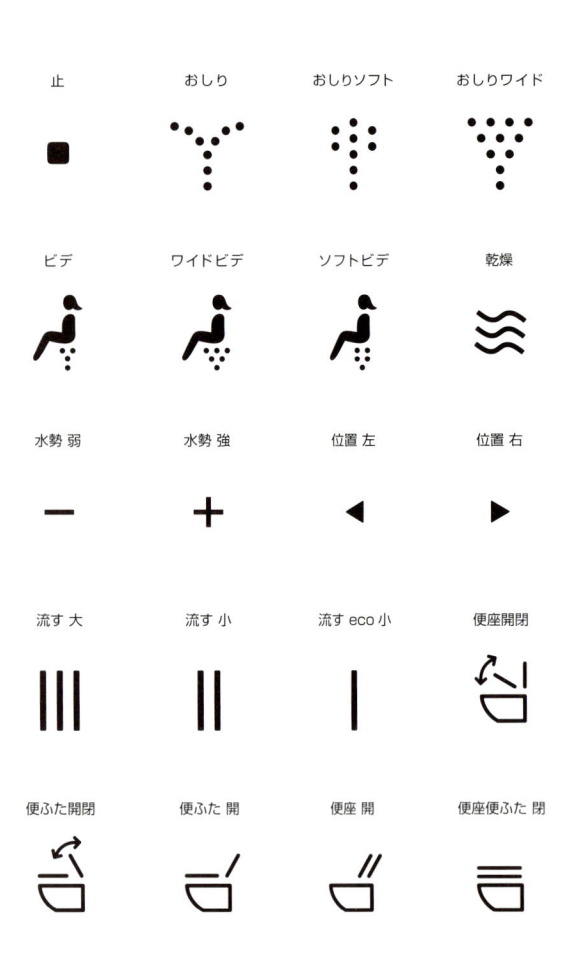

In the 1980's a TV commercial introducing WASHLET, TOTO's warm water spray toilet seat, made the product instantly famous. In 2010 the product reached 70% distribution across Japan and is aiming to enter overseas markets. Remote controls can be used much more intuitively than home appliances. To ensure easy usability symbols had to be clear and universally understandable.
(Pictogram for TOTO's WASHLET, 2013)

直感的なしるし

一九八〇年代「おしりだって、洗ってほしい」の名コピーで一気に知名度があがった「ウォシュレット」。TOTOの温水洗浄便座である。二〇一〇年に国内の普及率は七〇％を越え、海外に市場を求めている。リモコンでの操作は家電などより直感的に扱われることが多く、言葉や国別の習慣などを越えて理解されなくてはならない。

(TOTO ウォシュレット用ピクトグラム 二〇一三年)

Visual Labels

It is often said that Japanese people have a heightened sense of taste than those of other nations. I would say that we have more taste buds, we also have an expansive vocabulary to describe tastes. Kikizake, Japanese sake tasting, is a method to judge the quality of sake. Characteristics of sake are classified in many ways, to include the type of taste: Subtle can be described as Tanrei: Fresh and easy to drink. Noujun: Rich and concentrated. Or Shiripin: Strong with a sharp aftertaste. After a long aging process, sake becomes aromatic and more flavorful, with more elements to the taste. The abundance of flavors make it impossible to judge an aged sake with just one tasting. The labels on the bottle describe these various elements and characteristics in a condensed and simple manner via the typography used. The goal is to make the consumer almost taste the sake before they even purchase it. They may think, "this sake may be dry," or "this sake will be rich and sweet." Design provides us a way to understand and feel things prior to actually experiencing them.

("Junglin' by Masaaki Hiromura", published in AXIS, 2014)
 *First appeared in AXIS (June 2014) and revised for use in this book.

ラベルは語る

日本人の味覚が他国の人と比べて優れていると言われるのは味蕾（みらい・味を感じる器官）の数が多いということと、味に関する表現が幅広く豊かだということだろう。日本酒には利き酒という品質を判定する方法があり、「淡麗」「濃醇」「尻ピン」など独特の表現で微妙な香りも判別する。

長い時間をかけて育てた芳醇で複雑な味は、観察しただけではわからない。一升瓶に貼ってあるラベルは、その酒の特徴をタイポグラフィで端的に表現している。

「おっ、これはサッパリ辛口かな」とか「むむっ、まったり甘口だろう」と見ただけで喉が鳴るほど想像できるようにラベルは語っている。昔から理解する糸口にデザインが生かされているのである。もっと言うと、理解する手前の気配みたいなものを感じるためにデザインがある。

（アクシス「廣村正彰のJungjin'」（二〇一四年）
初出：『アクシス』（二〇一四年六月号）
連載「廣村正彰のJungjin'」を加筆修正

雑誌掲載作品のため非売品
Magazine display only, and not for sale

H

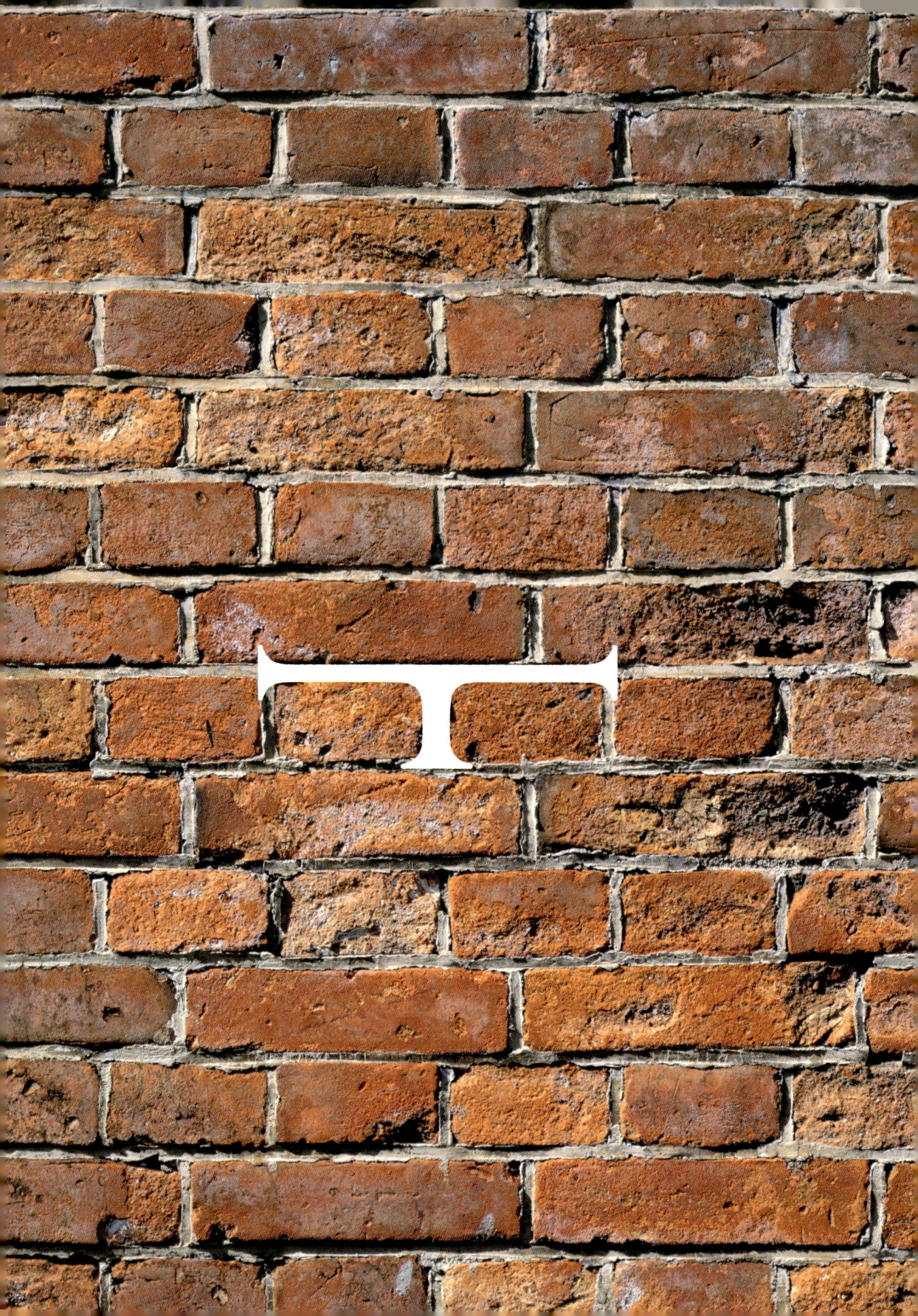

時間の記憶

一〇〇年前に東京の玄関、国のシンボルとしてつくられた東京駅。長い時間と多くの物語を紡いだ駅舎、記憶の象徴は赤レンガである。
東京駅の復元に伴いリニューアルした美術館「東京ステーションギャラリー」。レンガとレンガの間「目地」をTに見立てて美術館のシンボルとして提案した。
広く創造性を発掘、発信したいという美術館の思いを込めた。
一日の乗降客は新幹線も入れると五〇万人を越える。駅の内部には新しいショッピングゾーンも完成し、駅前の広場も整備されて玄関としての顔が整った。
復元された駅舎に訪れる人は傷んだレンガに時の記憶を想うかもしれない。
（東京ステーションギャラリー　二〇一二年）

Memory of Time

Constructed over a century ago, Tokyo Station is the main gateway of the capital and a symbol of Japan. Stories about the station building are countless, spanning years, and they evoke images of the station's iconic red brick façade. Coinciding with the restoration of Tokyo Station, TOKYO STATION GALLERY was also refurbished. As the station's red bricks are linked together by "joints" that resemble the letter "T," we proposed to use this as the museum's logo. The logo is symbolic of the museum's intention to extensively seek out and showcase new artistic talent. In a single day, including bullet train passengers, over half a million people pass through Tokyo Station. Inside, a new shopping zone is complete. The front of the station now features a space that serves as an entryway.
When visitors see the newly restored building, it may stir up nostalgic memories of the worn red brick station's bygone days.
(TOKYO STATION GALLERY, 2012)

"Brick Junglin'" Art Installation

This video installation titled, "Waiting for the First Train," was created for the inaugural exhibition that commemorated the restoration of Tokyo Station. A slow motion video of 12 male and female models is projected on the inner red brick wall of the station. They look appreciatively at the brick wall as if they were studying a painting. The projected image seemingly intermingles with the wall. The red brick theme was used to create exclusive products for the museum; these include book covers and memo pads.
(TOKYO STATION GALLERY, 2012)

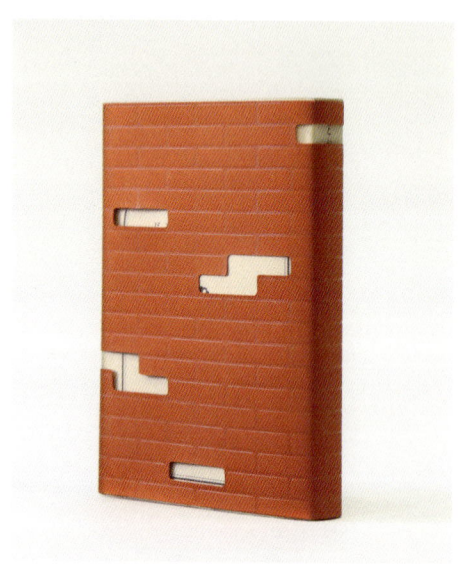

上段左：Brick Book Cover、上段右：Brick Envelopes, letters
下段：Brick Block Memo
Top left : Brick Book Cover   Top right : Brick Envelopes, letters
Bottom : Brick Block Memo

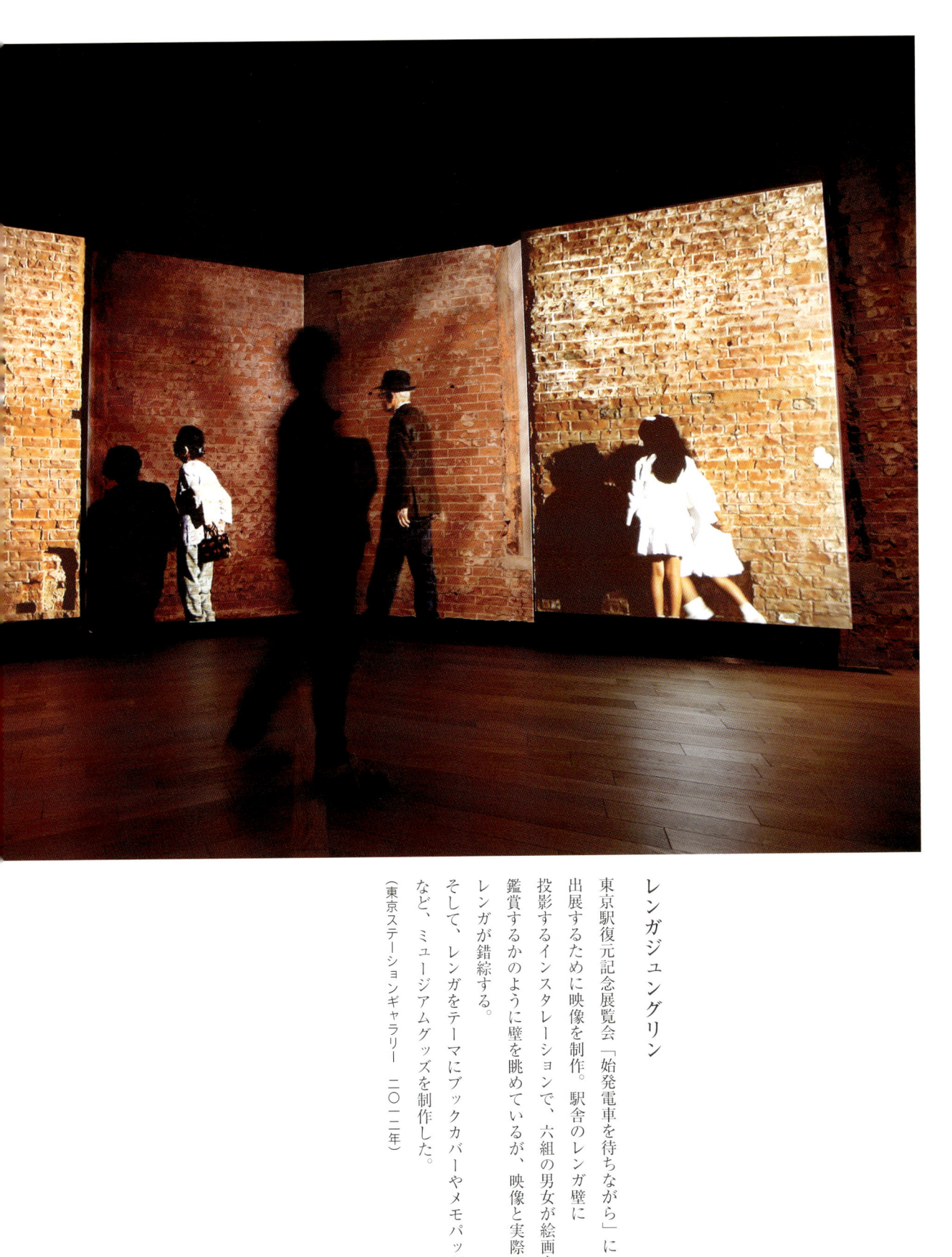

レンガジュングリン

東京駅復元記念展覧会「始発電車を待ちながら」に出展するために映像を制作。駅舎のレンガ壁に投影するインスタレーションで、六組の男女が絵画を鑑賞するかのように壁を眺めているが、映像と実際のレンガが錯綜する。
そして、レンガをテーマにブックカバーやメモパッドなど、ミュージアムグッズを制作した。
(東京ステーションギャラリー 二〇一二年)

Promoting Learning

The architectural design plan of a university should aim to create open spaces and the utmost transparency. This reflects an institution's commitment to uphold high standards of public transparency and to decrease the likelihood of problems. However, things can change gradually with time. To prevent people from accidentally walking into glass walls—and perhaps also out of a need for more privacy—glass walls separating classrooms and common areas have become increasingly opaque, and so that sense of transparency becomes blurred. At Ryukoku University's Fukakusa campus, big translucent signs in English are displayed on new glass buildings. The signs represent the significance of space. We hope the signs promote learning.
(Ryukoku University Fukakusa Campus, 2015)

うながす学び。

新しく建てられる大学は、なるべく開放的で透明性高く計画される。広く社会に開かれた学校であることの表明でもあり、多くのトラブルを避けるためでもある。しかし時が経つと状況は徐々に変化する。
パブリックと教室、教室と教室間を区切るガラスは、衝突などを回避するために、あるいはプライベートを守る？ためにどんどん非透過になって、透明性が損なわれてゆく。
「龍谷大学 深草キャンパス」の新しい校舎は空間の意味性を半透明の英文字で大きくガラスに表記した。学びの意識をうながすことができれば良いと考えた。
（龍谷大学深草キャンパス和顔館　二〇一五年）

AGRICULTURE INTERN
ECONOMICS BUSINES
TECHNOLOGY POLICY

063

4 | That Ish Feeling

Imagination and creativity are both processes of creation.

Whenever we imagine something and then go to create it, we never begin with a completely blank slate. All of our experiences and everything we've seen or heard since the time we were born is filed away on vast, infinite shelves in our hippocampus in the form of memories. In order to fit all of our memories onto these shelves, they are broken down into simple fragments, with the newest and most significant fragments stored at the forefront. Every now and then a fragment is recalled from the dusty recesses and coalesces with another fragment, forming a new idea. This is imagination.

Creativity is the act of giving form to this fusion of fragments. When we come across truly good design, we are struck by the freshness of it. But at the same time, we accept it without resistance. This is because the vast majority of us share similar fragments of memories. Even if we have not directly experienced something, we can use what we do know to combine those fragments into an idea and then give it form. As soft as a baby's bottom. Edges rounded like those of weathered wood. A honeysuckle-ish scent. These expressions are the fundamentals of creativity.

What we feel when we imagine something is packaged into the form we give it. Though design is simply form given to expression, countless underlying thoughts and feelings are bundled within. Regardless, succinct expression is often best.

四、っぽい、感じ

「想像力」と「創造力」、どちらも生みだすこと。

人が何かを想像し、そして創造しようとするとき、まったく無から生まれることはない。

人は生まれてから今まで、見たこと、聞いたこと、経験したことを脳の海馬という広大で無数の棚に記憶として仕舞っている。

その記憶の棚は大量に記憶するためにシンプルな記号のかけらとなり、最新で強烈な記憶のかけらから順番に納められている。

何かのきっかけで奥にあったかけらが呼び覚まされて、別のかけらと合体し、新しい想像（イマジネーション）が浮かび上がる。

創造（クリエイティブ）とは、そのかけらの群れをカタチにすること。

優れたデザインは出会った瞬間、新鮮な驚きと共にスッとカラダに入ってくるのは、多くの人に共通する記憶のかけらを持っているからだ。

「赤ちゃんのような触り心地」「木が風化した感じの丸み」「早春っぽい香り」、本当に体験していなくても記憶のかけらを組み合わせた知識が想像をカタチにする。

「〜のような」「〜っぽい」「〜な感じ」は創造の基礎であり、何かを思い描く気持ちがカタチに込められるのである。

デザインは単なる表現のカタチだが、その背景にある思いや気持ちがいっぱい込められているのである。

気持ちはいっぱいだけど表現は簡潔なほうが良い場合が多い。

記憶の破片でパズルを

東京スカイツリー®の足元に水族館をつくる計画に参加した。まさに都心の水族館である。

水族館に行く楽しみは、不思議な水生生物に出会い、その生態を間近に観察できることだろう。

シンボルを考えるにあたり、この多様な生き物たちをパズルのように組み合わせて表現する方法を提案した。

三角形を基本モデュールに、記憶をたどりつくってみる。エビ、カメ、ペンギン、カニ、クラゲ、スタッフと一緒に子どもたちも楽しく制作した。

メインのシンボルマークは水族館を象徴する「さかな」。記憶されているカタチの「原形」を見つけることは、誰もが理解できるルートを探すことである。

(すみだ水族館 二〇一二年ー)

Fragments of Memories in Puzzle Form

I helped plan the construction of an aquarium at the base of the TOKYO SKYTREE®—a truly urban aquarium. Encountering strange aquatic creatures and observing their environments is what makes going to the aquarium fun, so when choosing logos for the aquarium I suggested representing those creatures in puzzle-like collections of pieces. Using the triangle as my base shape, I set off recalling animals from memory and giving them form. Shrimp. Turtles... Penguins! The staff joined in. Don't forget crabs. Or jellyfish! We were like a group of big children just having fun. Being the aquariums most representative creature, the fish was chosen for the main logo. Discovering a memory's most basic form is about searching for that which is universally recognizable.

(Sumida Aquarium, 2012–)

ロゴデザイン案の数々
A selection of logo design options

SUMIDA AQUARIUM
すみだ水族館

すみだ水族館地勢仮想断面図
Cross Section of Virtual Geographical Figures of Sumida Aquarium

- 自然水景 / Natural Aquascape
- クラゲ / Jellyfish
- サンゴ礁 / Coral Reefs
- 東京湾・東京諸島 / Tokyo Bay and Tokyo Islands
- ペンギン・オットセイ / Penguins and Fur Seals
- イシサンゴ / Hard Coral
- サンゴ / Typical Co…

0 / -10 / -20 / -30 / -40

CO_2 / 炭素

Types
- 浮遊植物 / Free-Floating Plants
- 沈水植物 / Submerged Plants
- 浮葉植物 / Floating-Leaved Plants

クラゲの種類
Types of Jellyfish

- ミズクラゲ / Moon jelly / Aurelia aurita
- アカクラゲ / Brown jellyfish / Chrysaora melanaster
- タコクラゲ / Papuan jelly / Mastigias papua
- ハナガサクラゲ / Flower hat jelly / Olindias formosa
- カブトクラゲ / A kind of lobate ctenophore / Bolinopsis mikado

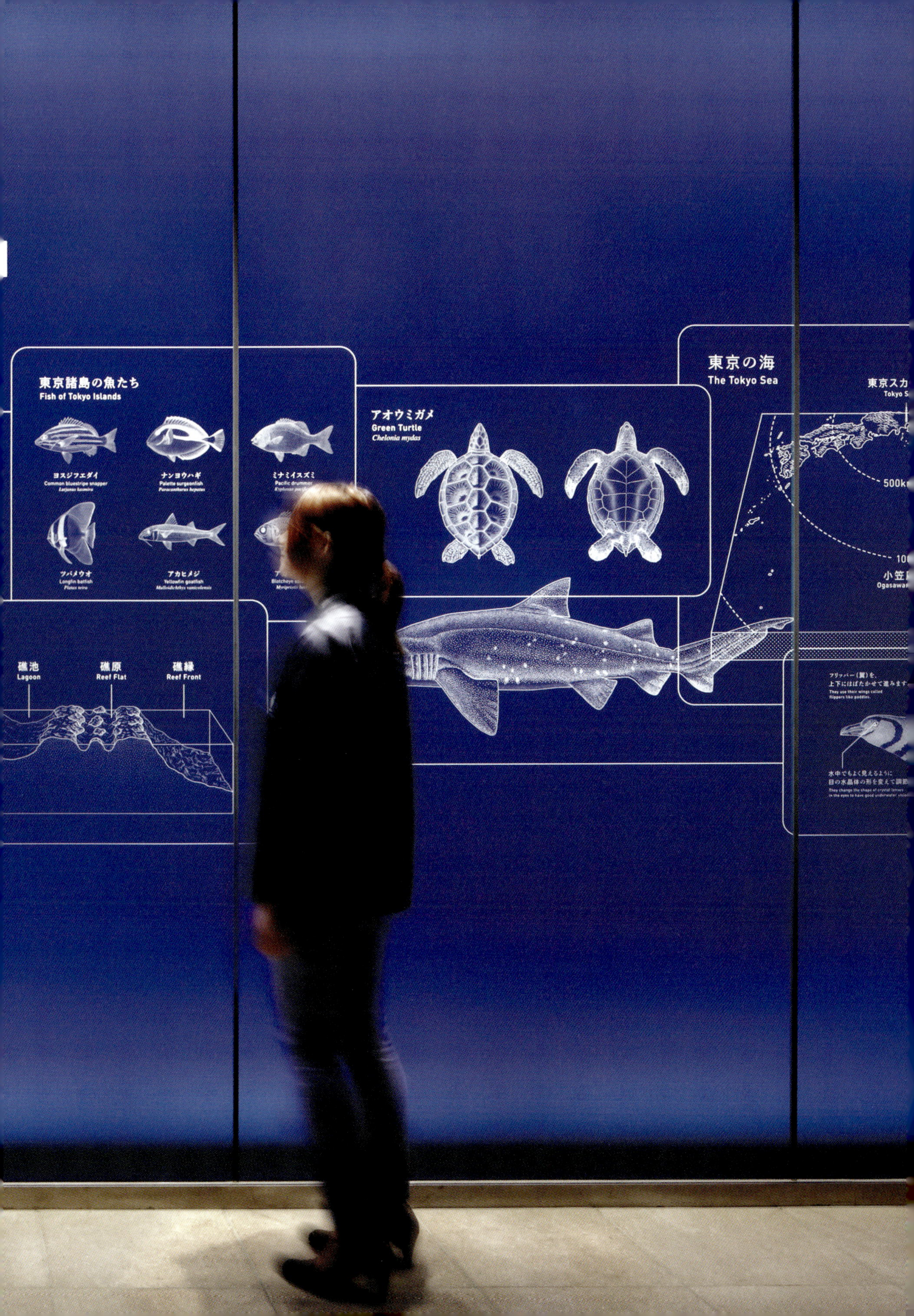

東京諸島の魚たち
Fish of Tokyo Islands
ヨスジフエダイ
Common bluestripe snapper
ナンヨウハギ
Palette surgeonfish
Paracanthurus hepatus
ミナミイスズミ
ツバメウオ
Longfin batfish
アカヒメジ
Yellowfin goatfish
アオウミガメ
Green Turtle
Chelonia mydas
東京の海
The Tokyo Sea
礁池
Lagoon
礁原
Reef Flat
礁縁
Reef Front

Unlike most seaside aquariums, Sumida Aquarium stays open until nighttime. Many of the visitors are adults stopping by on the way home from work or perhaps while out for an evening walk. With this in mind, I proposed a concept for the aquarium that I termed "Sense Knowledge." The goal would be to create an atmosphere that would stimulate the senses as well as the intellect. Descriptions on aquarium signage would include stippled illustrations. I envisioned visitors feeling as if they were flipping through pages of an old encyclopedia as they wandered around the aquarium, immersed in the vast world of the ocean's depths.

海辺の水族館と違い、「すみだ水族館」は夜も開館している。仕事帰りでも、夜の散歩がてらにも寄ることができるので、来館する客層も成人が多くなる。そこで水族館の考え方を「Sense Knowledge」と提案した。感覚的にこの空間を楽しんでもらうことに加え、知性も刺激できれば嬉しい。サインデザインでは、説明の図版を点描のイラストレーションにすることで事典のページをめくるように館内を回遊し、海洋の世界に浸ってほしいと考えた。

上段：すみだ水族館×葛飾北斎ポスター
下段左：ペンギン赤ちゃん誕生ポスター　下段右：「BLUE NIGHT AQUARIUM」ポスター
Top: Sumida Aquarium Posters (Hokusai Theme)
Bottom Left: Poster "A Penguin is Born."
Bottom Right: BLUE NIGHT AQUARIUM Event Poster

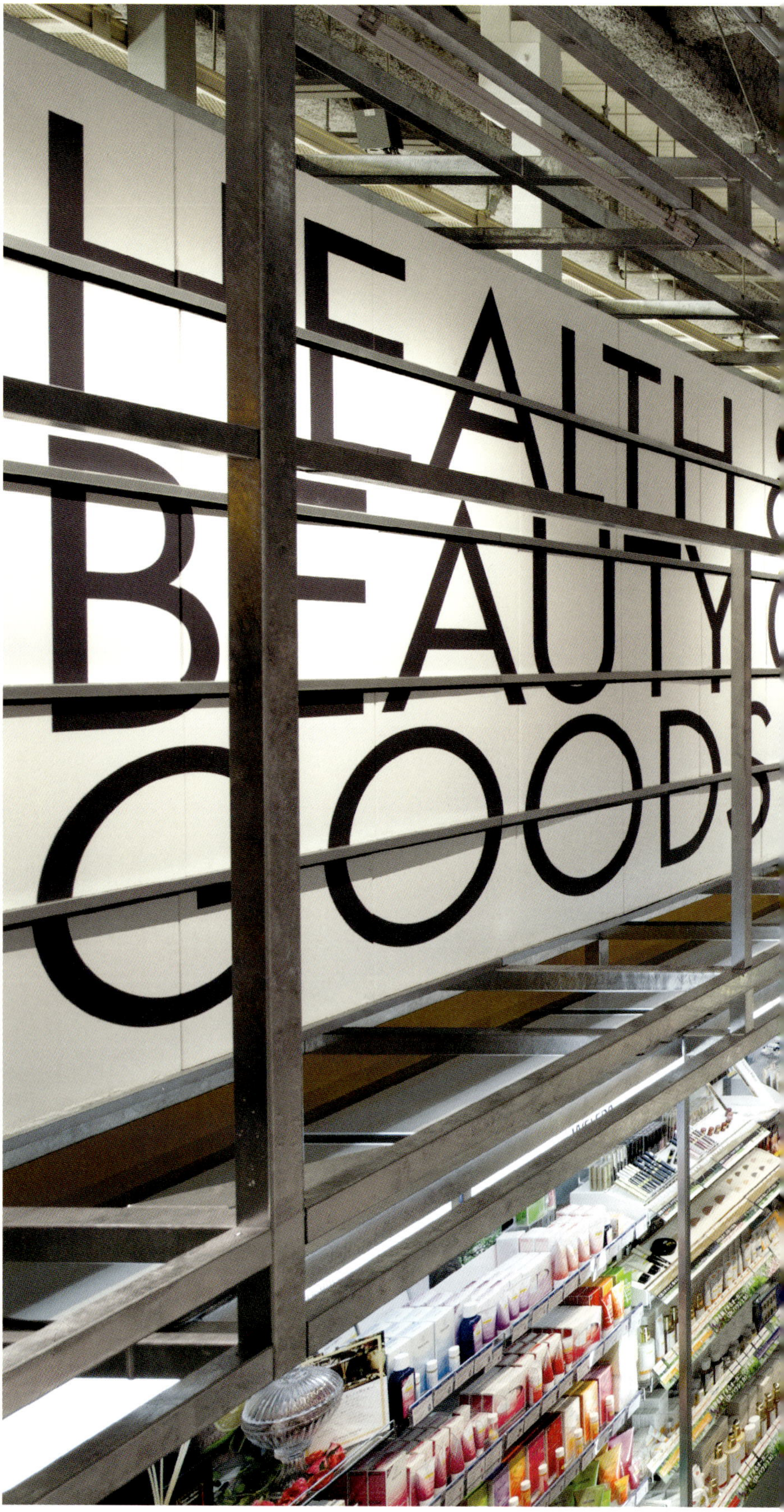
HEALTH
BEAUTY
GOODS

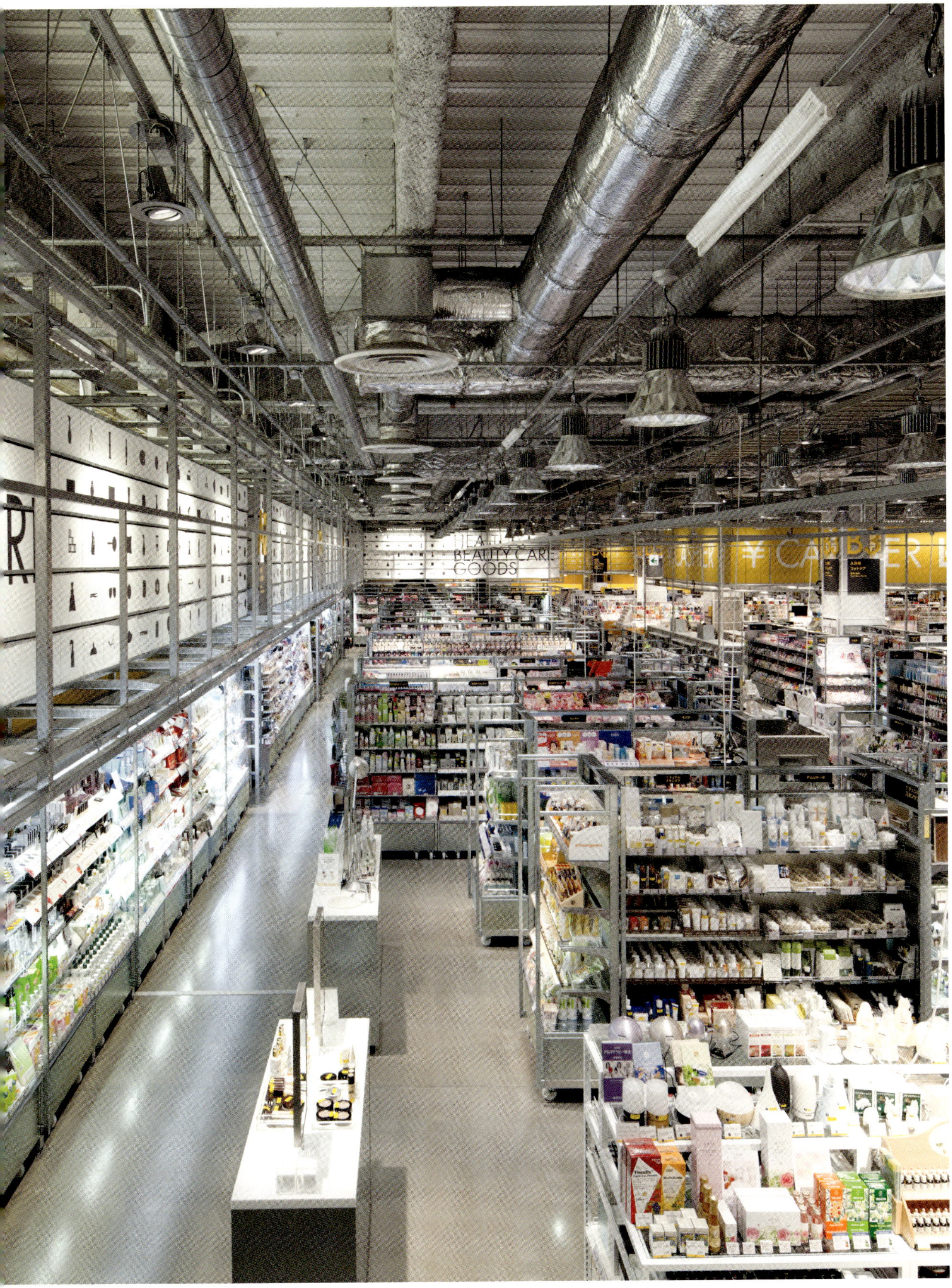
TEA
BEAUTY CARE
GOODS

蔵と市

新しいロフトが有楽町にオープンした。かつて東京宝塚劇場が改築のため仮に公演していたところだ。エントランスは元ロビー、客席だったところが売り場になる。天井高は六メートル以上、工場か格納庫のようである。そう言えばロフトができて二五年。はじめは「大人の屋根裏部屋」、売り場は「蔵と市」というコンセプトだった。だったらこの「蔵」のような空間に、二階部分の「屋根裏」をつくろうということになった。二階にはダンボールが積み上がり、ロフトの扱う商品がシルエットで描かれている。空間の意識化とサインデザインとしての効果を期待した。
（有楽町ロフト 二〇一一年）

Warehouse | Market

LOFT opened a new location in Yurakucho in a building that was once used as a temporary performance hall while the Takarazuka Theater underwent reconstruction. What was once a lobby is now the entrance, and what was once audience seating is now the sales floor. With a ceiling that stands at over 6 meters high, you might guess it was a factory, or perhaps a hangar. It's been 25 years since LOFT first opened. The original store concept was "a loft for adults" while the sales floor concept was defined as "Warehouse | Market." So we decided to take this warehouse-like building and transform the second floor area into a loft. Cardboard boxes with silhouettes of LOFT merchandise printed on them are stacked up on the second floor, calling attention to the area while also serving as sales floor signage.
(Yurakucho LOFT, 2011)

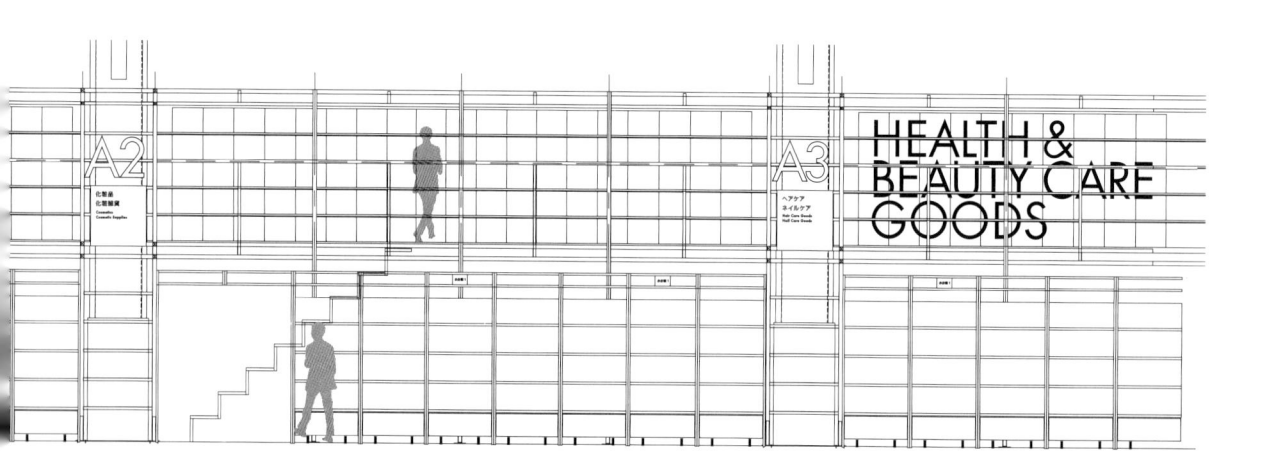

075

SYNQA
ITOKI Tokyo Innovation Center

A Space for Clouds

A reassessment of the value and importance of spaces is underway. We must seriously consider why we go to a place, and whether or not there is an actual need for that space. SYNQA is an innovation center created by ITOKI. The newly coined name SYNQA shares the same pronunciation with the Japanese words for "evolution" and "intensification." Rather than simply being an instrument to be used by businesses, the center was developed to facilitate the creation of new business through external cooperation.

While ideas and creativity are intangible, we often picture them taking form overhead. I imagined them floating in the air like fluffy clouds when I designed the center's glass partitions.

(ITOKI Tokyo Innovation Center SYNQA, 2013)

クラウドな空間

「場」の価値や、意味が問い直されている。なぜその場所に行くのか。本当にその空間が必要なのかをとことん考察しなくてはならない。

イトーキがイノベーションセンターとして開設した「SYNQA」。進化と深化を重ねた造語だ。事務機器だけではなく、外部との協業により、新しいビジネスを生み出す場としてつくられた。

アイデアや創造力は見えないが、生まれるイメージがある。ふわふわしたクラウド（雲）のように浮いている空間を想像してパーテーションのガラスにデザインした。

（イトーキ東京イノベーションセンター SYNQA 二〇一三年）

癒される時間

アヤナとは、サンスクリット語で「安息の地」。欧州名門ホテルのフランチャイズだったバリ島のホテルがリニューアルするにあたり、独自のブランドを開発したいとの話で始まった。新しい名称に含まれる意味。リゾートとは何か、癒される場所・時間とは何か、を考えた。たおやかに絡まるツタに思いを込めた。爽やかなブルーが白地に新鮮に映る。数年後、新たに森をテーマにしたリンバもできた。

（アヤナリゾート&スパ バリ 二〇〇九年／リンバ ジンバラン バリ by アヤナ 二〇一三年）

AYANA
Resort and Spa

RIMBA
Jimbaran
BALI

海岸へ降りるケーブルカー
Cable car descending to the beach below

Relaxing Time

Ayana is a Sanskrit word meaning "place of refuge." Previously a franchise of a distinguished hotel company in Europe, this Bali hotel approached me about developing its own unique brand to coincide with its impending renewal.
I thought about the meaning behind the hotel's new name, what a resort is, and what we envision when we talk about a soothing place or a relaxing time.
I felt like a gracefully entwined ivy plant was a fitting embodiment of these ideas, and I colored it a refreshing blue to lend it a vibrant presence on the white background.
Several years later I also designed the new RIMBA logo, for which I adopted a forest theme.
(Ayana Resort and Spa BALI, 2009 / RIMBA Jimbaran Bali by AYANA, 2013)

リンバ日傘
RIMBA Parasol

空のほとりで逢いましょう。

夢よ、もう一度

かつて、百貨店の屋上には遊園地があった。子どもたちの夢は休日に百貨店の屋上で遊び、大食堂でお子様ランチを食べることだった。日本全体が同じ夢を見ていた幸せな時代だったかもしれない。多様化が進み、ショッピングの方法も家族の楽しみ方も変わった今、百貨店の屋上が復活した。池袋の西武百貨店の屋上に、四季の植物を植え、壁面を緑化し、池や水盤を配して、まるで印象派の絵画のような空間をつくりあげた。かつての遊園地とは違う、憩いの場ができた。コピーは「空のほとりで逢いましょう。」
（西武池袋本店 九階屋上 食と緑の空中庭園 二〇一五年）

Return of the Dream

The department store rooftop was once a place for amusement parks. Children dreamt of spending their holidays playing on the rooftop before sitting down to a kid's meal in the food court. Perhaps all of Japan shared this dream, even. Those were the good days. Diversification has led to changes in how we shop and spend time with our families, but the department store rooftop is making its return. At the Seibu Department Store in Ikebukuro, we transformed the rooftop into something resembling an Impressionist painting. Seasonal plants spot the area and thick greenery covers the walls. Water basins and ponds are strategically placed throughout. The result—a place to relax and enjoy oneself—is similar to, yet quite the departure from the amusement parks of long ago. The accompanying tagline: "Meetings at the Edge of the Sky."
(SEIBU IKEBUKURO Roof Garden, 2015)

開拓のしるし

鉄道がもたらした効果は大きい。蒸気であれ、電気であれ、鉄の塊が力強く動くさまは心が踊る。鉄道博物館は子どもから大人まで人気の施設で年間約一〇〇万人が入館する。産業革命から始まった鉄道の歴史。新しい時代、新しい文化を開拓してきた証にシンボルマークは三つの車輪。シンプルで力強く、この博物館が常に進化し続ける運動体であることを示している。
（鉄道博物館　二〇〇七年）

The Mark of Progress

Trains and the railway changed just about everything. Whether steam-powered or electric, these huge masses of iron are overwhelmingly powerful and seeing them charge forth fills us with excitement.
THE RAILWAY MUSEUM is popular among both children and adults, with around one million visitors each year. The history of the railway began with the industrial revolution. It blazed the path for a new era and new culture. I designed a symbol consisting of three train wheels to represent this. Simple yet powerful, this logo mark would also signify the continued evolution of the museum itself as it blazes forward into the future.
（THE RAILWAY MUSEUM, 2007）

職人の魂

鍛冶の町として知られる新潟県三条市。
新しい包丁シリーズのシンボルを考えた。
職人が用いる「掴み箸」という道具をモチーフに
手づくりの和包丁を職人がていねいに、
ひとつひとつ使う人に届けたい、という
気持ちをカタチにした。
(庖丁工房タダフサ　二〇一二年)

Spirit of the Smith

I had set out to design a logo for a new series of kitchen knives forged in Sanjo, Niigata, known as "the city of smiths." I chose the smith's tongs as a motif to represent the smith's desire to provide each and every customer with carefully hand-crafted Japanese knives.
(TADAFUSA, 2012)

buchi

ふちを彩る

木のぬくもりを感じるおもちゃである。豊かなカタチは「ふち」が彩色され、木の素材感とのバランスがすばらしい。ネーミングは「buchi」。おもちゃのシルエットを想像させるロゴタイプとカラーリングにした。
(buchi 二〇一二年)

Coloring in Edges

The wood construction of this toy lends it a sense of warmth. Each of the toy's many shapes has colored edges that contrast beautifully with its wooden material. The name: buchi. For the logo I chose a design and coloring scheme reminiscent of the toy's form.
(buchi, 2012)

084

Great Circle of Unification, Flags Flown for the Future

The Great East Japan Earthquake may very well have changed the lives of all the people of Japan. We were forced to reevaluate the meaning of life, our values, and what our hometowns, work, and family meant to us. When designing the layout for an event promoting revitalization after the disaster, I decided to organize it so that everyone there would form a single circle—representing cooperation—and flags of hope would be flown to introduce local products. Together we are strong.
(TOHOKU DESIGN MARCHE, 2012)

おおきな輪と旗印

東日本大震災はすべての日本人の生き方を変えたのかもしれない。命、価値、ふるさと、仕事、家族、あらゆる意味が揺らいだ。復興のためにイベントが開催されることになり、みんながひとつの輪になって、力を合わせるカタチをつくった。希望の旗を立て、地元の産品を紹介する。気持ちがひとつになって力が湧いてくる。
（東北デザインマルシェ　二〇一二年）

Shape with Meaning

Graphic design is two-dimensional. The world of one's imagination is brought to life on paper, which can then be taken anywhere in the world. It uses words and mixtures of colors in order to convey information. Architecture is the thing that graphic design aspires to. Architecture is real, existing right there before your eyes. Though years or decades may pass, it remains. And there is a reason behind where it stands. From the outer appearance to the innermost corners, there is intent behind every piece of the design. From the positions of the door handles to the joints of the tiles, there is a reason for every detail.
And the reason for its existence defines how people use it. There is a reason for a piece of architecture's shape. And because of this, graphic design can represent the meaning behind its existence in illustrated form.

カタチの意味

グラフィックデザインは平面のデザイン。紙の上に想像の世界をつくり、世界中どこでも持ち運べる。文字を使い、色彩を調合して情報を操ることが役目である。そしてグラフィックデザインが憧れるのが建築。すべてがリアルにそこに在る。何年も何十年もその場所にある。その場所でなくてはならない理由がある。だから設計の意図は外観から内部まで行き渡る。取手の位置からタイルの目地まで理由がある。そして存在の意味は人との関わり方を示している。グラフィックデザインは、建築の存在する意味を図にすることができる。建築のカタチに理由があるからだ。

今治市伊東豊雄建築ミュージアム（2011年）
Toyo Ito Museum of Architecture, Imabari, 2011

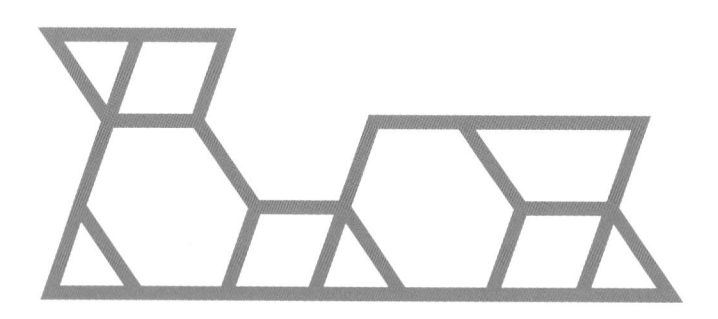

愛媛県今治市大三島町にある美術館。伊東豊雄さんの建築作品が展示されている。
The architectural works of Toyo Ito are on display at this Omishima museum, located in Imabari, Ehime.

今治市岩田健母と子のミュージアム（2011年）
Ken Iwata Mother and Child Museum, Imabari City, 2011

愛媛県今治市大三島町にある美術館。母と子をモデルにした岩田健さんの彫刻作品が展示されている。
Ken Iwata's sculptures, modeled after mothers and children, are on display at this Omishima art museum, located in Imabari, Ehime.

ヤオコー川越美術館 三栖右嗣記念館（2009年）
Yaoko Kawagoe Museum Yuji Misu Memorial Hall, 2009

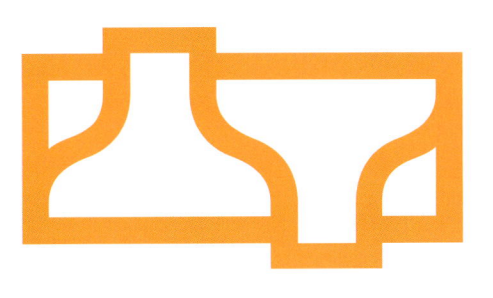

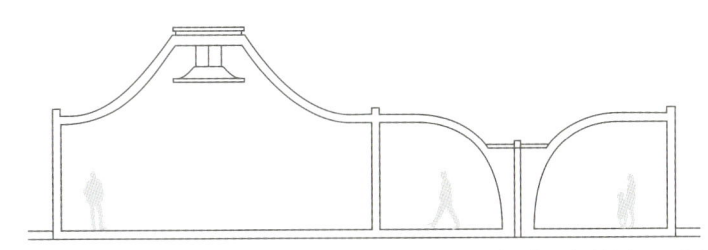

埼玉県川越市氷川町にある美術館。埼玉県に所縁の深い洋画家 三栖右嗣さんの作品が展示されている。
The works of painter Yuji Misu, who had strong ties to Saitama, are on display at this Hikawa art museum, located in Kawagoe, Saitama.

5 | Inviting Decorum

Am I right or wrong? We ask ourselves this question countless times. What you think is right is not always accepted. Changing values in society dictate what people judge as acceptable or unacceptable. National norms and values become the rule of law. At the family level, those norms result in moral principles. Social norms differ with geography and evolve with time, so they are variable.

During the initial launch of mobile phones, people were often found using the phone on the train or while driving, because they wanted to show off their new piece of technology. However, the influence of law has changed how people use their mobile devices due to safety concerns. When a society-changing device, such as a mobile phone, is introduced, new norms are also introduced.

Some norms are not necessarily enforced by laws, such as morals. So the only consequences are at the social level. The influence of morals can be seen in many aspects of our lives from daily activities to religious practices. Moral principles provide peace and order in our communities.

Design does have a role in this aspect. For example, peace and order is promoted at busy places such as airports or train stations with the effective support of clear and easy to understand signage. This allows for the efficient and safe flow of pedestrians. Visitors can easily find the toilet, destination, departure time, etc., without having to read or speak the local language.

Design can also create the joy of experiencing something new. It can be likened to, an efficient security system that does not require the stress of requiring a complicated line. Design should enhance the positives of spending time in a new place. In that sense, design is different from reinforcing regulation. It aims to ease tension and minimize the stress of encountering an unfamiliar culture. Design creates a sense of discovery and joy, which in turn, introduces peace and order.

五、秩序を誘う

自分は正しいのか、間違っているのか、人は常に自問を繰り返す。自分の正しさは社会の正しさではないときもあるからだ。そのような社会的な判断をするときの尺度として「基準」が生まれた。国家の基準は法律になり、家庭の基準は家訓になる。正しさは地域によっても変わるし、時代によっても変化するので、絶対的ではない。

携帯電話が世の中に出始めた頃、自慢げに電車の中やクルマを運転しながら会話をする人を見かけたが、今はほとんどいない。周りに迷惑をかけ、事故が多発するので法規制されたからだ。新たに経験するモノごとには新たな基準が発生するのである。

基準ではあるが、規制がないのがモラルである。モラルはルールではないので、罰則がない。毎日の生活から宗教的な思想まで、私たちは多様なモラルの中で暮らしている。モラルはコミュニティの秩序なのだ。

そしてデザインは秩序を見えるカタチにすることができる。駅や空港など多くの人々が利用する場所では、素早く速やかに行動をサポートするためにサインデザインが有効に機能している。行き先、ゲート、出発時間、トイレなど言葉が分からなくてもスムーズにたどり着ける。

そしてデザインは新たに体験する喜びも生む。争って並ぶ必要のないセキュリティのシステム、特別な場所で過ごす楽しみや期待の演出、他国の文化に交わる多少の緊張感など、秩序は規制して整えるものではなく、ストレスを軽減して誘発するものである。デザインによる発見や喜びが新しい秩序をつくる。

9h

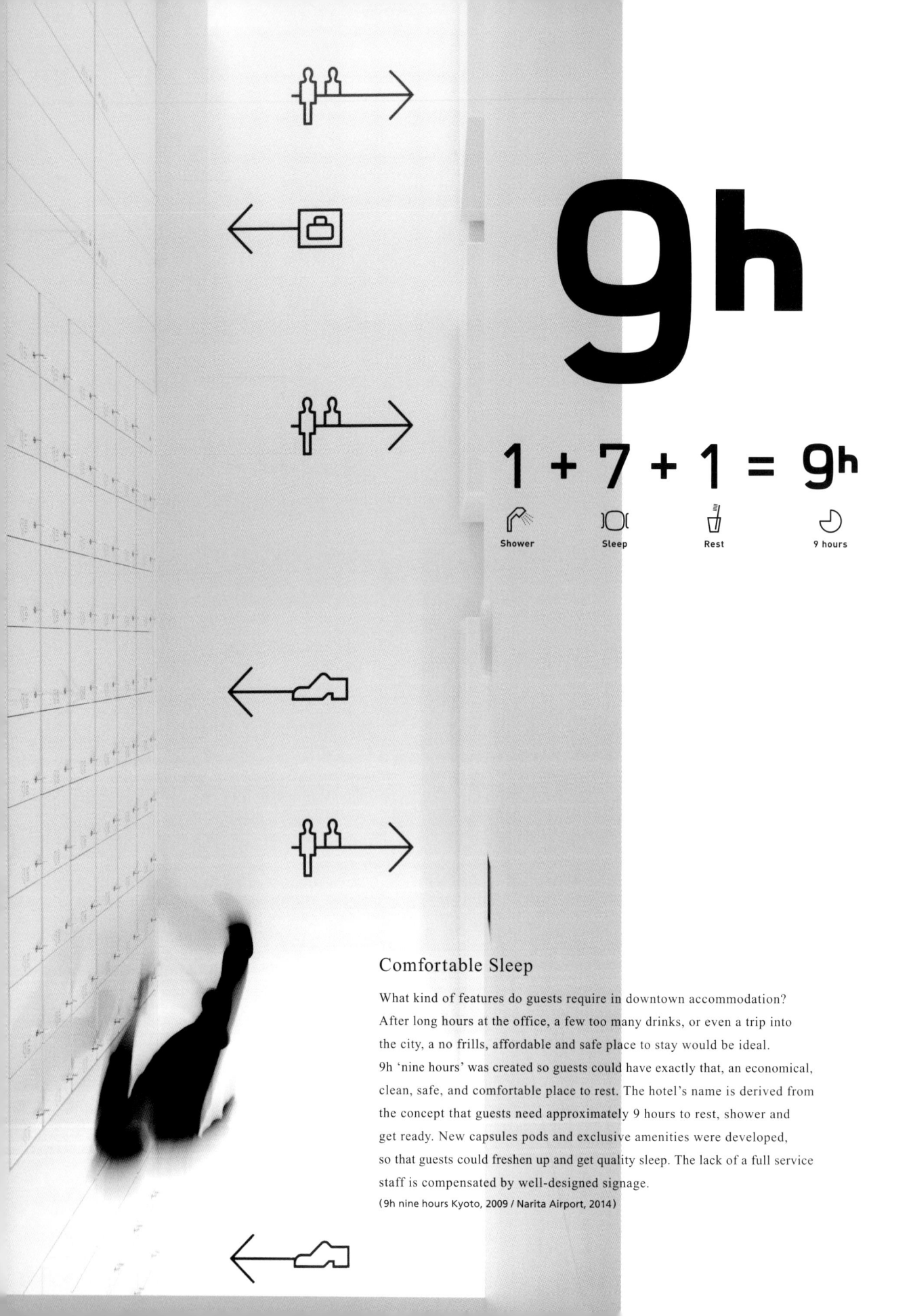

$1 + 7 + 1 = 9^h$

Shower Sleep Rest 9 hours

Comfortable Sleep

What kind of features do guests require in downtown accommodation? After long hours at the office, a few too many drinks, or even a trip into the city, a no frills, affordable and safe place to stay would be ideal. 9h 'nine hours' was created so guests could have exactly that, an economical, clean, safe, and comfortable place to rest. The hotel's name is derived from the concept that guests need approximately 9 hours to rest, shower and get ready. New capsules pods and exclusive amenities were developed, so that guests could freshen up and get quality sleep. The lack of a full service staff is compensated by well-designed signage.
(9h nine hours Kyoto, 2009 / Narita Airport, 2014)

快適な眠りだけ

都市の宿泊にはどのような機能が必要だろう。高級を競うホテルではなく、残業や飲み会で遅くなり仕方なく泊まる時、あるいは都市を楽しむ旅行で安く泊まりたい時。清潔で安全で快適な眠りを安い価格で約束する宿泊を考えて「9h（ナインアワーズ）」はつくられた。汗を洗い流す、眠る、身支度をする。この三つの行為を時間に置き換えてネーミングにした。快適な眠りを実現するために新しいカプセルが開発され、それに付随するアメニティも開発し、清潔さ、快適さを追求。そのかわり人的なサービスは無いので、サインがその役割を担う。

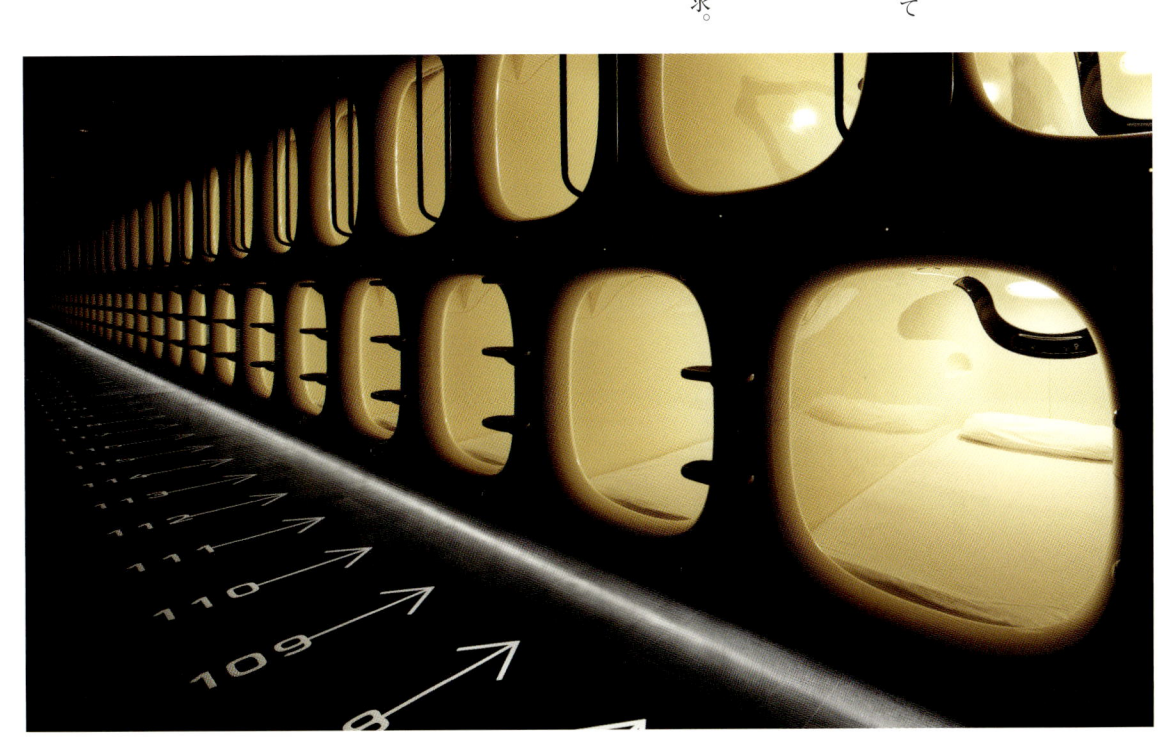

（9h ナインアワーズ 京都 二〇〇九年／成田空港 二〇一四年）

A beneficial aspect of public signs is that they relay information that can be understood by people of different ages and races. At airports or stations, or on the street, even without detailed directions, by following signs people can find their way. At '9h', we incorporated signs to help guests navigate their way around the hotel, in the same manner that pedestrians at a station depend on signs to direct them to where they want to get to. The signs guide guests to gender specific facilities and capsule pods. They also illustrate locker and shower room use. Orientation is smoother and consequently, guests have more time to rest.

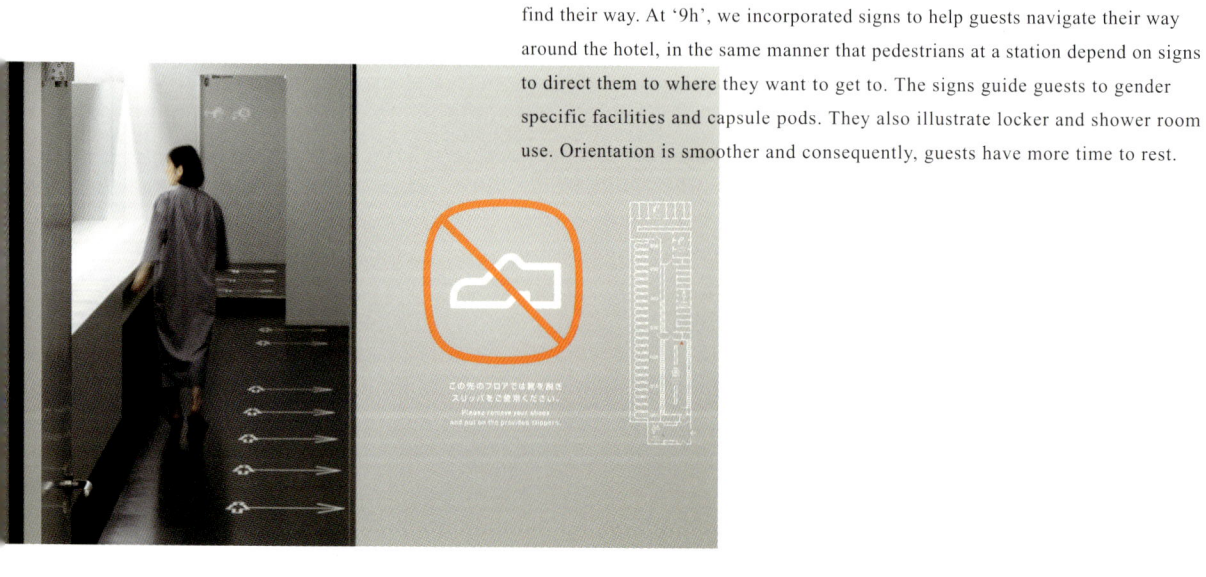

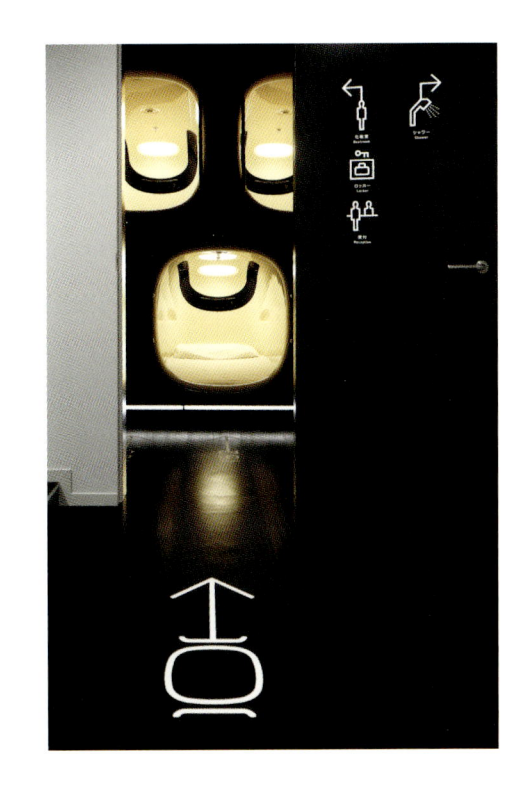

公共のサインデザインが良いところは、年齢や国籍を越えて同じ情報を共有できるところにある。空港や駅、道路など細かくわからなくても大体予想できる。「9h」も、まるで駅のような感覚で人が行動し、目的に導かれることを目指した。男女の振り分け、ロッカーの使い方、シャワーのマナー、自分のカプセルへの誘導。間断なくシームレスに行動し、豊かな眠りをなるべく長く。

093

094

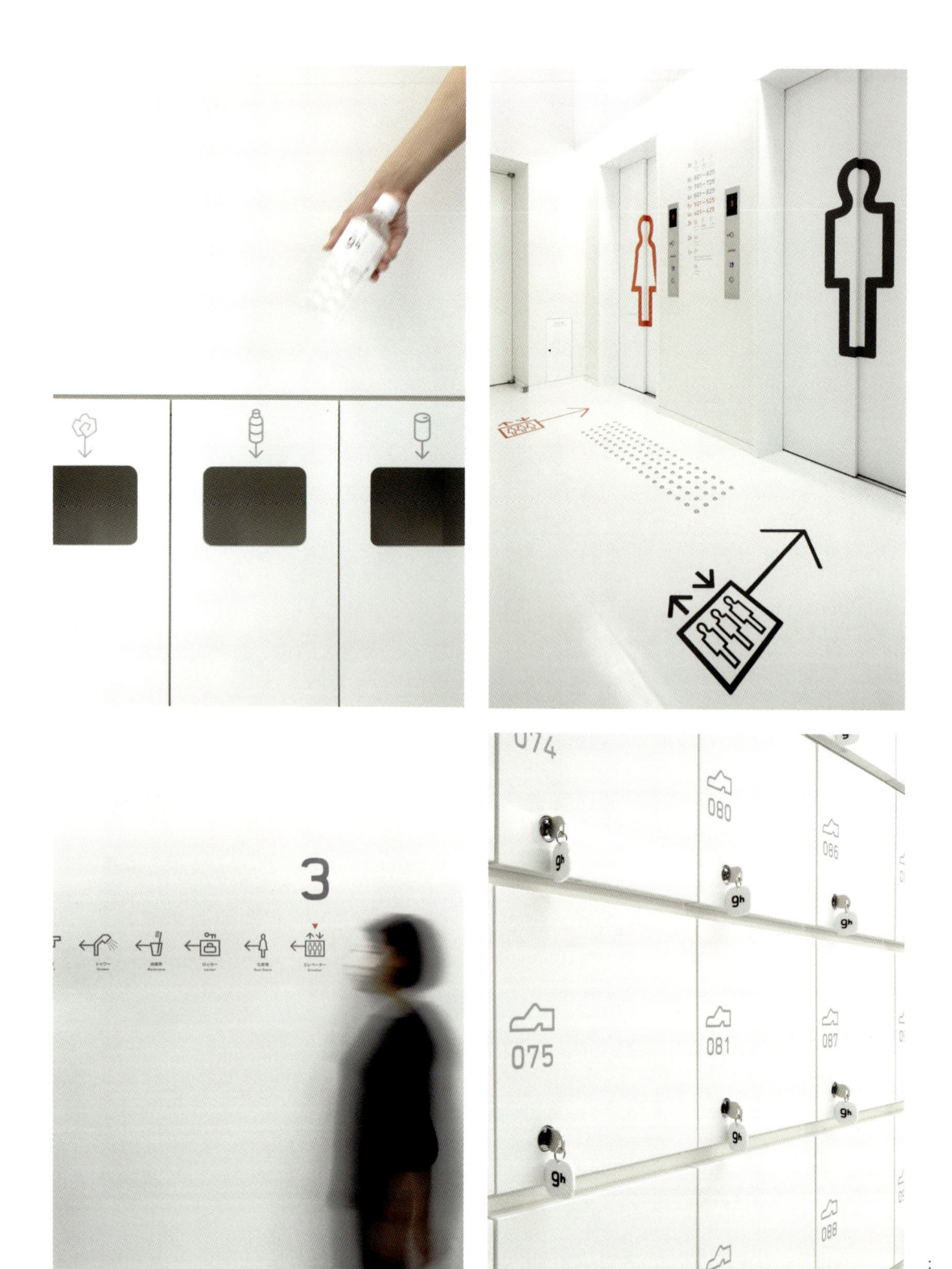

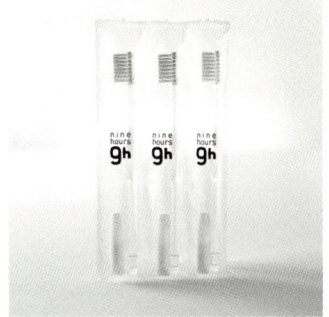

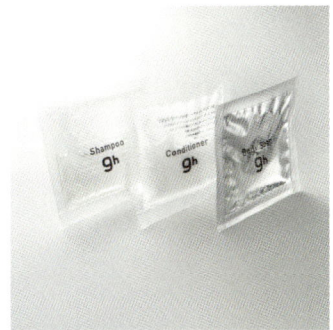

上段左から：スリッパ袋、ミネラルウォーター、歯ブラシ
下段左から：ハンドソープ、シャンプー・コンディショナー・ボディソープ、ルームウェア
From top left to right: Slipper bag, Mineral water, Toothbrush
From bottom left to right: Hand soap, Shampoo / Conditioner / Body soap, Lounge wear

Viewing Order

As online shopping becomes increasingly more integrated into everyday life, consumers have grown to expect next-day delivery. After clicking and ordering a product online, have you ever considered, what the delivery process of receiving your package entails? It is said, in this age of globalization, logistics plays a leading role. The Yamato Group's "Haneda Chronogate" is one of the largest logistics terminals in Japan. To manage the constant flow of delivery trucks within the colossal terminal, clear signage depicting route, location and position, is essential. By applying the stripe themed signs, orderly and seamless movement is accomplished.

(Yamato Group's Conventional Logistics Terminals Haneda Chronogate, 2013)

見るルール

ネットショッピングが一般化し、翌日に品物が届くのがあたりまえの時代になった。クリックした商品がどのような経路をたどってたどり着くのか想像したことがあるだろうか。

今、時代を制するのは物流だと言われている。

この「羽田クロノゲート」はヤマトグループ最大級の物流ターミナル。

ひっきりなしに到着するトラック。サインに必要とされているのは正確な「位置」「経路」「動き」である。連続するストライプにより、この物流ターミナルでのルールを示している。ストライプによって導かれる秩序がシームレスな流れをつくっている。

(ヤマトグループ 羽田クロノゲート 二〇一三年)

和の里
Wanosato

ストライプのサインシステムは、巨大な倉庫では位置を、オフィス棟では行動のルートを示している。また、この物流ターミナルには地域貢献エリア「和の里」という周辺住民に解放した空間がある。ストライプのパターンはここでも共有され、点在する時間にまつわる名言を彫り込んだストライプが、散策する際の楽しみになっている。

In the large logistics terminal, a stripe themed signage system directs workers to different areas, signs depicting work conduct are also on display in the office building. On the premises of the logistics terminal there is a green community area, known as "Wanosato."

As a symbol of co-existing with the community, it is open to the public. The consistent stripe theme extends to the park. Additionally, wise quotes inscribed on the stripes enliven the experience of taking a walk in the park.

上・中央：オフィス棟
下：ヤマトフォーラム（スポーツ施設）
Top & Middle: Office building
Bottom: Yamato Forum (Sport facilities)

情報の建築

人類最高の発明は文字と本だろう。
だから図書館は知の象徴として地域に存在している。
天津図書館は市の文化エリアに、延床面積五五〇〇〇平米五〇〇万冊収蔵という規模で建てられた。
大きく吹き抜けたエントランスホールの上空には壁梁が渡り、本棚が配置されている。
本棚で構成された大空間は、はじめて体験するダイナミズムである。
サインデザインはホールのどこからでも視認できるように壁面に沿って表記されている。
本は情報の建築とも呼ばれている。
立体的な思考で編集デザインを行わなくてはならないからだ。
この建築もまさに情報の知が造形になっていると思う。

（天津図書館　二〇一二年）

A Building of Information

The greatest inventions of mankind are surely writing and books. Libraries exist all over the world as a symbol of knowledge. Tianjin Library, located in the culture district of Tianjin City, is colossal. It has a total floor area of 55,000 square meters and houses 5 million books. Above the reception area, a large clear glass atrium is flanked by book shelves, the shelves are incorporated into the wall beams.
One experience's a new sense of dynamism in this voluminous space filled with books. To ensure visibility, signage is displayed on a wall and can clearly be seen from anywhere in the hall. It has been said, books are a form of architecture as they are constructed with information. Additionally, similar to architecture, the process of publishing a book, from editing to designing a cover, requires three dimensional thinking. The building is an exact architectural depiction of information and knowledge.
(Tianjin Library, 2012)

Modern Design and Photographs

Charles Eames made groundbreaking contributions to the field of modern industrial design. His Aluminum chair and Shell chair still remain popular pieces. Coupled with designing furniture, he also produced films including the well-known "POWERS OF TEN." Work took him extensively around the world and he left behind many photographs documenting his travels. We held an exhibition at Axis Gallery, showcasing Charles Eames's photography and philosophy. From a central perspective in the gallery, photographs were aligned to the left and right, and suspended in midair. To encourage visitors to circulate around the exhibition space, his philosophical quotes were displayed along the outer walls of the gallery.
(CHARLES EAMES Photo Exhibition 100 images × 100 words—A Message from a Great Designer, 2008)

モダンデザインと写真

二〇世紀の工業デザインに大きな影響を与えた人物にチャールズ・イームズがいる。シェルチェアやアルミナムなど現在でも人気の家具である。イームズは家具以外でも、映像作品で有名な「Powers of Ten」などを制作していた。また仕事で世界を巡りながら、多くの写真も残していたのだ。アクシスギャラリーにてイームズの写真と言葉の展覧会を開催した。中央に立つと写真が左右の中空に並び、外周を廻りながら言葉を読む展示演出である。
（チャールズ・イームズ写真展 100 images × 100 words ——偉大なるデザイナーのメッセージ 二〇〇八年）

告知ポスター
Announcement poster

色と紙

紙と暮らしの関わりは長くて深い、いくら社会のデジタル化が進んでも紙のアフォーダンスを再現するのは難しい。特種東海製紙の「Ｐａｍ」をリニューアルした。紙の歴史は日本の歴史と深く関わっており、戦時中の軍のための開発品、東京オリンピックの専用ポスター用紙、証紙や商品券などの偽造防止技術、最近では放射能のセシウムを吸収する紙も開発している。印刷用紙やパッケージ用紙も多く開発しており、「ＴＡＮＴ」という名前のファンシーペーパーは現在一三一色という世界一の色数を持っている。全紙の「ＴＡＮＴ」をすべて並べて展示してみると、それだけで圧倒的な開発力を体感することができる。

（Pam 二〇〇四年）

Paper and Color

Paper plays an integral role in life; therefore the two have a long and intertwined relationship. Despite the rapid digitization of our society, paper is not so easily replaced. We refurbished Pam, owned by Tokushu Tokai Paper Co., Ltd. The history of paper has evolved along with the history of Japan. Paper has been developed for a variety of purposes in Japan, to include military use, Olympic advertising, and even anti-counterfeit products for use with stamps and gift certificates. More recently, paper has been used to absorb radioactive cesium. Furthermore, a wide variety of printer paper and packaging paper have been developed. The premium paper brand TANT comes in 131 colors.
TANT boasts the widest color range in the world. The museum illustrates the company's outstanding progress in the paper making industry.
(Pam, 2004)

Life Changing Packaging

Package design plays an important role in modern markets. Initially, packaging was only used to protect or preserve products. The emergence of mass produced and consumed commodities altered that notion and package design began to be developed.
Generally, the design of the packaging should aim to be eye-catching and thereby enhance the sales factor. However, we were given the opportunity to design packaging with a completely different objective. "Sysmex" produces medical products that enable health analysis through in-vitro testing. We were tasked to design packaging for reagents. Strict instructions had to be relayed on the packaging as correct handling is crucial.
As the reagents are distributed all over the world, given the differences in language; we used icons, colors and symbols which could be universally understood.
(Sysmex, 2011)

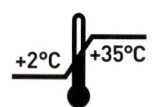

生命に関わるパッケージ

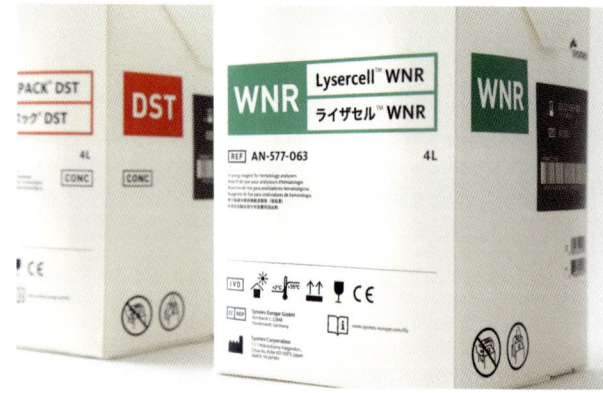

物々交換だった時代は、パッケージにデザインは必要なかった。パッケージは物を保護するために存在していたからだ。大量生産し大量消費する時代になり、パッケージデザインは発達した。商品の差別化、目立って売れることがデザインの目的なのだ。しかしまったく別の目的のパッケージデザインをすることになった。「シスメックス」という医療メーカーが販売する検査用試薬のパッケージデザイン。商品を取り違うことは絶対に許されない。全世界に発送されるので言語共通で理解できるアイコンを利用し、色彩と記号でわかりやすい表記を目指した。
（シスメックス　二〇一一年）

清潔で機能的

東北の震災以降、電気の使用について日本全体が少し敏感になり、オール電化と叫ばれた住宅環境も、多様的に考えられている。トイレで手を洗った後、送風で乾燥する機器が定着したが、ペーパータオルの使用も徐々に増えてきた。今やペーパータオルは手拭きだけではなく、キッチンで生鮮品の水切りや保湿に使われている。「タウパー」の新しいパッケージは印刷面積を少なくすることで、従来問題になっていた印刷のこすれを解消しつつ、コストの軽減をした。各銘柄の特徴と使用用途を共通のアイコンで記号化し、ブランド全体の統一感を図った。
（タウパー 二〇一二年）

再生紙使用　二枚重ね　食品使用可能　手ふき使用可能

Clean and Functional

Following the Great East Japan Earthquake, the nation has shifted their awareness regarding energy use. Given the amount of electronics in the home, there has been more consideration concerning how these products consume energy. An example of this can be seen in restrooms, many people use electric hand dryers but a growing number of people are opting to use paper towels. Further, paper towels can be used in the kitchen to wipe the counter or clean off fresh produce. As a solution to minimize smudging caused by printing, Towper's packaging was redesigned to contain less print. This also had the added benefit of cost reduction. Icons representing product features and usage were used consistently, resulting in a more unified brand identity.
(Towper, 2012)

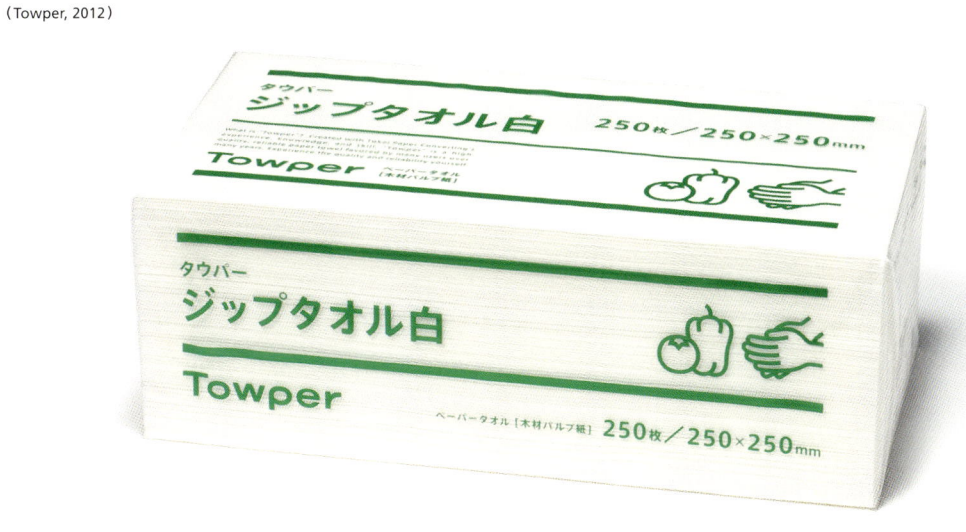

6 | Awakened Memories

Measurements and sizes always have a reason or origin behind them. Take for example the traditional English measurements of inches and feet; the former originally defined as the length from the tip of the thumb to the first knuckle joint, the latter as the length between the tip of the toe and the heel. There are also similar examples of traditional units of measurement in Japan: the tsue (total body length, or height), hiro (the width of both hands spread apart), and ata (the length between the tips of the thumb and the index finger). The ideal length of chopsticks was traditionally standardized to 'one and a half ata', or approximately 24 centimeters.

There are also accurate methods of measurement memorized internally by the body. For example, a traditional Edo-style piece of sushi is just the right size to eat in one mouthful. It is said that a well-trained sushi chef can press each piece into shape with a consistent weight of 20 grams and 240 grains of rice. We find an easy and immediate affinity with designs that are born from physical experience and memory, without resorting to any logic or theory. Physicality in industrial design or costume design is obvious, but it is also an important part of graphic design.

Japanese notepaper and posters have their own unique standardized system of sizes, divided largely into A-ban and B-ban. These are based on what is known as the hakuginhi, or silver ratio, which has been favored by the Japanese for centuries as a formula for design, from ancient monuments such as Horyuji temple or classical bodhisattva statues to the modern animated characters of Doraemon or Anpanman. Just as sizes based in nature or the human form feel comfortable to us, the shapes and colors of emblems and logotypes too have their own stories of origin that are based on our collective memories and experiences, and therefore appeal to our emotions and seep into our consciousness with ease. They are new visual experiences, and yet they are etched into our memories so effortlessly. An identity that has a visual balance compatible with its origination and upbringing becomes a design that we hold dear and utilize for a long time.

六、呼び起こされる記憶

寸法やサイズには必ず理由がある。いちばん分かりやすいのが体のサイズから生まれたもので、イギリスの「インチ」は親指の先から第一関節までの長さ、「フィート」はつま先からかかとまでの足の長さ。日本では「つえ＝身長」、「ひろ＝両手を伸ばした長さ」、「あた＝親指と人差し指を開いた長さ」などがある。箸の使いやすい寸法は「ひとあたはん」といい約二四センチを基準にしていた。

身体が記憶する正確な計測もある。

江戸前の寿司職人はひとくちで食べるのにちょうどいい大きさ。熟練した寿司職人は一貫二〇グラム、四二〇粒の米で握る。

身体性、体験や記憶から生まれるデザインの親和性は理屈なく素直に入ってくる。

工業デザインや衣装デザインでの身体性はもちろんのことだが、グラフィックでも身体性は重要なポイントである。

日本のノートやポスターはＡ判Ｂ判という独自のサイズ規格。白銀比と呼ばれ、日本人が好んで採用してきた。古くは法隆寺や薬師三尊像からこの白銀比でつくられている。

自然や身体から生まれたサイズが心地よく感じるのと同じように、マークやロゴタイプにもストーリーがあり、多くの人に共通の記憶や体験から呼び起こされたカタチや色は、素直に馴染み、すぅっと気持ちに入って来る。

新たな視覚体験だが心地よく記憶に刻み込まれる。そのように視覚的バランスと生い立ちの相性が良いアイデンティティは永く愛されるものになる。

107

HEALTH & BEAUTY CARE GOODS
TRAVEL ACCESSORIES
美容・健康雑貨　トラベル用品

The Power of the Graphic

Graphic design is planar design, and cannot win against real materials or overwhelming spaces.
However, the two-dimensional is not without its own unique world of possibilities. LOFT in Tachikawa had to be built in a multistoried old building with low ceilings. Furthermore, it had to be a prototype for future stores in its cost-effectiveness. What we proposed was to display large black and white photographs of various products offered by LOFT all around the store space. While clearly defining each section of the store, they were also striking visual props for customers.
(Tachikawa LOFT, 2012)

グラフィックのチカラ

グラフィックデザインは平面のデザイン。
リアルな物質感と圧倒的な空間の感覚には勝てない。
しかし二次元だから可能な世界もある。
立川にロフトを出店する条件は、古いビルで多層階、天井も低い。
そして、今後のプロトタイプになるようにコストも抑えたいということ。
サインデザインで提案したのは、
ロフトで扱う商品をモノクロームの写真で大きく空間に配置するというもの。
各売り場の領域を示すと同時に、ダイナミックな演出を試みた。
(立川ロフト 二〇一二年)

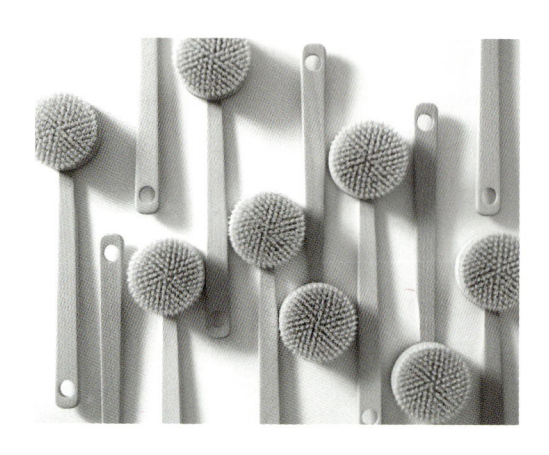

LOFT reportedly has around 100 thousand items on offer. From stationery to household goods to novelty items, around 100 were chosen for photographing. People often think of LOFT's goods as very colorful, but presenting them in black and white imbued them with a new and playful sense of rhythm.

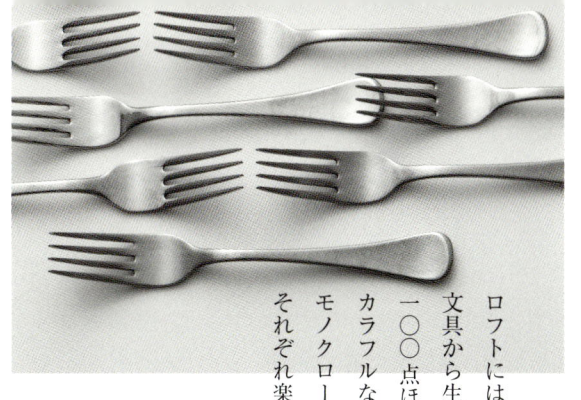

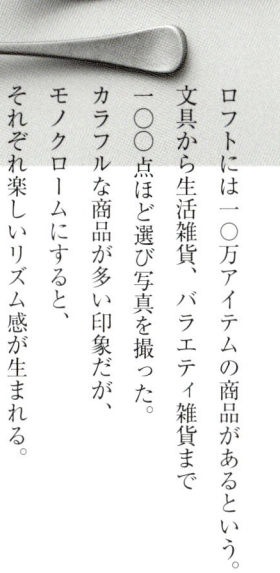

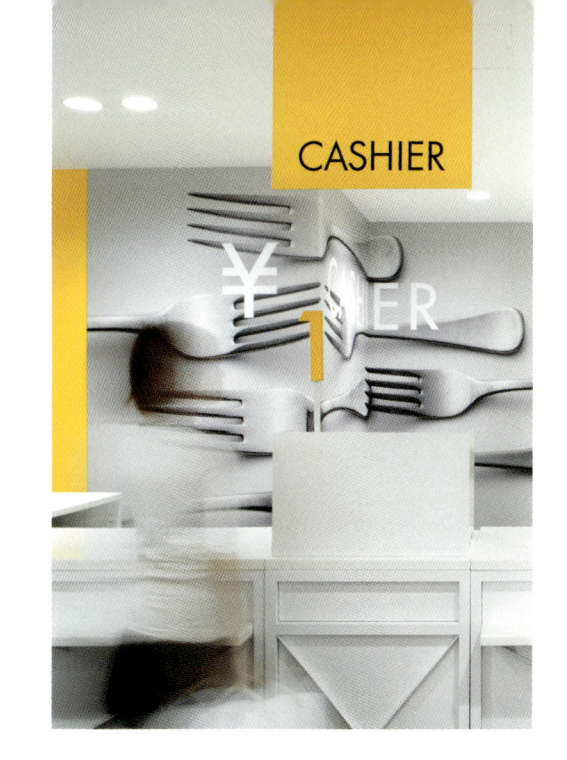

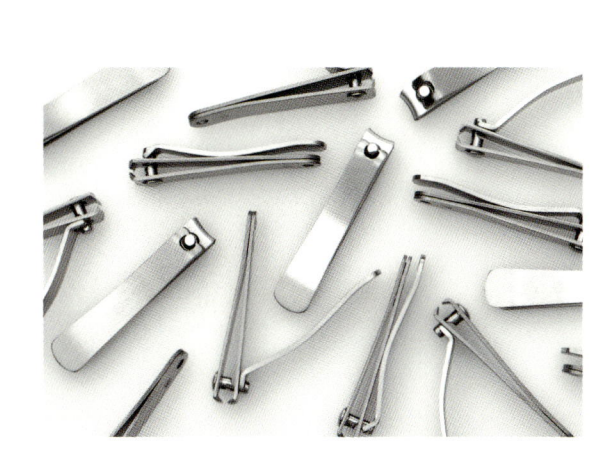

ロフトには一〇万アイテムの商品があるという。文具から生活雑貨、バラエティ雑貨まで一〇〇点ほど選び写真を撮った。カラフルな商品が多い印象だが、モノクロームにすると、それぞれ楽しいリズム感が生まれる。

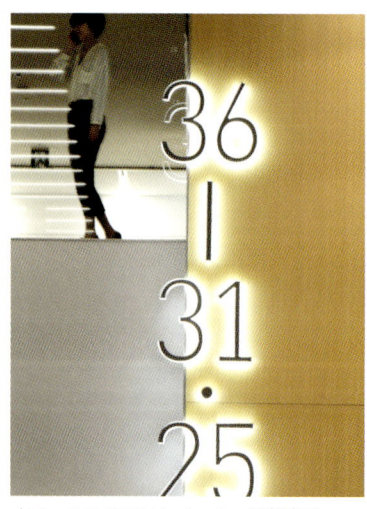

オフィスエリアエレベーター階数表示
Elevator floor display in office area

共用部エレベーター
Shared elevator

時を刻むアイコン

昔から駅には待ち合わせ場所があった。
東京駅の「銀の鈴」、渋谷駅の「ハチ公」、池袋駅の「いけふくろう」、待ち合わせの標が駅のシンボルにもなっている。
大阪の近鉄大阪阿部野橋駅は天王寺駅と地下で繋がる複合ターミナル。地上の再開発に伴い新しい待ち合わせのシンボルを開発した。
「半分の時計」だ。光る天井には巨大な時計の左半分をデザインした。右半分は吹き抜けているので、時計の針だけが空中を廻る。
みんな本当に時間が知りたいわけじゃない、携帯だって持っている。時計という、時を刻むアイコンは意識の発火を生む。
自然に時計の下に人が集まって来るのだ。
その上にそびえるのは「あべのハルカス」。日本一高い。空に向かって伸びるタワーは六つの要素が積み重なっている。
地下の駅部から百貨店、美術館、オフィス、ホテル、展望台。それをサインデザインは段階的な濃度のブルーで表している。
(あべのハルカス 二〇一四年)

Icons Marking the Passage of Time

Train stations have always had meeting spots. The 'silver bell' at Tokyo Station, the Hachiko dog statue at Shibuya Station, or the Ikefukuro owl statuette at Ikebukuro station; all of these landmarks have become definitive symbols for their respective stations. Abenobashi Station in Osaka has now built a terminal building with an underground connection to Tennoji station, and in doing so it has combined the redevelopment of the area with the construction of a new meeting place and symbolic landmark. It is, literally, "half a clock." The illuminated ceiling has been designed in the shape of a giant clock with just the left-hand face. The right-hand side is an atrium, and the clock-hand simply glides across its open space. Of course, people do not congregate here to find out the time; most of them have cellphones. The clock is an icon marking the passage of time, and it is a symbol that kindles our consciousness. People are naturally drawn to the spot underneath this clock. And towering above it is ABENO HARUKAS, currently the tallest building in Japan. This skyscraper has six distinct functions layered on top of one another; from the underground station at the bottom, to a department store, to an art museum, to offices, to a hotel, and finally to an observation deck at the very top. In our 'sign design', we chose to express each of these tiers with a different shade of blue.
(ABENO HARUKAS, 2014)

触れてみたい

遺伝子の反応なのか、幼児体験からくる追感覚欲求なのかわからないが、見ると触れてみたくなる質感がある。フワフワしたぬいぐるみは、子どもでなくてもぎゅっと抱きしめたくなるし、チクチクするブラシの毛先はずっと撫でていたいものだ。渋谷公園通りにあるモヴィーダ館の新しいサインデザインは膨らんだ風船か、お餅のようにプクプクした質感の数字が壁から飛び出すことを考えた。
触感を刺激して思わず触れてみたくなるサインは脳を発火させ、新しい体験の欲求を加速する。
（西武渋谷店 モヴィーダ館 二〇一三年）

The Urge to Touch

Whether it is built into our DNA by nature or acquired from childhood experiences in our nurture is not clear, but there are certain textures that we instinctively feel like touching with our hands. The urge to caress or squeeze a cuddly toy is not an instinct unique to children, for example, and most of us get a distinctive sense of pleasure from stroking the bristly tips of the hairs on a brush. In our new 'sign design' for the MOVIDA Bld. on Shibuya Koen-dori, we came up with the idea of having numbers with a balloon-like, puffed-up texture, protruding from the walls.
Signs that urge us to touch them also stimulate our minds and stir our senses, accelerating our desire for new experiences.
(SEIBU SHIBUYA-MOVIDA Bld., 2013)

7 Loft &
LOFT & Creation
6 Loft &
LOFT & NatuLife
ロフトセレクション
5 無印良品
こども服・マタニティ
4 無印良品
メンズウエア・ステーショナリー
お直し工房
Menswear, Stationery
3 無印良品
レディースウエア
ヘルス＆ビューティー
2 MUJI
カフェ
デリレストラン
Cafeteria & Delicatessen
1 無印良品
自転車
トラベル用品
Bicycle, Travel goods
B1 無印良品
食品・リビングルーム・ベッドルーム
キッチン&ダイニングルーム
Food, Living room, Bedroom
Kitchen & Dining room, Household goods

Narrative Pole

In Native American communities, we find the totem pole. Images of animals, birds, human faces and imaginary beasts were once carved into these wooden poles, as a record of a particular tribe's history and its notable events. Deciphering these engravings provides us with a narrative of the people who used to inhabit the area. We designed a pole sign for Taipei New Horizon, a multipurpose facility located in the Songshan Cultural and Creative Park in central Taipei. The result was a truly modern totem pole, made up of icons signifying various cultural facilities such as cinemas, concert halls, hotels, and offices. Icons piled on top of one another to form a singular objet d'art and symbol of the city, passing on a narrative to future generations.
(Taipei New Horizon, 2014)

物語の柱

アメリカ大陸の先住民が暮らす部落にはトーテムポールが立っている。動物や鳥、人間の顔や想像の怪物などが柱に彫られており、部族の歴史、特別な出来事の記録として立てられていた。ポールの彫像を読み解くと、その土地に暮らした人々の物語が浮かび上がる。台北市の松山文創園区にできた複合施設「臺北文創」で、ポールサインをデザインした。映画館やコンサートホール、ホテルやオフィスなどいろいろな施設のアイコンを積み上げたら現代のトーテムポールになった。アイコンは重なってオブジェになり、街のシンボルとして未来に物語を紡いでいる。

（臺北文創　二〇一四年）

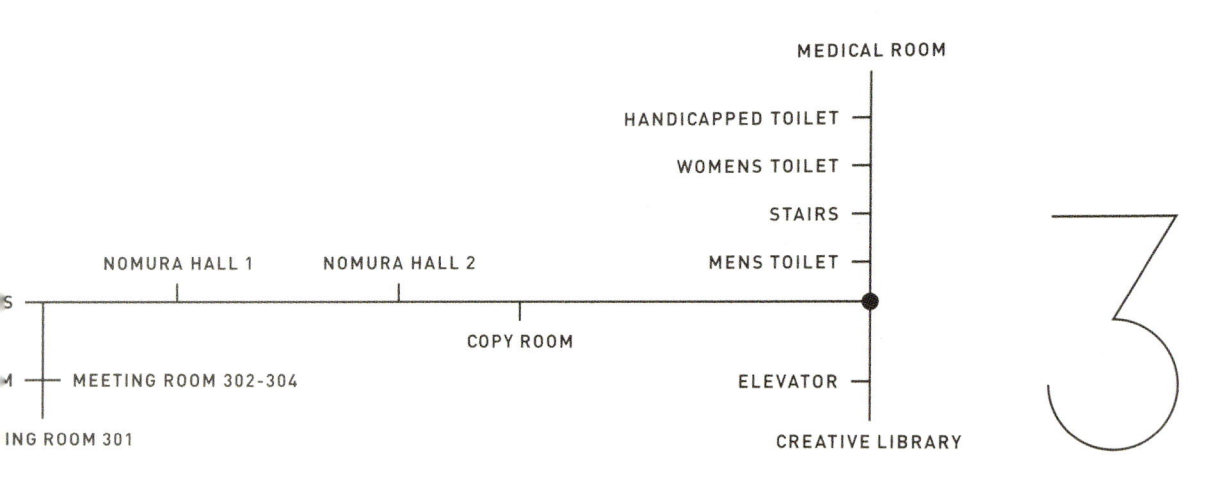

地図を読む

地図が読めるかどうかは、空間把握能力の差だという。男性の方が優れていると言われるが、それは男女の脳が別々の進化をしてきたからなのだ。狩猟の経験から遠方の位置関係など空間感覚が発達した男と、木の実や果実を採り子どもを育てて、周辺視野が広がった女の違いである。誰でもわかるマップを中心にデザインしたのは「乃村工藝社本社ビル」。ニューヨークの地図は碁盤の目になっていて、南北に走るアベニューと東西に走るストリートをたどればわかりやすい。そんな感覚でフロアを把握してもらいたくて考えたサインデザイン。男女の差は関係なく理解できる。
（乃村工藝社本社ビル　二〇〇七年）

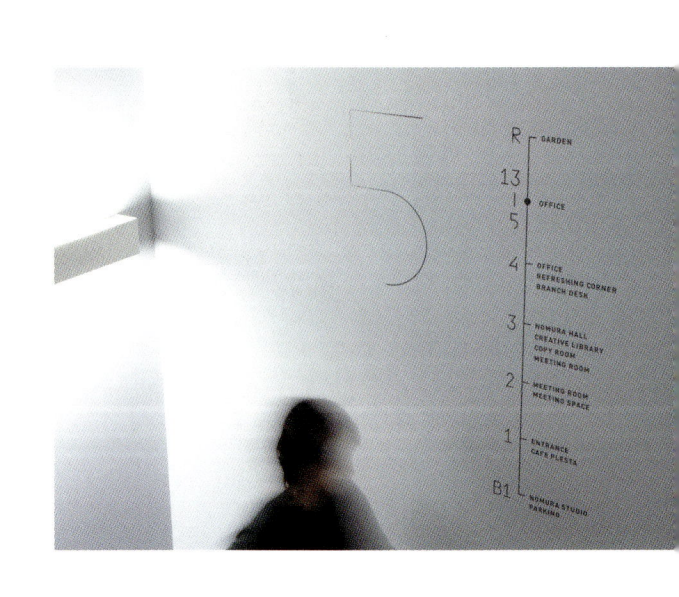

Reading Maps

Whether one is good at reading maps or not is said to depend on one's spatial skills. In general, men are said to have better spatial skills than women, and this can be explained by slight differences in the evolutionary development of our brains. Men have developed spatial visualization abilities over greater distances due to hunting, while women have a more holistic view of their immediate surroundings due to gathering and childrearing. NOMURA Headquarters Building was designed with the central theme of a map that anyone can easily read. A map of New York is easy to follow because of its grid-board formation, with the avenues running vertically south to north, and the streets running horizontally east to west. In a similarly straightforward fashion, we wanted this visual design to allow the viewer to get a simple and immediate grasp of what was on each floor, absolutely irrespective of gender.
(NOMURA Headquarters Building, 2007)

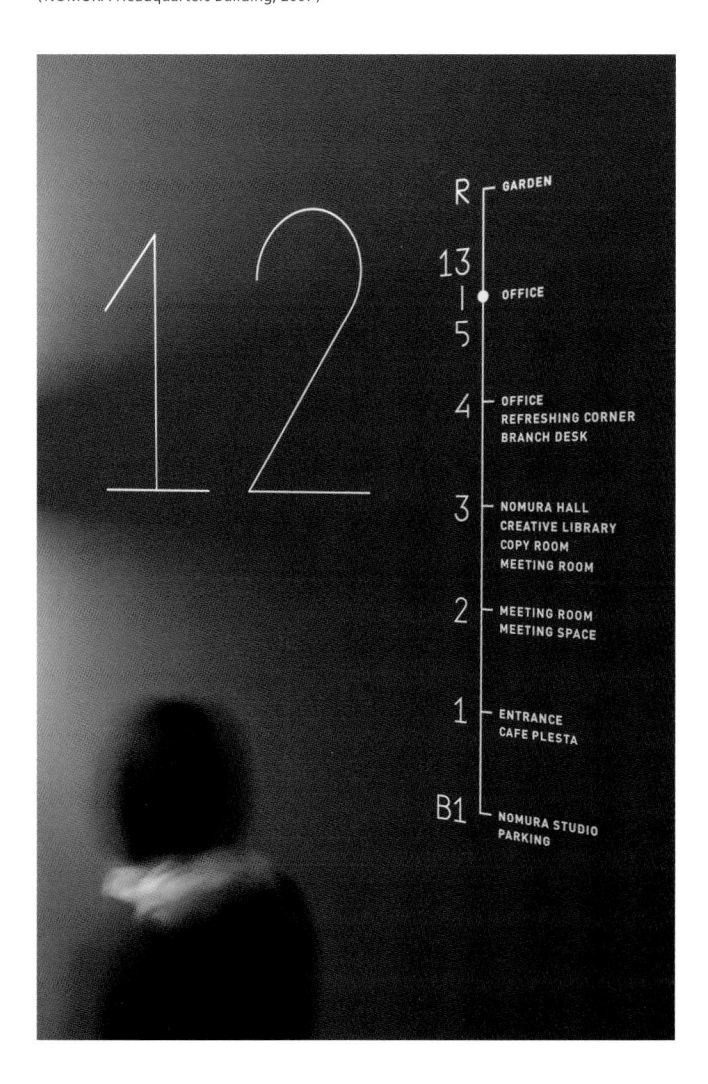

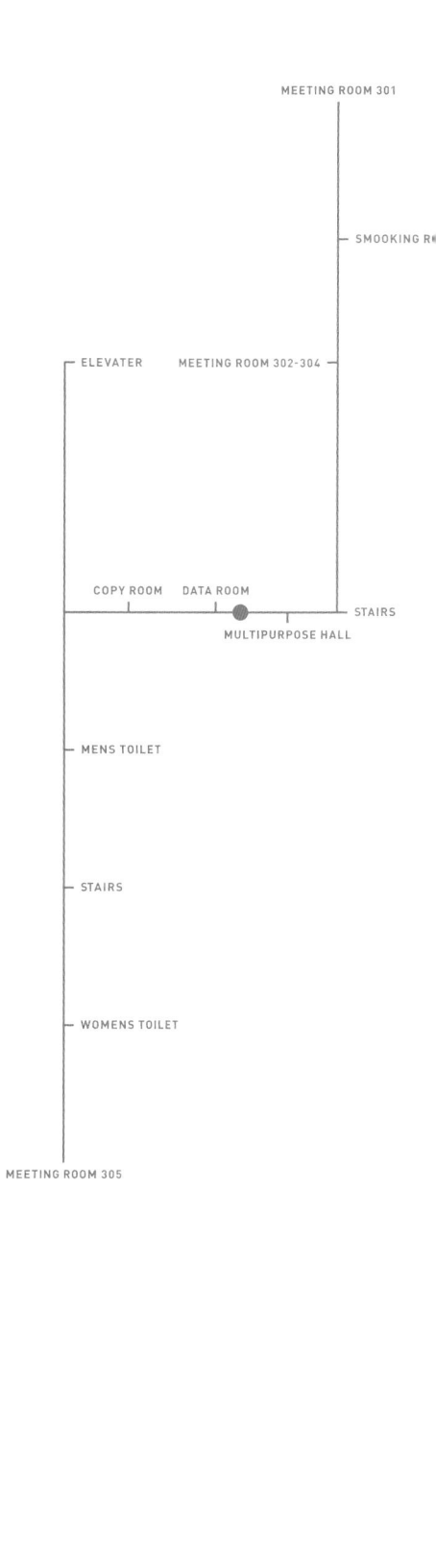

想いを送るしるし

切手デザイナーと飲み屋で偶然隣り合わせた。

彼は総務省（郵政事業庁）の所属で、技芸官と呼ばれ、日々切手のデザインを考えている。記念切手を含めるとかなりの切手が年間に発行されているが技芸官は四〜五人、精度を高く発行し続けていることは驚異だ。

数ミリ角の空間に、テーマごとのアイデアを考えてデザインする。絵画のような表現から幾何学模様まで、送る人の想いをカタチにする。

郵便が民営化されたことを記念してオリジナル切手をデザインして展覧会を開催した。

私は一円から一〇〇円までの切手を金額に合わせた蟻の数で表した。原寸大の蟻は何度見ても胸がざわざわする。

また、展示物が小さいので、かがまなくても良く見えるように細い台を浮かす展示を試みた。

（POST 切手 郵便が変わり始めた。切手のデザインはどう変わる。二〇〇七−二〇〇八年）

A Seal to send your Thoughts

I happened to sit next to a stamp designer in a bar. He was employed by the Ministry of Internal Affairs and Communications, working in its Postal Agency arm as an 'Arts Officer', whose daily job it is to come up with new designs for stamps. If one includes special commemorative editions, there are a great number of stamps issued every year. But that there are up to five so-called Arts Officers continuously and meticulously involved in the process was a surprise to me. With just a few millimeters of space to work on, they come up with ideas for designs based on various given themes. From painting-like expressions to geometric patterns, they each give shape to the thoughts of the sender. To commemorate the privatization of the postal service in Japan, we organized an exhibition of original stamp designs. I designed a series of stamps with an ant motif, valued from 1 yen to 100 yen, conveying the monetary value of each stamp by differentiating the number of ants in the designs. I have always been fascinated by ants, and particularly by their full-scale representations. Also, as the objects exhibited were very small, I tried displaying them on suspended narrow stands, in order to allow the viewer to inspect them without crouching down.

(Post Stamps: The Japanese postal service has begun to change. But how will postage stamps evolve?, 2007–2008)

A Mille-feuille of Air

Paper was created to transfer information and leave records. Papyrus, from which the English word 'paper' is derived, was invented by the ancient Egyptians and made from the pith of plants, first soaked in water to make them soft, then layered on top of each other and dried to make a paper-like material. Strictly speaking, therefore, it is not the same as paper. Paper was invented 2000 years later in China, and it is made by pressing together fibers of cellulose pulp from cotton and wood into thin sheets. Throughout the ages, paper has continued to evolve alongside civilizations and their cultures. It is closely related to printing in particular, and in recent times, we have developed paper that can undergo very large amounts of printing at high speeds. New forms of paper are always in demand as society modernizes. This particular paper is made from adding thin air pockets in between the fibers, just like a mille-feuille, which results in softer and thicker sheets that still feel very light. And with uniformly applied coating techniques, it also has a very high level of printability. Named "airus", it is a paper-type for a new era.
(airus—mechanism and quality, 2015)

空気のミルフィーユ

紙は伝えるため、記録を残すために生まれた。

Paperという言葉の起源になったパピルスは古代エジプトで植物の皮を水で柔らかくして重ねて乾燥したもの。厳密には紙ではない。

パピルスから二〇〇〇年後の中国で紙は発明された。コットンや木などの繊維質が絡まり一定の厚さで面状に広がったものを紙と呼ぶ。

紙はどの時代でも文明や文化に寄り添いながら進化してきた。特に印刷との親和性は高く、近代では高速で大量の印刷に対応した紙がたくさん開発された。

常に時代は新しい紙を求めているのだ。

いままでは両立しなかった軽くて高精細な新しい紙の開発に関わることができた。

この紙はミルフィーユのように繊維と繊維の間に空気をはさみ、ふわっとして厚みがあるが軽い。

そして均一なコーティング技術で高い印刷再現性を可能にしている。

新時代の紙の誕生、「エアラス」と名付けた。

（エアラス・性能と品質　二〇一五年）

一冊の写真集との出会いが始まりだった。世界中の一〇〇歳を撮り続けているドイツの写真家、カルステン・トーマエレン。彼の「Happy at Hundred」と名付けられた写真集の中の人々の笑顔が素敵すぎて虜になってしまった。新しい紙「エアラス」には一本一本の皺が経験した時間を語り、人生はこれからだ！と微笑む彼らの写真が最適だと思えた。日本の一〇〇歳一〇人を北海道で撮りおろし、彼らの一〇〇年を「エアラス」に刷り込めた。

It all began with a single photography book. It was by German photographer Karsten Thormaehlen, who has continued to photograph hundred-year-olds from all over the world. Named "Happy at Hundred", I was absolutely captivated by the wonderful smiling faces within its pages. Each wrinkle, finely printed on this new "airus" paper, tells of these people's lives and times, their smiles beaming as if to shout out "Life begins at 100!" These photographs seemed like perfection to me. I decided to travel to Hokkaido to photograph 10 Japanese centenarians, and committed their 100 years of life to "airus."

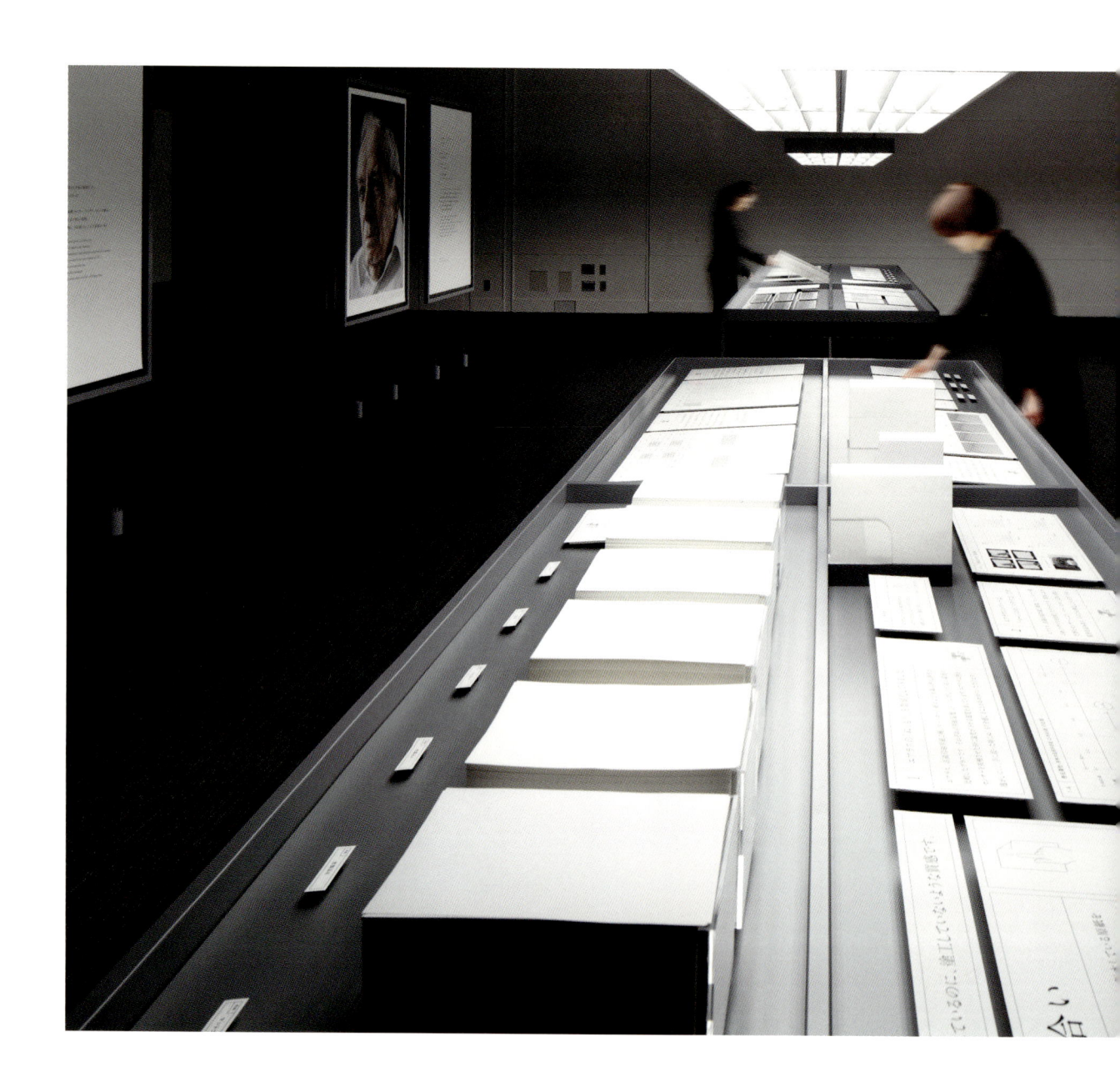

Differences between types of printing paper are hard to understand. When specifying
printing options, there is a dizzying array of choices available, and you always has to look
for the right balance between the cost and characteristic properties of a given type of paper.
It is not uncommon to just end up choosing the paper that you are most accustomed to
using. Yet, the most important thing is how much of an emotional reaction you can evoke
in the viewer, and the slightest variation can sometimes have crucial consequences. We held
an exhibition entitled "airus—mechanism and quality", in order to explain the new paper's
properties as clearly as possible so that potential users could make an informed decision
about it. Physically comparing and contrasting things with our senses enriches
our understanding of them.

印刷用紙の差異はわかりにくい。印刷指定の時、毎回多くの種類の中からコストや特性のバランスを吟味しなくてはならないのだ。つい、いつもの使い慣れた紙を選んでしまう。しかし、届けたい人の心をどれだけ動かせるかが重要、微差が決定的な差になる時もある。新しい紙を徹底的にわかりやすく理解して判断してもらえるように「エアラス・性能と品質」という展示会を開催した。体感的に比較し、見くらべることで理解が深まる。

廣村正彰の頭の中をのぞいてみる

2015 年 7-8 月　収録
インタビュアー　飯田彩

廣村正彰の「言葉」

飯田　今回の出版は、グラフィックデザイナー廣村正彰がどのようなことを考え作品を生み出していくのか、そのデザイン思考を読み解くということをテーマにしてきました。これまでお話を伺ったり原稿を拝読していて、廣村さんは、「言葉」にとても意識的なデザイナーだと感じたのですが、ご自身としてはいかがでしょうか？

廣村　僕がデザインを志した頃は、カッコイイことを生み出すのがデザインだと思っていました。時代がどんどん変わっていって、カタチはもちろん、プロジェクトの文脈を組み立てたり、仕組みをつくるということもデザインになっています。またそのためには、考えていることを説明して周辺の人を巻き込んでいかなければならない。そのときに「言葉」はとても重要だと思っています。

実は、僕は子どもの頃からしゃべるのが苦手なんです。失敗談はいろいろありますが、いちばん強烈な記憶はクライアントから言われたひと言でした。30代半ばの独立直後の頃で、一生懸命つくってきたプランをとうとうと説明していたら、相手から「何を言っているかわからないよ」と。すごくショックでした。うすうす自分でも何を言っているんだろうと思うことがよくあって（笑）、自分でもこれはまずいなと思っていたところだったので、自分の気持ちを見透かされたような気がしたんですね。

それから、思いつくままに口に出すのではなく、いったん自分で理解してから口に出すように、常に相手に理解されるための言葉を選ぶように気をつけています。デザインは、まず伝えて理解してもらうところから始まりますから。

文章を書くのも同様に苦手意識があって毎度四苦八苦しながら書いているんですが、もし書いたものを褒めてもらえるようになったのだとしたら、わかりやすくなってきたのかもしれません。そこには、師匠の田中一光先生の影響もあるかもしれない。田中先生は、普通の言葉を使って、ものすごく感動的な文章を書いていました。こんな文章を書く人になりたいという気持ちはずっともっていました。

飯田　事務所のスタッフとのやりとりも、スケッチを描くのではなく言葉でされると伺いましたが、何故でしょうか？

廣村　絵で伝えるということは、カタチや色などのイメージを言葉よりもリアルに正確に伝えられると思うんです。一方で、言葉というのはあいまいですよね。僕が彼らに対して使う言葉は、抽象的で「あそこで見たあんな感じ」とか非常に不確実なんです。アイデアを思いついた瞬間に電話で伝えることもありますね。そういう言葉を彼らなりに解釈して、自分の頭の中にあるボキャブラリーで視覚化して制作しなければいけないので、スタッフはすごく大変だと思います。その大変さを乗り越えるということは、僕たちがかつて田中一光デザイン室でやってきたことなんですが、初期段階では他者の美意識も入るので新鮮な感動があるんですよ。それを丁寧にブラッシュアップして次のステージに乗せていくことが楽しいですね。それから、プロジェクトの過程では、私とスタッフで同時にクライアントの話を聞き、その後でディスカッションをすることにしています。それは、同じ話を聞いても私とスタッフでは捉え方が若干違うのではないかと考えるからです。その解釈の違いにデザインの種があるのではないかと思っているんです。

飯田　違いを擦り合わせていくのではなく、差に注目されるのが面白いですね。

廣村　デザインは、基本的には意識の共有化、最大公約数みたいなものですね。自分が思っている範囲と他人が思っている範囲の合わさったところにデザインがある。しかし、合わさらないところにこそ、実は重要なポイントがあるのではない

かと思うんです。あたり前だと思っていた理解が、話してみると違う、話してもわかり合えないということが起こるのは面白いですよね。しかも、大きな違いではなく、若干の違いであるということがポイントで、こういうものにデザインの種を見つけて、それを育てていくと面白いものが生まれることがあるんです。

そもそも、相手が誰でも僕は聞き役だと考えていて、常に聞き上手でありたいと思っているんです。デザイナーは自己主張が強いと思われがちだけれど、僕は逆に自己主張がゼロで「自分」がない、自分では真っ白という感じがしています。

特に自分自身の生活に関しては、まったくこだわりがないんです。当然、美しいものは美しいし、整った空間で生活したいと思いますが、それ以上のこだわりはない。けれど、デザイナーとしてはそれではよくないという気持ちもあります。仕事の相手に対しては、あるこだわりのレベルをもたなければならない。それは自身のこだわりではなく、課題や要望を理解するためにある程度のレベルが必要だということです。

いつもを疑うことから始まる

飯田 第1章のテーマは「いつも、を疑う」ですが、これは廣村デザインにとって重要なキーワードのひとつですね。

廣村 僕は、デザイナーとして常に疑い深くいなければと思っているんです。仕事がきたときに、限られた時間のなかでどんどん進めていかなければならないわけだけれど、そういうときでも常に、なぜこれをやっているのだろうか？ とか、これで本当にいいのか？ とか考えます。そういう一瞬思考を止めた空白のときに起こる化学反応があるので、疑うということで起こるデザインへの作用があると思って意識的にやっています。

デザインというのは、求められる目的地はひとつでも、そこへのルートは無限にある。デザインとは、そのプロセスのなかのディテールの部分をいかに楽しむかということだと思うんです。

難しいのは、必ずしも良いデザインが、売れるデザインではないということです。だからといって市場が求めているものをそのままつくればいいかというと、そうでもない。マーケティングどおりに市場が求めている価値観をそのまま商品化すれば、成果として70点くらいはつくでしょう。けれど、90点を求めているクライアントにその方法は通用しません。そうでない結果を生み出すところに、デザインのダイナミズムがあると思っています。

飯田 デザインの命題と良いデザインとの関係のお話は、「コープさっぽろ」（012頁）のプロジェクトに繋がってきますね。

廣村 そうですね。2015年に50周年を迎えるコープさっぽろのCI（コーポレートアイデンティティ）を整えていきたいという依頼がありました。そのためにいくつかのデザインをしていますが、まだまだこれから続いていくプロジェクトです。

コープさっぽろは北海道全域をカバーしているのですが、札幌以外は、高齢化が進んだ地域も多く、全体に過疎化しています。生活協同組合は全国にありますが、特に北海道では雪に閉ざされた時期に食事や必要な生活品を届けるライフラインになっています。

コープの配達車に同乗して配達先でヒアリングをしてわかったのは、ご老人がみんな、荷物を届けるスタッフと話をするのを楽しみに待っているということです。やはり日々の暮らしの中で人と話すことはとても大切で、組合員にとってもはや単なる宅配サービスではないのだということがわかると、そこから新しいビジネスの可能性が生まれてきます。そのひとつとして、市町村と連携した高齢者見守りの取り組みがあります。田舎に高齢の親を残して都市部に出て来ている子世帯が、

親のために必要なものを毎週注文して、配達の際にスタッフが様子を見て子どもに報告をするというものです。
また、食料自給率200%という環境を生かして、できるだけ100%北海道産のもので商品をまかなおうという指針の元に商品開発を行っています。ただし、本当にすべての商品を北海道産にしてはダメだということもコープの方から教わりました。北海道産の果物がどんなに充実していても、北海道では採れないバナナが食べたいというお客さんがいるかぎりは地域外から仕入れて販売する。その根底には、「組合員ひとり一人のためのコープ」という理念があります。組合員と言っても、一口1000円以上の出資金なんです。その考えが素敵だなと共感しました。

飯田 プロジェクトの一環に、プライベートブランド（PB）のパッケージデザインがあります。商品の写真を使わず、コピーのみが大きく入ったパッケージはとてもユニークですね。

廣村 普通のPBであれば、統一性や、パッケージの華やかさが求められるんですが、コストを抑えるために、文字だけで商品を理解してもらうことを考えました。あえてコピーだけのパッケージにしたことが差別化につながり、消費者に選ばれるようになっています。
店頭で商品を見るのは一瞬ですから、シズル感をビジュアルで見せるのがいちばん効果的なので、多くのナショナルブランドでは写真を使います。今回はあえてそのセオリーを捨てて、ちょっと時間は必要だけどメッセージを読んでもらうことに賭けたんです。北海道にこだわったこのPB商品には価値があって、手に取ってもらえれば十分納得してもらえる自信があります。
さらに最近では、カーボンフットプリントや、アレルギーやカロリーの表示をして、それを見て消費者が選べるようにしていこうとしています。

日常の中にあるデザインの種

飯田 第2章に収録している「Junglin'（ジュングリン）」（024頁）は、廣村さんのライフワークとも言える継続的なプロジェクトですね。

廣村 これは、池袋西武のリニューアルが完成した記念に何かやりませんかと声をかけていただいて、2011年に開催した展覧会がはじまりです。当時、デザインは「意識の発火」だという考えが頭の中にあり、それをテーマにした作品をつくってみようと思いました。そのタイトルとして、「順繰り」という、無意識的に行っている日常の行動のなかで、なにかのポイントにハッと気がつく瞬間があるのではないかという意味を込めて「Junglin'」と名付けました。
日常的な動きを表現するには、グラフィックのような静止画ではなく動くものがいいと考えて、映像を選びました。動きの中から発見する何かがあると思ったんです。映像と言っても先端的な映像をつくりたいわけではなく、パラパラ漫画のようなものがいいなとイメージしてつくりました。しかし、初回の入館者数は惨憺たるもので、展覧会としては完全な敗北だと思いました。一方で、ものすごく面白いと言ってくれる人もいて、しばらくして雑誌『AXIS』の編集の方からこのテーマでコラムを書いてみませんかと声をかけていただいたんです。結局それが20回、3〜4年続くことになりました。
毎回テーマを探すのが大変なんですが、次は何にしようと考えることがものすごく勉強になりました。私たちは何に対して無意識の中から意識をしているのだろうということを、本を調べたり人に聞いたりしながらテーマになりそうなものを見つけるという作業を繰り返し行いました。そのうちに、それらをまた次の映像にしてみたいと思ってやったのが、2014年にAXISギャラリーでやった展覧会「Junglin'2 無意識の中の意識」です。

扱っているテーマは実にさまざまなので、「ジュングリンってなに？」と聞かれると困ってしまうんですが、「ずっと連続して動作をしているものの中から何かを発見する」ということだと思います。今回の金沢21世紀美術館の展覧会（2015年–2016年）では、金沢で撮りおろした映像を使った「ジュングリン」を展示する予定です。

グラフィックデザインがすべての起点

飯田 廣村さんの仕事は、グラフィックから空間やブランディングなど他分野にわたっていると思いますが、一貫して「グラフィックデザイナー」と名乗っていらっしゃいますね。
廣村 僕は、どんな仕事をしていても、一生「グラフィックデザイナー」と名乗りたいと思っています。デザインにおいての起点、オリジンが、僕の場合はグラフィックデザインだと思っていて、どんな仕事をしてもいいけれど、グラフィックデザインが基本にあって常にそこに帰るという感じがしています。
なので、ものを考えるときには、空間であろうが、ものづくりであろうが、まずグラフィックデザインを基準にして考えています。グラフィックデザインのいいところは平面であるところ、つまり一瞬にして宇宙まで描けるということです。絵や写真であればどんな世界観でもすぐに表現できるけれど、これを立体で具現化しようと思ったら大変ですよね。そういった想像の翼を広げることによって、限界をつくらずに自由にものごとを考えることができます。
だから空間をデザインする時には、空間に入った時の体感的な印象だけではなく、写真に撮られたときにどう魅力的に写るかという視点でもデザインを考えています。同時にその視点は、たとえばお客さんがエスカレーターで上がってきた瞬間のフロアの印象でもあるわけですから、とても重要なポイントになるんです。
建築家がよく使う「アクティビティ」という言葉がありますが、これは空間に対しての仕組みをどうつくるか、それによって人はどう動くのかということだと思います。この考え方をはじめて知った時にはものすごく感動して、僕はそれを平面で考えたいなと思っているんです。

飯田 グラフィックデザインやエディトリアルデザインでも、廣村さんならではの視点があると思いますが、たとえば今回の本はどのようなことを考えてデザインされたのでしょうか？
廣村 デザインには、セオリーやルールに則ることから生まれる心地よさのようなものがあって、特にエディトリアルデザインでは、そういったシステムをもとに考えていった方がいいと思っています。ただ、僕にとっては、学校で学んだセオリーよりも田中事務所で教えられたことの方が強く残っていて、そのせいなのか、僕のデザインは、箱組みの仕方や行間の取り方について、おかしいとか、何でこうなっているのかと他のデザイナーから聞かれることがあるんです。
今回の本では、縦組みの和文と横組みの英文を併記して組んでいくということにチャレンジしています。縦書きなのに左綴じだし、はじめて見た人はかなり違和感があるんじゃないかと思うし、普通はあまりこういうことはやらないかもしれない。なので、その解決策として見開きで完結するように、少なくとも日本語の本文とその訳文が同じ見開きに納まるように紙面をデザインしています。日本人は多様性をうまく受け入れていく土壌をもっているので、その包容力をデザインに取り入れていくのはいいかなと思って進めてみました。ひとつの言語の中で4種類もの文字を使っている許容力の高い民族はそんなにはいないですよね。だから、こういったイレギュラーなデザインも上手にそしゃくしてくれるのではないかと思っています。

「わかりやすい」サインとは何か

飯田 次にサインデザインについてうかがいます。これまでにさまざまな施設のサインデザインを手掛けられていますが、どのような思考から生み出されているのでしょうか？

廣村 サインデザインでクライアントから求められることは、ほとんどの場合「わかりやすく」という1点ですよね。その度に、一般的な「わかる」と同時に、この場所での「わかる」とはどういうことだろうかと違いを考えます。

クライアントにとっての「わかる」とは、場所や順路などの情報がはっきりと示されるということなんですが、僕が考える「本当にわかる」ということは、この施設がどういう場なのか、どういう成り立ちでできたのか、どんな人がつくったのだろうか、あるいはどういう思いでつくったのだろうか、ということが伝わることがいちばん重要だと思います。大きな空間の意思が受け取れたら、あとは「行って探せばあるよ」くらいのラフな感じでいいのではないかと思っているんです。

たとえば、海外に行くと、サインは日本ほど親切じゃないし、セキュリティに関してもそうで、使う人に優しくない。かたや、日本は親切で丁寧だけれど、過剰だと感じる場合もあります。一概にどちらがいいというわけではないけれど、僕たちがやっているサインは、あまり説明しすぎず、その場所で体験する時間を豊かにするために有意義に働けばいいなと思っているんです。

具体的なポイントのひとつとして、その空間に入っていく最初のところに、全体のサインのシステムや雰囲気がわかる仕掛けをするようにしています。最初に何かが起こると、訪れた人はここはそういう場所なんだなと意識のスイッチが切り替わります。そうやって、その後の空間を楽しんでほしいと思っているんです。

また、できるだけシンプルで簡素な仕掛けをするように心がけています。シンプルなもののなかで、見る人が感情を込められるような、あるいは何かを受け取ってもらえるようなことがあるといいなと思います。

飯田 「TOTO ミュージアム」（158頁）では、まさにエントランスにたくさんの水滴がサインとしてつけられていますね。

廣村 TOTO は水に関わる会社で、「水と地球の、あしたのために」という環境のスローガンを掲げています。そこで、水をサインのモチーフにして、とにかく水滴をいっぱいつけるサインを計画しました。視界の中に水滴がたくさん入ってくることで、訪れた人に「やはり水に気を遣っている会社なんだな」と感じとってもらえるといいなと考えたんです。

エントランスの正面のガラスには水滴がたくさん散っていて、文字やロゴもなく、これ自体は何も示していない。けれど、その場所自体のアイデンティティを示すサイン。もはや、これをサインデザインと言っていいのかわからないんですが。（笑）

飯田 「すみだ水族館」（066頁）は、図鑑のようなサインデザインが特徴的で、従来の水族館とはかなり雰囲気が違いますね。

廣村 クライアントは新江ノ島水族館の実績があったのですが、海辺にある水族館とは違う都心にある水族館の在り方を議論しました。最終的に「Sense Knowledge」というコンセプトと、それに追随するデザインをセットで出しました。最初はサインデザイン単体の依頼でしたが、結果的に全体のコンセプトから、シンボルマーク、グラフィックデザインなどを一体でデザインしています。このような施設は、エンタテインメント性が大切なので、最先端の3D映像とか、4Kハイビジョンとか、新しいことをしなければいけないと多くの関係者が思っていました。けれど、新しい技術というのは、一度見た瞬間から古くなってしまう。この水族館では、はじめて見る時の新しさよりも

リピーターを増やすことを考えたいと思いました。街の中にあるという立地を生かして、近所の人たちがふらっと寄ってくれるような場所、夏場だったら夕涼み感覚で来て、館内のバーでちょっとお酒を飲んでもらえるような場所になるといいなと思いました。

僕は、大英博物館やルーブル美術館に行く度に感動するんです。展示は何度も見ていて目新しさはないはずなんですが、天井が高くて、廊下がだーっと長くて、そういう空間を歩いていきながら古い絵画なんかを見ているだけで、物語の世界に入っていける。だから、水族館もそういった美術館や博物館のように、物語を紡いでいく場所になればと思いました。そこで、展示の説明などをモノトーンのエッチングで表現しています。

スローなサイン

飯田　第7章「デザインのスピード」では、駅や空港などのファストなサインに対して、スローなサインをテーマにしました。

廣村　本当は僕自身はせっかちな人間なんだけど、僕がやりたい「スローなサイン」は、理解するプロセスに時間をかけたい、あるいは時間をかけてもわかりたいと思えるデザインにするべきだと思っています。サインを見る時間は瞬間だと思うけれど、それでも0.1秒が1秒になるとしたら、それは大きなことですよね。理解するまでの1秒間のプロセスの中に感情が生まれるんだと思うんです。それはたとえば、愛おしい、可愛い、あるいは、爽やかだなと感じるかもしれない。そういう感情が呼び起こされることが重要で、それが見る人に寄り添う、わかってもらうということに繋がるんじゃないかと考えています。

サインはもともと、人が案内すればいいのだけれど、できないので案内板をつける、という成り立ちで発生したものです。だから本当は、みんなはサインを読みたいわけでも指示されたいわけでもなく、優しくおもてなしされたいのだと思います。そのときにいちばん大切なのは人ですね。旅館の女将だったり、学校の先生だったり、案内をしてくれる人の印象が相手には強く残ります。そういうことをサインデザインでも大切にしています。デザインは人のためにあって、人が中心にあります。だからちゃんと人に向けて言いたいし、受け取る人にも人から受け取っているように感じてもらいたいんです。

実際に人と会話をしているときにも、相手の反応が面白いですよね。今、一瞬目が輝いたなとか、表情がほころんできたなとか、面白くて笑いたそうだなとか、そういうことをサインからも感じてほしい。ただ事務的に場所や順路を示すということではなく、サインを見た人が思わずニコニコしながら目的の場所に行ってくれたら嬉しいですね。あとは、自分が楽しみたいということがあります。サインデザイナーは、病院とか、学校とか、公共建築とか、得意分野がそれぞれあると思いますが、そういうノウハウが蓄積すると、だんだんと無駄が削ぎ落とされてピュアな状態、つまり「速い」サインになっていってしまう気がするんです。その点では、僕の場合ははじめて来る仕事が多い。それに対してどうしたらいいのだろうと面白がりながら試行錯誤していることが、そのままサインに出るといいなと思っているんです。

飯田　「横須賀美術館」（150頁）は、「よこすかくん」が館内を案内してくれるスローなサインデザインですね。廣村さんのサインデザインのキャリアのなかでもひとつのポイントになる作品だと思います。

廣村　たしかに横須賀美術館のサイン計画はとても高い評価をいただきました。では、なぜこれをいいと思うのかなと考えてみると、ひとつは文字に依存していないということ、もうひとつは動きがあるということなのではないかと思うんです。

サインに使っている「よこすかくん」は、ピクトグラムでもアニメーションでもないその中間にいるものだと思います。このサインは、パラパラ漫画のひとコマのように、動いている動作の一瞬を切り取ったものなのです。たとえば階段のサインでは、よこすかくんの仕草で上りと下りの違いもわかります。そういう要素をサインにもちこみ、それがサインシステムのなかで機能しているという点が評価されたのだと思っています。まずきちんと機能することが重要で、そのうえで感動を与えるものだという点で、横須賀美術館や「9h」（090頁）が評価されるのだと思います。

飯田 9hの場合は、一見、横須賀美術館と同じように文字を排したスローなサインでありながら、無駄なくツーリストを導くという点では、非常にファストなサインですよね。

廣村 そうですね。9hの場合は、駅のサインなどのファストとは違っていて、合理性をつきつめた結果のファストだと思います。この施設自体が、眠ることに特化した何のトッピングもない合理的なカプセルホテルなんですね。だから、それをピュアに表現することが大切だと思いました。宿泊などが低価格で人的なサービスはできないし、自分の判断で行動することが徹底している。この徹底しているというところが面白い。外国人観光客が興味をもって利用するのもその点だと思います。合理的といっても決してギスギスしているわけではなく、あくまで面白がっているということがポイントです。9hは、僕がこれまでやってきたなかで最もサインデザインらしいサインデザインだと思っています。

同じく、「ヤマトグループ 羽田クロノゲート」（096頁）も合理性のサインデザインです。物流ターミナルという機能と速さが求められる施設の必要に迫られたサインというのはやはり強いです。ここではストライプのシステムでデザインしていますが、必要性という点で考えれば、ここまでは必要ない。けれど合理性を過剰なまでに徹底的にやることで、サインとして面白くなるんです。

飯田 なるほど。廣村さんのサインデザインにとって、素材や質感も大切なポイントですね。

廣村 実は、2、3年前までは、自分がつくるサインには質感と物量はいらないと思っていたんです。極端に言えば、サインという情報を受け取るためのものなのだから、素材感や厚みは必要ないという考えです。だから、ほとんどのサインに粘着シートを使っていました。

この考え方は今も変わっていないのですが、最近は、うまく質感を取り入れたいと考えるようになりました。たとえば、「西武渋谷店 モヴィーダ館」（114頁）では、数字のサインをちょっとぷくっとさせています。人に優しい感じを出したいと思って、真っ白なお餅が膨れたようなイメージで、思わず触りたいなと思うものを目指しました。そういう表現を、意識のスイッチを押して、サインを理解するきっかけにしたいなと思ったからです。だから、素材を使うといっても、ピカピカのステンレスを用いて文字を切り抜いて、すごくきれいでしょ？ というのとは意味が違っています。素材は、個々の空間がもっているコンテクストにタッチするポイントだと捉えているんです。それが「ぷっくり」だったり、「ざらざら」だったり、受け手の記憶の中にあるものを呼び起こすようなものを使いたいなと思っています。

色に心を寄せる

飯田 グラフィックデザインにとって「色」も非常に重要な要素だと思いますが、廣村さんはどのように考えていらっしゃるのでしょうか？

廣村 色の話をするのは本当に難しいですね。無限にあり、無限のマッチングがあるから、知れば知るほど怖くなります。なるべくなら使いたくないくらいです。（笑）

田中一光先生は「色の魔術師」と呼ばれていたんですが、田中先生の色使いはやはり素晴らしいです。田中一光デザイン室には「色の箱」というものがあって、頂きものの包装紙や海外のパッケージなどの一部を田中先生が切って、箱にストックしているんです。色を検討するときには普通は色見本を使うと思うけれど、田中先生は、この色の箱から色を考えるんです。いわば、世の中に溢れているものの中から、田中先生の目を通して選ばれた色が詰まった箱というわけですね。

六本木の 21_21 DESIGN SIGHT で「田中一光とデザインの前後左右」展をやったときに、「His Colors」（180 頁）というインスタレーションをしました。展示室の一角の床と壁一面に、100 色のカッティングシート®と 150 色のタントという紙の中から組み合わせて、田中先生の色で空間をつくりました。縮尺 1/50 くらいの模型のなかで延々と自分でカラーチップを組み合わせながら考えて、最終的には素直にいいなと思うものができました。実は、今回収録した作品のなかでこれがいちばん好きです。

飯田　他にも、特に色が重要な意味合いをもつ作品はありますか？

廣村　「あいちトリエンナーレ 2013」（172 頁）がそうですね。この VI（ビジュアルアイデンティティ）はカタチに目が行きがちだと思うんですが、最大のポイントはブルーで統一していることなんです。

ここで使っているブルーは、印刷の基本になるシアン 100％です。真夏のイベントだということもあり、人々がシンクロしていくことを目指した「シンクロするブルー」という色なんです。市民や県民みんなで盛りあがるアートイベントだから、はためくフラッグが街中に現れると、ああ、始まったんだなと地元の人たちが心を寄せていくものになるといいなと考えました。

それから、ロフトの「SELF&SHELF LOFT」（206 頁）では、めずらしくカラフルなロゴをつくりました。ロフトの VI は、田中一光デザイン室時代に担当したものです。赤みのある黄色に黒い文字を合わせていますが、その当時、黄色は商業施設では禁じ手のようなところがあったのをあえて提案したもので、鮮烈な印象がありました。

この VI は、社長が変わっても代々ずっと守られてきて、内部の人が守っていかなければならないと思うものがブランドというものなのだとあらためて実感しました。時代が巡ってたまたま自分がロフトのディレクションをすることになったときに、この VI は守りたいと思う自分といつか崩してやろうと思う自分がいました。そこで、派生のブランド SELF&SHELF LOFT ができたときに、一気に多彩にしてみました。小さい店舗ながら商品が多彩なので、カラフルでもいいかなと考えて。ティーンをターゲットにしたブランドで、白を基調としながらカラフルな色がロゴや店内に入ってくるようにしています。

日本的デザイン志向

飯田　『Japan Creative ジャパンクリエイティブ』（ハースト婦人画報社）のなかで、日本人は古来、窮屈さなどのマイナス要素を愛でる要素に変えていく力があるとおっしゃっていますが、そのような日本的な思考を廣村デザインのなかにも強く感じます。そのような思考をするきっかけはあったのでしょうか？

廣村　やはり、田中一光先生の影響が大きいと思います。田中先生は「現代の琳派」と呼ばれた人で、奈良や京都という古都で生まれ育って無意識に吸収したものはあったと思いますが、先生自身は最初から日本のことに興味があったわけではなかったそうです。1960 年代にポップカルチャーが盛んな時代、自分はついていけない、時代に取り残されていると感じていたときに、科学史家の

吉田光邦先生から『日本の文様 花鳥風月』（淡交社）という本の編纂のデザイン協力を依頼されたことがきっかけだったそうです。デザインだけではなく一緒に日本の文様について勉強をすることになって、そのなかでの出会いや学んだことから深く日本のことを考えるようになったと聞いたことがあります。

一方で、事務所に入った頃の僕にはまったくそんな思考はなくて、ただそういう古風なデザイナーの事務所に入っただけで、当時憧れていたデザインはまったく違ったんです。ただ、田中先生が素晴らしい才能の持ち主だということはわかりました。その才能に圧倒されながら多感な時期を10年も過ごしましたから、やはり影響は受けたんだろうなと思います。

たまたま機会があり、ジャパンクリエイティブ（以下、JC 214頁）に参加することになったのは、不思議な巡り合わせだなと思うんです。1980年代に田中先生がやられたことを、現代にもう一度違うコンセプトで進めることになりました。それから少し勉強をしていますが、日本的な思想にいつかちゃんと触れてみたいと、どこかで思っていたのかもしれません。

田中先生じゃないですが、僕も現代のデザインについていけないなと思うことが、特に40代の頃にありました。30代の独立したばかりの頃はバブルの最後の方で、まだ時代が華やかで仕事もあったし、若かったのでみんながちやほやしてくれました。いくつか賞も取って、何かものをつくればみんなが喜んでくれると思っていました。ところがその後、暗黒の40代と呼んでいますが（笑）、何をやっても響かないという苦しい時期がありました。ただ仕事はあるから、自分としてはただ仕事をこなしているだけという時代でした。

そんな頃に建築家との出会いがあり、空間のデザインをやるとこで、あらためてグラフィックデザインを考えるきっかけができました。師匠である田中先生が2002年に亡くなったこともあって、それ以前と以降ではいろいろなことが変わりました。当時、僕は48歳だったんですが、日本全体でみると失われた20年の途中だったし、いろいろなものが閉鎖的になってきていました。日本のグラフィックデザインは、1980年代にガラパゴス化と言われ、いちばん華やかだった時代で、日本は技術も含めて世界に名だたるグラフィックデザイン大国でした。それが、経済が下向きになるとともに、グラフィックデザインも減速していった。なんとなく面白いものをという依頼が少なくなって、もっと実質的に売れるとか、人が入るとかということについて考えなければならない、アメリカの商業デザインに近い方向になっていくわけです。その一方でデジタル化の波がやってきて、2000年頃からどこの事務所にも1台はMacがあるようになっていきました。

ところが、僕はそういう華やかなりし時代のデザインには乗り切れないところがあり、デザインとは、もう少し生活のリズムの中から見つけ出すものなんじゃないかなと思いはじめていました。日本の閉鎖的な時代のなかで生み出されていったものづくりの思想とちょっと似ているんですが、受け継がれていくなかで、工夫をして少しずつよくしていくというような考え方です。毎日の通勤で歩く道を変えるだけで何か新鮮な気持ちになるというような、普通の毎日のルーティーンのなかから気づきを見つけることによって、デザインは少しずつ生まれていくんじゃないか、そういうデザインを考えていきたいなと思った。そういう日本的な考え方というものが、田中一光先生から、ジュングリンやJCへと結びついて、今に繋がっている気がします。

飯田 そういったデザインは、受けとる側、使う側にも日本的な繊細な感覚が必要ですね。

廣村 僕は、最初がいちばん良くて、そこから鮮度が落ちていくデザインはつくりたくないと思っ

ています。使ううちにすぐに古びてしまうような新しい技術は極力使わないようにしています。
それから、「畳む」とか「縮む」という概念も、日本的でいいなと思います。韓国の李御寧先生が1980年代に『「縮み」志向の日本人』（学生社）という本を書かれていて、そこでは縮み志向とは日本人の能力が開花した部分だとおっしゃっています。かつての日本には「大きいことはいいことだ」と歌っていた時代があったけれども、実はその時代はそんなに良くはない。もっと限られた条件、限られた材料の中で最大の能力を発揮するというのが日本の技術力ですよね。その力が「ウォークマン」を生み、「プリウス」を生んできたわけです。

飯田　「仕舞う」という言葉に「舞」という字を使っているように、日本人はそこに美学を感じているところはありますよね。

廣村　そうですね。単純にコンパクトになればいいということではなくて、所作と全部関係してくるのだなと思うんです。さまざまな用途を兼ねるという考え方もそうで、たとえば和室を居間として使ったり、書斎として使ったりするということも所作に関係してくる。その都度、まっさらな状態に戻すということが素敵だなと思います。そういう清貧の思想に近いものもあって、自分自身も制御してコンパクトに生活をしたいなという気持ちがあります。
JCをやって本当に良かったと思うのは、つくり手と話をする機会を得られたということです。彼らは長い間受け継いできた技術を信じてものをつくっていて、そのもののつくり方へのこだわりが面白い。それが今、壁にぶつかっています。生活や価値観が変わっていくなかで、これらの技術が生きながらえていくにはどうすればいいのだろうかという大きな課題があります。JCの活動を通して見つけた面白いもの、技術は、再度世の中に花開かせたいと思っています。

飯田　JCは、具体的にどのようなことを目指しているのでしょうか？

廣村　JCの事業は、伝統工芸だけではなく、産業や先端技術も含め、日本の良いところを見つけて海外に向けて知ってもらうためのものです。ボランティアの仕事だけれど、関わっている人たちは新しい繋がりができたり、自分の興味が満たされることに魅力を感じて自発的に参加していると思います。
実際に、これまでに協力をお願いしたつくり手の方に断られたことは1度もありません。海外からデザイナーに来てもらい、何日か技術の研究をしてもらって、プロトタイプをつくって海外にもっていくということにかかる労力と経費は、持ち出していただいています。それでも、もし数％でも可能性があるならば、自分たちは新しいことに挑戦してみたいと言われました。それはJCだからではなく、誰かから声をかけられたことによって新しい扉が開く可能性があるのなら賭けてみたいということですね。だから僕たちは、扉をちゃんと開いて階段を上り、舞台に立ってもらわなければいけないと思っているんです。
多くのジャパンブランド振興の事業は、展覧会や展示会をやっておしまいというのが多いですが、本当はそこから先を考えるのが大切なので、一緒に考えることで継続的に活動しています。コストを合わせるとか、量産する体制などハードルが高い。途中でもういいよと諦めてしまうつくり手もいるけれど、なんとか続けていきたいと思っています。
日本にいると自分が日本人であるアイデンティティを感じることは少ないけれど、逆に海外の人達が真面目で勤勉な日本人の気質に大きく期待してくれている時代になっているのではないかと思います。それは、これまでちゃんとそういう文化をつくってきた日本人のおかげです。それがわかっているから、その期待に応えたいと思います。

テクノロジーは目的ではなくプロセス

飯田　最終章は、「おさまり、で納まる」というテーマです。廣村さんがアイデアを定着させる手法は多種多様ですが、さきほど「すぐに古くなる技術は使わない」とおっしゃっていましたね。

廣村　おさまり、ディテールが、デザインの質を決定します。プロジェクトごとにさまざまな方法を検討しますが、基本的に最新のテクノロジーはなるべく使わないことにしています。デジタル全般を使わないということではなく、デザインの中心に技術があるのではなく、デザインのプロセスを見せるために、デジタルやネットワークの技術を使うようにしているんです。たとえば「ブッククロック」（036頁）は映像をモニターで映し出しますが、手で本をめくるというローテクさを織り込んでいます。そこに最新の映像技術や高精細のモニターは必要ないわけです。

エアラスの展示会「エアラス・性能と品質」の展示計画（122頁）で今年のDSA大賞をいただきましたが、最後まで残った3作品のひとつに、横浜の象の鼻パークで行われたプロジェクションマッピングがありました。「たてもののおしばい」というタイトルで、公園を取り囲む5つの建物にそれぞれ顔が映し出されて、その人（建物）たちが会話をするというものなんです。それを見て、プロジェクションマッピングもひとつの分岐点に来たなと思いました。つまり、最初は新しい技術がもの珍しく、見たこともない新しい映像を見ることが目的になっていましたが、バキバキの最新のCG画像を使わなくてもコンテンツ次第で面白いことができるんだという証明になったと思ったんです。そうやって使い方がもっと発展していくわけで、技術はそのように使われていくべきです。

飯田　では、エアラスの展示会が評価されたポイントは何だと思いますか？

廣村　エアラスは、かさ高でありながら、高い再現性をもつという相反する機能を実現した紙です。ポスターなどよりも、本のように手で触って読んでもらうものに適した紙だと思いました。そこで、展示の最初に、「タッチ・エアラス」というインスタレーションをつくって、見る人が必ず紙に触ることからはじまるようにしたんです。棚から紙を取るというアクティブな行動を求められるインタラクティブな仕掛けをつくることで、紙の展示でありながら、五感で感じさせるという展示であるということが評価されたのではないかと思っています。

2つめのエリアでは、16人の100歳の方の笑顔の写真を展示しているんですが、この写真には本当に感動しました。70、80歳くらいだとまだまだ欲望みたいなものがあるけれど、100歳になると、毎朝起きたときに生きていることに感謝するんだそうです。そういうことがこの微笑みに表れているので、そういう無垢な微笑みを再現することが重要だと思いました。しわもシミも、白髪もすべて再現するんです。それによって100歳の価値がもういちど実感として立ち現れる。エアラスはそういうことに耐えられる紙だなと思って、やってみたいなと思いました。イベントが前に出がちですが、紙の性能と品質をしっかりと理解してもらうということができたのではないかと思います。

そもそもデザインとはなにか？

飯田　第8章で「受け取る個人の想像をどれだけ広げられるかがデザインの価値」だと書かれていて、デザインとは何かという問いへのひとつの答えだと思いました。たとえば「西武渋谷店A館エントランス」（238頁）では、抽象的なグラデーションのストライプから、見る人によってさまざまな風景、イメージが広がる仕掛けになっていますね。

廣村　デザインは情報を扱っていて、受け手に届けたいというのがひとつの目標になります。だけど、今の時代は情報が多すぎて、かえって本当に求める情報にたどり着けない状況になってしまっている。多くの人は、流れるように入ってくる情報を整理もできないまま詰め込んでいくだけ、あるいは、電流のようにただ体を流れているだけで、後には何も残らないという状況になっていて、それはもはやデザインではない。デザインがもたらすものは、伝わる、理解してもらうということのなかに、ある価値観が生まれるということだと思うんです。つまり、価値観を生まないデザインは、もはやデザインではないと考えた方がいい。受け取ったときに何かの感情が生まれて、記憶に留るということが大事だと思います。それを、我々デザイナーは、ビジュアル、色、あるいは文字を使って伝えている。ただし、一方的に届けるだけのデザインにはならないようにしたいと思っています。西武渋谷店のリニューアルは、エントランスを活性化して集客しようという商業施設の理論からスタートしていますが、単に目立たせるということでなく、街行く人たちが少しだけ感情を揺さぶる何かを共有することに意味があります。特殊なアルゴリズムによって生み出される、うつろい、にじむ、一期一会の色彩のなかに人々は何を思うか、それが見た人の感性にゆだねられているのが面白い。これこそインタラクティブの醍醐味です。

デザインの未来を考える

飯田　最後に、これからのデザインは、どのようになっていくと思われますか？

廣村　僕が学生の頃と比べて、デザインという言葉がさらに一般化してきたと感じています。デザイン家電とかデザインホテルという言葉を耳にしますが、「デザイン」というものが、どのような効果があって、どのようなものを指すかも常に揺れ動いて、領域もあまり定まらない状況になっています。だからこそ、デザインとは何なのかをそれぞれが考え直すいい機会だと思います。

以前、高校生に訪問授業をしたときに、「デザインとは、新しい体験をつくりだすこと」と定義したんです。新しい体験といっても、まったく今まで想像もしなかったことというのではなくて、少し視点を変えるだけで新しい体験ができるということを目指しています。グラフィックもプロダクトも空間も同じことで、デザインが新しい体験をつくり出すことで新しい生活が生まれ、意識が改善されていく。なので、デザインの未来というのは、常に新しい体験をつくり出すということが目標になるのかなと思っています。

一方で、「新しい」という言葉は不確実で、その言葉のプレッシャーをいつも感じながら仕事をしているわけですが、それをどこにもないものと捉えるとデザインなんてできなくなってしまう。そうではなく、誰もが気がつかなかった隅っこにあるものと考えたら、あるかもしれないなと思いますよね。そういう気づきが集まってくると新しい体験になるんだろうなと思います。

たとえば、音がせずにスムーズに閉まるドアのヒンジとか、引き出しがゆっくり閉まる機構なんかを見ると、ものすごく感動するんです。引き出しなんて閉まればそれでいいんだけど、この機構を見ると、閉まる動作自体が質感をもっているという感じがする。ささいなことだけれども、こういうものも生活を豊かにする良いデザインですよね。いろいろな企業と話をしていると、グローバル化を目指すとよく聞くけれども、もはや充分にグローバル化していると思うんです。IT化によって、もう勝手に世界は繋がっているしね。それよりももっと自分たちの足元を掘り下げていったほうが面白い。一見地味かもしれないけれど、そういうことからデザインの未来は開けるのではないかと思います。

A glimpse into the mind of Masaaki HIROMURA

An interview by Aya IIDA
July/August 2015

Masaaki HIROMURA on words

IIDA In the book, you share what you, as a designer, think about when creating something new and you delve into the subtleties of the thought process behind design. I've noticed that as far as designers go you seem to be very conscious of the words that you use.

HIROMURA When I first became interested in becoming a designer, I thought that design was about creating things that were cool. As the years passed and times changed, design has come to include not only creating physical form, but also bupilding context and structure. In order to do that, you need to be able to convey your ideas and get people around you involved. This is where words become very important.

Speaking has been a weak point of mine. For example, when I was in my mid-30s and had just started out on my own. I was going on and on explaining this plan that I had worked on so hard to a client, when he said to me, "I have no idea what you're trying to say." It totally threw me off.

From that point on, I decided to stop just saying whatever came to mind, and instead choose my words deliberately with the goal of always making myself understood.

Similarly, I've never felt writing to be a strong point of mine. But perhaps having my writing praised means that it has become a bit more intelligible. That probably has something to do with my mentor Ikko Tanaka. He would use plain words to produce incredibly moving prose.

IIDA I've heard that even when dealing with your office staff you rely on words rather than sketching things out.

HIROMURA Using images allows you to communicate ideas about things like form and color much more vividly and accurately than using words. But words allow you to be ambiguous. *Something like that thing we saw at that place.* Kind of like that, even on the phone. They have to interpret this in their own way, using their own unique vocabulary to visualize and create. The aesthetic senses of multiple individuals are incorporated into a project from the very beginning stages and the result is something fresh and exciting.

When working on a project, my staff join me during the consultation with the client because I assume that there will be slight differences in how we interpret the client's words, and I feel like it is within these differences that we can find the seeds from which design sprouts.

IIDA What's interesting is focusing on those differences, rather than trying to resolve them.

HIROMURA Design is basically the sharing of consciousness. It's like a common denominator. Design exists in the overlap between our own scope of thought and that of others, but I think that some very important pieces actually lie outside of this overlap. We may think that our understanding of something is completely obvious, but when we talk it over with someone it may turn out that's not the case. This is where we can discover the seeds of design, and if we cultivate those seeds they may grow into something fascinating.

I consider my role to be that of the listener and I always aim to be a good one. Designers are often thought of as very self-assertive, but on the contrary I try to be completely nonassertive.

This is especially true in my daily life. I have no real preferences. Of course I like things to look nice and I enjoy living in a clean, organized space, but beyond that I have no preference. I do feel like this may not be optimal as a designer, though. It's necessary to have some level of preference when dealing with others in business, in order to understand their wishes and issues.

It begins with questioning the ordinary

IIDA The theme of chapter one is "Question the Ordinary." I assume that this concept is a critical part of your design process.

HIROMURA As a designer, I feel that I must always remain skeptical. I am continually considering why I am doing something, whether it's good enough, and so on. There is a reaction that occurs during these brief moments of silence when thought ceases. I make a point of being skeptical because I feel it brings something to my design.

When it comes to design, even if there is only one goal destination, the paths leading there are limitless.

To me, design is about how you choose to enjoy the details along the way.

What's difficult is the fact that good design is not necessarily design that will sell. If you were to adopt a pure marketing perspective and just produced exactly what market values demand, that might take you 70% of the way. But when a client is looking for 90% or more, that won't cut it. The challenge of design lies in creating something that doesn't stop there.

IIDA   Speaking of the challenge of design and what makes good design, these are topics you tackled with the CO-OP Sapporo project (p.12), aren't they?

HIROMURA   That's right. 2015 marked the 50th anniversary of CO-OP Sapporo and they approached me about making some adjustments to their corporate identity.

CO-OP Sapporo serves all of Hokkaido, but many areas outside of Sapporo are dealing with aging of the population, and pretty much the whole prefecture is seeing decreases in the population. Consumer cooperatives can be found all throughout Japan, but they are truly a lifeline in Hokkaido, delivering food and the daily necessities at times when consumers are snowbound.

It became evident that all of the elderly customers really looked forward to talking with the staff delivering their goods. This meant that there were new business opportunities to be explored. One of these includes efforts to check in on the elderly in cooperation with local municipalities.

The CO-OP is founded on a philosophy of valuing each and every co-op member, and members only require a minimum investment of 1000 yen per person.

IIDA   Part of the project involved designing packaging for CO-OP's store brand. It was incredibly unique how you used only large written descriptions on the packaging and didn't include product pictures.

HIROMURA   Normally store brand packaging would call for consistency and flashy design, but we were interested in reducing costs so it occurred to me that we could rely on writing only to convey what the products were. Purposely creating packaging with nothing but descriptions has actually served to set the products apart and they now attract the consumers.

Consumers may only spend a fraction of a second looking at a product in the store, so many of the big brands use pictures on packaging since this is the most effective way of really catching the consumer's eye. I purposely avoided this strategy and took a chance on delivering a message to the customer even though it might take a moment to read.

Recently we've also been moving toward displaying carbon footprint, allergy, and calorie information.

Seeds of design in everyday life

IIDA   *Junglin'* makes an appearance in chapter two (p.24). I understand this is an ongoing project that could be considered your life's work.

HIROMURA   It all began with an exhibition that I held in 2011 after Seibu Ikebukuro approached me about doing something in commemoration of the department store's renewal. At the time I was playing with the idea that design "kindles the consciousness" so I decided to create something based on this theme. I titled it *Junglin'*. This is a play on the Japanese word junguri, which means "by turns." The name represents the idea that we can suddenly make important realizations amidst just unconsciously going about doing our normal daily thing.

In order to express our everyday actions, it seemed more appropriate to use something that moved rather than a still image, so I decided to use video. That said, I wasn't interested in creating a fancy, cutting-edge video. I had in mind something more along the lines of a flip book comic.

But the number of visitors for this first exhibition was pitifully low. But there were a few people who told me they really enjoyed the exhibition and shortly after one of the editors of *AXIS* magazine contacted me about writing a column for the magazine based on the same theme. That ended up lasting three or four years, with a total of 20 columns.

Searching for a theme to write about each time was tough, but it was a real learning experience. What is it that we are conscious of in unconsciousness? I searched for possible themes, and eventually I felt compelled to turn these themes into a new video, which became the *Junglin' 2 Consciousness in the Unconscious* exhibition that I held in 2014 at the AXIS gallery.

It really spans a truly broad range of themes. I think Junglin' is about discovering something from within continual movement. I plan on presenting a *Junglin'* that uses video shot in Kanazawa at an upcoming exhibition at the 21st Century Museum of Contemporary Art, Kanazawa in 2015–2016.

Graphic design, a starting point

IIDA You specialize in a broad range of design. Still, you always refer to yourself as a "graphic designer."
HIROMURA Whatever kind of work I do, for the rest of my life I would like to continue referring to myself as a graphic designer. I began with graphic design, and I feel graphic design plays a fundamental role in anything I do.

Therefore, whenever I size up a space or think about manufacturing a product, I always use graphic design as my guideline. An advantage of graphic design is that it is two-dimensional, so you could produce a likeness of the universe in seconds. It would be much more challenging to reproduce in a 3 dimensional format. With graphic design we can think more freely and let our imagination flow uninhibited.

When I design a space, I consider the first impression and I also design by picturing the space from the perspective of how it would look in photographs. Because the moment visitors step off the escalator, that is what they will see.

Architects often use the word "activity" to refer to the way they plan a layout by anticipating how people will move within that space, and I thought of how to incorporate that in a two-dimensional format.
IIDA I think you have a unique design approach. What did you take into consideration in designing this book?
HIROMURA When designing there is a certain sort of comfort achieved by following theories or rules. But, rather than the theories I learnt at school, I was much more strongly influenced by my time at Tanaka Design Office. My designs are different. Other designers find my spacing between lines and layouts perplexing.

In this book, I set out to typeset the Japanese text vertically and beside it, horizontally, the English translation. The book is bound on the left with the text running vertically. This sort of format is not typical, so at first glance one might find it rather strange.

I went ahead with my experimental design as Japanese people are open to diversity. Therefore, I believe they will indulge this irregular design.

What exactly is "an easy to understand" sign?

IIDA I would like to ask you about signage design. Can you please tell us your thought process of creating those signs?
HIROMURA In most signage design projects, clients typically request that the signs be easy to understand. I try to figure that out, and at the same time consider what would work in that specific environment.

Clients think their request refers to how clearly a place or route is displayed for customers. In my opinion, the truer sense of "easy to understand" is a more genuine understanding of the facility. Once the intention of the facility is communicated, the rest can be left to customers.

Compared with Japan, signage and security systems overseas are not as user-friendly. In Japan they are user-friendly and meticulous but also sometimes a little excessive. So, it is hard to say which is better. Either way with our signage, we avoid over directing.

One specific thing we do is to display a sign at the entrance depicting the entire signage system. In this way, customers are able to enjoy experiencing the whole space as it unfolds.

Additionally, we try to do this as simply and casually as possible. When we receive something nice, we are filled with happy feelings. It is a simple emotion, and this is what I want people who see the signs to feel.
IIDA For "TOTO Museum" (p.158), you designed signage that uses water drops as a motif.
HIROMURA TOTO is a company that develops water-related products. Their corporate slogan is "Water, Earth and Better Tomorrow." Therefore, I designed signage that uses water drops as a motif. We wanted visitors to see the water drops and recognize that the company truly values water.

At the entrance, there is nothing but numerous water drops. The water drops themselves do not show anything in particular, as they simply indicate the identity of the venue. I am not sure this can be called signage design anymore. (laughter)

IIDA   Regarding "Sumida Aquarium" (p.66), the signage makes the viewer think of an encyclopedia, making the aquarium look very different from the usual.

HIROMURA   We needed to discuss the concept of an aquarium located in the center of the city, which is different from an aquarium located on the seaside. As a result, I proposed a concept coined, "Sense Knowledge." Initially, I was asked to design only signage, but actually ended up on a concept that integrates the whole project. This includes symbology markings and graphic design.

Facilities like this aquarium should serve as an entertaining venue, therefore, many people involved believed that cutting edge technology was essential to the facility. However, new technology becomes obsolete once people take an initial look at it. Therefore, rather than impress visitors with new technology, I opted to focus on capturing many repeat visitors. Taking advantage of the urban location, I wanted the aquarium to be a place where people could just drop by for a drink at the bar, or just enjoy cool air in the summer.

I wanted Sumida Aquarium to be a place where stories are told. To express this idea, I used monotone etching for descriptions of the displays.

Slow Design

IIDA   In Chapter 7, "Speed of Design", you focused on designs for a slower pace versus designs for a faster pace.

HIROMURA   Actually, I am an impatient person, but design wise, I want to create slow designs. I think I should make slow designs so that people feel like taking time to understand what they mean. If designs make us see signs for 1 full second instead of 0.1 second, I think that would mean a lot, as we feel emotions during the process of understanding signs in 1 second. I think it is very important that signs evoke our emotions, because we then feel comfort and care, which in turn enhances our understanding.

Signs were developed to take the place of an actual person giving us directions. When we want gentle guidance, we need a person offering such considerate hospitality. This is what I try to infuse in my sign designs. Design exists for people, and should be people-oriented and more interactive. So, I want to convey this meaning through these signs that people look at.

Additionally, I want to enjoy myself when I am creating signs, and I want my enjoyable experience to be reflected in the design.

IIDA   For "Yokosuka Museum of Art" (p.150) the signage features "Yokosuka Kun," which directs visitors around the museum, this is a slow design. This design marked a turning point in your work as a sign designer.

HIROMURA   It is true that the signage designed for Yokosuka Museum of Art was highly commended. In my opinion, for one thing, the signs do not feature any words. Additionally, the signs appear to have movement. "Yokosuka Kun" is neither pictogram nor animation, but rather something in between. In fact, this sign is just like a page out of a series of pictures in a flipbook. Through his gestures we can tell if he is going upstairs or downstairs. By incorporating these elements the overall sign system functions very well. I believe that is why the signage for Yokosuka Museum and "9h" (p.90) were lauded.

IIDA   The signage for "9h" is a seemingly slow design without words similar to the Yokosuka Museum. But at the same time, in the sense that the signage should guide guests quickly, it is a fast design.

HIROMURA   I agree. 9h became a fast design due to the pursuit of rationality. 9h is a place to have a good rest, but without the conventional services expected at a traditional hotel. Because of this, I thought it is important that the signage should express information in the most simple and purest manner. 9h requires the customer to decide what actions to take, which is interesting and non-traditional. Even though the design is rational, it does not mean the place isn't warm or friendly. 9h represents my purest expression of sign design.

Likewise, the sign design for "Haneda Chronogate" (p.96) embodies rationality. Distribution terminals require functionality and speed, which demands the signs be pure. The sign design uses a stripe system, which is an extremely rational design. In this context, excessive rationality can work well to make signs very interesting.

IIDA   Materials and textures are also important elements in your design.

HIROMURA   To be honest, until a few years ago, when I created signs, I thought it was not necessary to utilize materials or textures. I believe the purpose of a sign is to relay information, therefore, though extreme, I felt it was unnecessary to consider the texture or thickness of materials.

I still continue to think this way, however, recently, I've wanted to use the texture of materials more effectively. For instance, for the Movida Section at Seibu Department Store in Shibuya, we came up with an idea of having numbers with a puffy rice cake texture. The texture encourages people to touch the numbers and by doing so their minds and senses are stimulated.

By touching materials we can identify the context of a space. Whether they are "puffy" or "grainy," I want to use materials that evoke a reaction from deep within our minds.

Directing one's attention to color

IIDA   What are your thoughts about the very important role that color plays in graphic design?

HIROMURA   Talking about color is incredibly tricky. The numbers and combinations of colors are practically infinite, so the more you know, the more intimidating it becomes to think about how to use them. Sometimes I think I'd rather not use any colors at all. (laughter)

Ikko Tanaka was often referred to as "the sorcerer of color", and he was certainly deserving of that name. There was this thing called "the color box" in his design studio. It contained bits of wrapping paper and packaging from abroad that he had cut off from various gifts he had received. Usually, you consult some kind of sample book or chart when choosing colors, but Mr. Tanaka selected his colors from the pieces of paper stocked in this box.

I created an installation called "His Colors" (p.180), in conjunction with the *Ikko Tanaka and Future / Past / East / West of Design* exhibition held at 21_21 DESIGN SIGHT in Roppongi. I selected materials from Cutting Sheet of a 100 different colors and TANT of 150 different colors, fixing them to the floor and walls in a corner of the exhibition room, trying to create a space made out of Mr. Tanaka's (use of) colors, and I ended up with something that I was genuinely pleased with. Of all the works recorded here, this is my personal favorite.

IIDA   Are there any other works in which color plays a particularly important role?

HIROMURA   That would be "Aichi Triennale 2013" (p.172). People will probably be drawn first to the shape of this VI (visual identity), but the most important thing about it is that it is uniformly blue. I wanted a "synchronizing blue" that expressed the coming together of people there. I wanted all the flags fluttering in the streets to signify and remind the locals of this event.

I also designed an unusually colorful logo for Loft's "SELF&SHELF LOFT" (p.206). It combines a black font with a slightly red-tinged yellow background. I suggested this color precisely because yellow was considered to be practically taboo for retail stores at the time, and so it felt very daring, almost extreme.

As CEOs have come and gone, this VI has continued, and this brought home to me the fact that a brand truly becomes a brand when the people within it feel a desire to protect and conserve it. When they created "SELF&SHELF LOFT", I decided to rework the original VI, this time using an array of colors. Although the stores are quite small and quaint, the items they stock are very colorful, so I felt it was apt.

A Japanese design orientation

IIDA   In *Japan Creative* (JC; Hearst Fujingaho, 2012), you stated that, historically, the Japanese have been good at taking negative elements, such as lack of space, and turning them into positive and desirable aspects. I feel that this Japanese way of thinking is strongly present in your own design too. Is there a particular reason or cause that triggered this approach of yours?

HIROMURA   I think Ikko Tanaka was a big influence in this regard. Mr. Tanaka used to be referred to as a "modern successor to the Rinpa school", and

I do think that growing up in old cities like Nara and Kyoto did rub off on him to some extent. But he himself claimed that he wasn't particularly interested in Japan to begin with. Around the 1960's he was asked to work on the compilation design of the book *Patterns of Japan: the beauties of nature* by the science historian Mitsukuni Yoshida, and this was apparently what triggered an interest in Japanese culture for him.

I, on the other hand, had no such inclinations when I first joined his office. But I was aware of the incredible talent that Mr. Tanaka possessed. I was constantly in awe of his creative talents, and so I suppose I was influenced by him considerably.

I thought it was a strange coincidence that I ended up participating in Japan Creative (JC, p.214). It led to me essentially revive what Mr. Tanaka was doing in the 1980's, only in a modern setting with a different concept.

I also had similar feelings of not being in sync with modern trends in design, especially during my 40's. I set myself up as an independent designer during the end of the economic bubble in Japan. There was a lot of lucrative work, and I was getting a lot of attention due to my relative youth. But after that came a difficult period, which I like to call "my dark 40's" (laughter), where nothing I made seemed to create any kind of significant impact.

It was around then that I met a certain architect and this led me to rethink and reevaluate my graphic design. My mentor Mr. Tanaka passed away in 2002, and this also brought about significant changes in my life. I was 48 at the time, in the midst of the long recession of the 90's, and things were becoming more and more closed and protectionist in Japan. As the economy declined, so did graphic design. The majority of clients stopped requesting what was interesting creatively, and began to move more in the direction of American commercial design, focused above all on sales and popularity. At the same time, everything was becoming digitalized.

But I was somewhat ambivalent about that glamorous and flamboyant era for design in the 80's, and I was starting to think of design as being something that you find from the routines of everyday life. It was an approach to design that had some similarities with the more inward-looking side of Japan, whereby you take a pre-existing idea and try to modify and improve it bit by bit. I began to think that design is probably created gradually, by observations and fresh perspectives on our everyday routines. I think this kind of Japanese way of thinking on my part came from Ikko Tanaka, via my work with Junglin' and JC.

IIDA That kind of design would seem to require a certain Japanese delicate sensibility, both on the part of the spectator and the user.

HIROMURA I don't want to come up with designs that are at their best when new, and then lose their sense of freshness with time. I try as much as possible not to use any kind of new technology that looks as if it's going to be quickly outmoded.

I also like the "Japanese-ness" of the concepts of "folding" and "shrinking". The Korean writer O-Young Lee published a book called *The compact culture— The Japanese Tradition of "Smaller is Better"* in the 80's, in which he cites the preference for minimization and miniaturization as a great achievement of Japanese sensibility. The distinction of Japanese technology lies in its ability to get the maximum level of efficacy and capability from much more limited conditions and materials.

IIDA Just as the characters for the word *shimau* (meaning 'to put away' in Japanese) also includes the character meaning "dance", Japanese people tend see a certain aestheticism in these kinds of concepts.

HIROMURA I think so. It's not just a matter of making things more compact, but relates to an entire manner or way of thinking about design. There is a connection with the idea of 'dignity in poverty' here, and I find myself wanting to apply this kind of economizing to my own life, in order to make it more manageable and compact.

The great thing about being involved with JC was that I got a chance to speak to various artisans. These people really believe in the skills and techniques that they've inherited, and I was impressed by their meticulous attention to detail and the great pride they had in their work. As lifestyles and values change, there is the problematic issue of how to preserve and boost the longevity of these traditional skills and methods. I'd like to take the intriguing art forms and techniques that I've encountered through the activities of JC and reintroduce them to the world.

IIDA   What are the specific aims of JC?

HIROMURA   JC is an organization that seeks to highlight and promote Japanese traditional manufacturing, as well as the latest in industrial design and technology, overseas. Its work is largely dependent on volunteers, but they're motivated by the opportunities to make connections with people all over the world and fulfill their artistic interests.

In actual fact, we've never had a single manufacturer refuse an invitation to collaborate. They've told me that they're absolutely dedicated to making something new, even if the chances of success are relatively low and costs are incurred. That has less to do with the reputation of JC and more to do with their willingness to take risks and create opportunities. We therefore have a sense of responsibility to these manufacturers to try and give them the best chance to develop and expose their work to the wider world.

JC has been able to continue its activities for this long because of its ability and foresight. Making everything cost-effective and creating the systems required for mass production is incredibly difficult, and there are some artisans who give up halfway, but we'd like to continue with what we're doing for as long as possible.

I think we're in an age when people coming from abroad are keen to learn from Japanese arts and crafts and have high expectations of its industrious and meticulous aesthetic. That is largely thanks to the Japanese people who have conserved and developed this culture. And because I'm aware of that, I'd like to live up to those expectations as far as possible.

Technology is a process, not an aim

IIDA   The last chapter is "Settled in Harmony". You finalize your ideas in a variety of different ways, but you mentioned earlier that you don't want "to use any kind of new technology that looks as if it's going to be quickly outmoded."

HIROMURA   I believe that the final harmony and detail determines the quality of a design. I consider a number of different methods for each project, but I tend to avoid using the latest technology. I don't want the technology to be a central feature of the design itself. Rather, I try to use technology to show the process of design. For example, "Book Clock" (p.36) uses monitors to display its images, but it has a distinctly low-tech aspect.

My planning for the 'airus' exhibition *airus— mechanism and quality* (p.122) received the DSA Grand Prize this year, but of the three pieces shortlisted for the prize, there was one that involved projection mapping in Zonohana Park in Yokohama. It was called "Buildings Acting"; people's faces were projected onto five buildings surrounding the park, and these people (or buildings) would then proceed to talk to each other. What this piece proved to me is that you can do something interesting with the technology just by having a novel concept or unique content, without relying on the latest computer graphics technology. That's how the functions of a particular technology widen and develop, and I believe that's how technology ought to be used.

IIDA   So why do you think the airus exhibition was so critically acclaimed?

HIROMURA   'airus' is a paper-type that has the opposing qualities of being both bulky and having a high degree of reproducibility. Rather than being used for posters, I felt it was a kind of paper best suited for things that you touch while reading, such as books. So I created an installation called "Touch airus", and made sure that people could touch the paper at the exhibition. Although it was essentially an exhibition showcasing paper, installing this interactive feature gave the impression of an experience that stimulated a multitude of senses, and I think that may have had something to do with its critical acclaim.

I also displayed photographs of 16 smiling centenarians, and these were very striking to me. If they had been aged 70 or 80, there would still be a sense of desire in their expressions, but when you reach a hundred, it seems like you're just grateful that you still get to wake up every morning. It's that gratitude and contentment that comes across in these faces. All the wrinkles, spots, and grey hairs had to come across clearly, to reinforce the innate value of living to a hundred in the minds of the viewers.

I thought that airus could handle this feat, and that's why I used it. With this one, I think we managed to get across the properties and quality of this paper very well.

What is design in the first place?

IIDA   In Chapter 8, you write that "the value of a design is determined by how much it can stretch the imagination of its individual recipients", and I thought that this was a good answer to the question "what is design?" For instance, in "Seibu Shibuya entrance" (p.238), your use of abstract gradating stripes manages to conjure up a variety of different sceneries and images depending on the viewer.
HIROMURA   Design deals with information, and one of its aims is to transfer that information to the recipient. But there is so much information out there these days that people often find it difficult to find the information they really want. Or the information is just like an electrical current that flows through the body, with nothing of any real value retained, and that's not got anything to do with design anymore. Design has to communicate something in an intelligible way, and create a sense of value in a person. We designers try to do this by manipulating visual images, colors, or text. However, I do try to make sure that my designs don't just transfer information in one direction.

The original concept behind "Seibu Shibuya entrance" was of a purely commercial and practical nature. But it had to instill some kind of emotional reaction in the passersby to truly grab them. The evanescent, blurring, one-and-only color combinations created are perceived differently from person to person, and it was interesting to leave the effect of this installation up to the individual sensibilities of each viewer. After all, that's the very essence of "interactive".

Thinking about the future of design

IIDA   Finally, how do you think design will evolve in the future?
HIROMURA   The word "design" is far more prevalent now compared with when I was a student. I think that what design" refers to, and is effective for, is constantly changing, without a clearly fixed definition.

I once defined design as "the creation of new experiences" in a presentation for a group of high school students. By "new experiences", I don't mean something that has never even been conceived of before, but a slight alteration in perspective. This applies to all forms of design. By altering the way we experience a particular thing, design also alters our behavior and reinvigorates our awareness. So I think the future of design has to be based on the aim of constantly suggesting new ways of experiencing.

On the other hand, the word "new" is considerably open to interpretation. The weight of pressure that comes with this word is something that all designers struggle with, but if you set off with the premise that there's no such thing as "new", then you can't really *do* design. But if you consider "new" to be something hidden in the corner, hitherto gone unnoticed, then the idea of finding it becomes a realistic prospect. I think that the act of creating new experiences is just a succession of these kinds of "finds" or discoveries.

For example, when I look at the mechanism that allows a drawer to be closed slowly, I really get inspired. I get the sense that the very action of closing has itself a kind of texture. It might be a small thing, but a solid and good design has a significantly beneficial effect on our lives. When I speak to different companies, I often hear the word "globalization" being thrown about, but personally I think the world is globalized enough. What's more interesting is taking a closer, deeper look around your own backyard, so to speak, and digging for new ideas there. I think that it's these kinds of things that'll pave the way for the future of design.

7 | Speed of Design

Do we perceive "Time" as it should be perceived?

    Time passes quickly in good times, conversely, it seems to pass very slowly during difficult times. We shouldn't pass this off as a silly saying, because it is referring to our frame of mind. Our sense of time seems to vary depending on our age. This has been analyzed logically by "Janet's Law." According to this theory, how a person feels about the passage of time is inversely proportional to our age. As we grow older, we gain more experiences. We develop a sort of immunity; things are less surprising, leading to us feeling as if time gets shorter. There is an equation to calculate effective time in integral value, showing that a person with a lifetime of 80 years would hit the halfway point at the age of 10. I think that this idea is not completely wrong.

    In the design industry, however, the speed of time is perceived differently. Advertisement or web design is much faster. Whereas, book and package design tend to have a slower pace. This represents the perception of time, it can also be considered as the speed the information is consumed. At stations or airport, recognition must be as quick as possible. At museums or hotels, a slower pace is favored. This is a concept of time developed by the space. In some spaces, we walk and talk at a slower pace. Our outfits or facial expressions seem gentle and slow. Designs for those types of spaces encourage quietness and thinking. Whereas, fast design pace works better for something functional or stimulating. Designs for a slower pace are suited for objects that relay a story. Personally, if asked, I prefer to be a person who does things at a slower pace.

七、デザインのスピード

「時間」はちゃんと捉えられているのだろうか。

楽しい時間は早く過ぎ、辛く苦しい時間は長い。そう感じるだけ、とバカにしてはいけない。体感する時間の感覚は人によって、年代によって違う。

これを論理的に分析した「ジャネーの法則」がある。

人が感じる時間の長さは自らの年齢に反比例するという説で、大人になると既に経験した事柄が多くなり、刺激が減るので体感時間が短くなる。体積体感時間という計算式では八〇才の人生の折り返しは一〇才くらいになるのである。あながち間違っていないな、と考えてしまう。

デザインの領域でも時間の速度は違う。

広告やWEBは早く、本やパッケージは遅いと感じてしまう。

これは主に認知する時間の感覚だが、情報を消費するスピードと考えてもいい。

サインデザインでは、駅や空港など認知する速度が重要な場所と、美術館やホテルなど、ゆっくりと理解や価値を深めるほうが良い場所がある。

それは空間がつくる概念時間と考えてもいい。

歩く速さや会話の速度、服装や表情までゆったりと感じる空間は、デザインのスピードも静かに深く進むのである。

機能的で刺激的にはファストが、おだやかで物語的にはスローなデザインが似合うような気がする。どちらかと問われれば私はスローな人になりたい。

とろとろ時間の過ぎる場所

海を眺める一等地だと思った。
三浦半島の突端、観音崎公園の中に
この「横須賀美術館」はある。
東京湾の入口に位置し、
海上はひっきりなしに大小の船が往来する。
一日中眺めていてもあきない風景、
そんな美術館では時間がゆっくり過ぎていく。
海を眺めて食事をとり、アートを鑑賞する。
とろとろ時間が過ぎるところには、
ゆっくりしたデザインが良い。
多言語で案内するのではなく、ここでは人の動作を
アイコンにした「よこすかくん」が誘導してくれる。
読むのではなく、眺めるサインである。
(横須賀美術館　二〇〇七年)

A Slow-paced Spot

I think Yokosuka Museum of Art's location is perfect, with a breathtaking view of the sea, where time slows down. From the museum, which is in Kannozaki Park, on a point of the Muira Peninsula, a continuous stream of large and small vessels are visible, sailing to and from Tokyo Bay. It is possible to spend a whole day looking at the view and never tire of it. Also within the museum, time seems to pass deliberately slower. Whether savoring the scenery while dining in the museum restaurant or looking at art, the museum's slow design, makes one appreciate the value of a more leisurely pace. Instead of multilingual information, a male pictogram referred to as "Yokosuka kun," guides visitors. The design of the signs can be visually interpreted, without any text, reading is not required.

(Yokosuka Museum of Art, 2007)

よこすかくんはちょっとコミカルである。
階段を上り、遠くを眺め、本を読みながらこの場所が何か、
この先に何があるのかを教えてくれる。

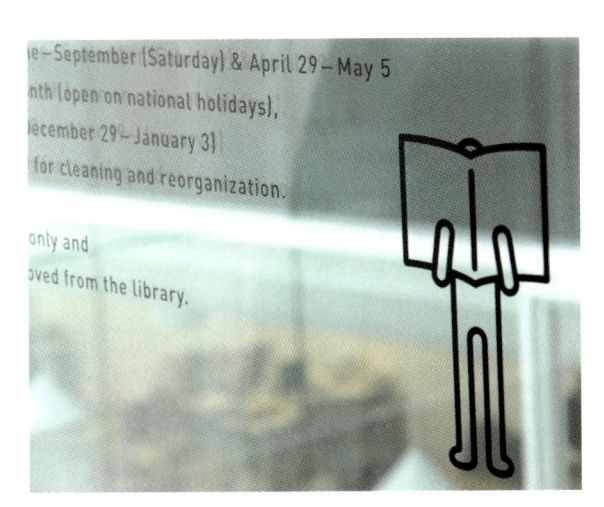

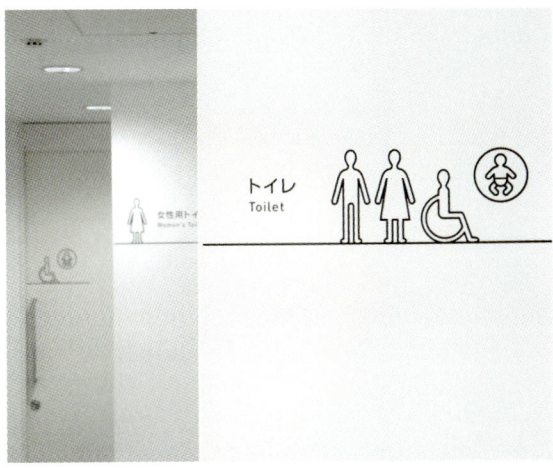

Yokosuka-kun has a slightly comical appearance. He is represented doing various actions such as climbing stairs, looking into the distance and reading. Through this format, he relays direction and information.

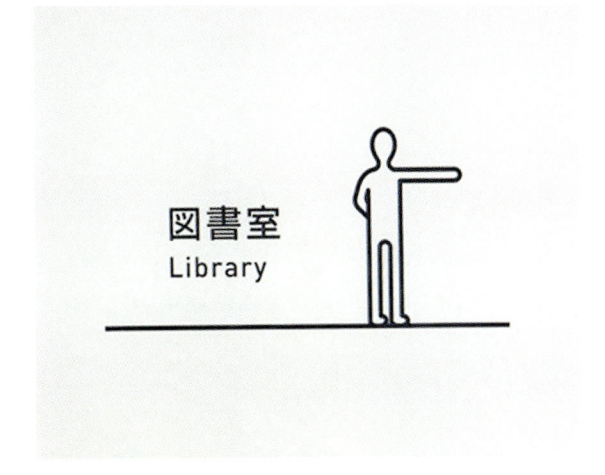

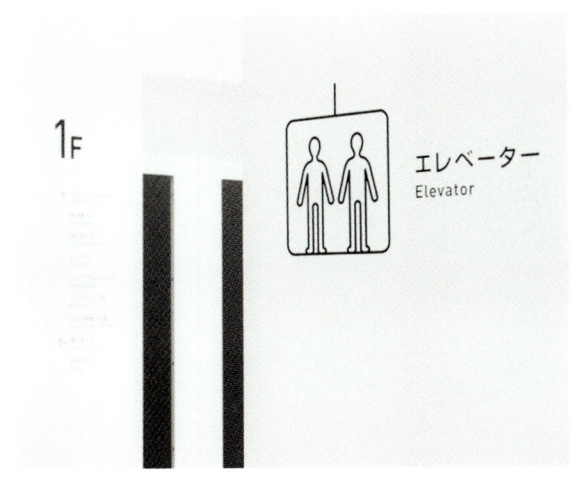

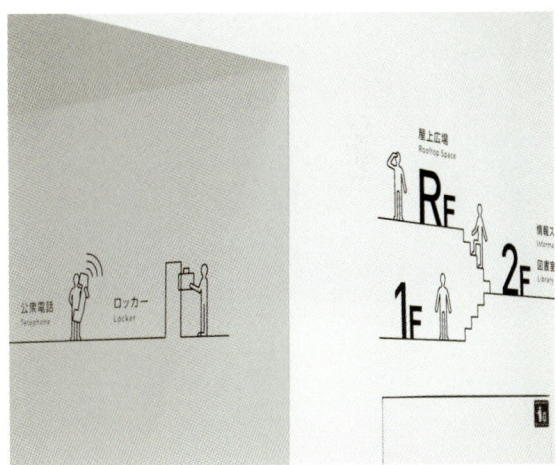

153

Not Sick

In concluding a long journey, ships dock for maintenance and refueling, similarly, people need to stop and get medical checkups to maintain their health. Medical checkups are not limited to those who are sick; people in good health can also get a checkup as preventative health care. Located in Chiba Prefecture, Shinwa medical resort is a progressive medical and wellness resort. Similar to conventional medical institutions it provides medical checkups, additionally; it also has a spa, fitness facilities and a restaurant that serves traditional Japanese cuisine. We used a metal hanger, as the design motif for the signs. Identifying icons were placed in front of each room.
(Shinwa medical resort, 2011)

病気ではない

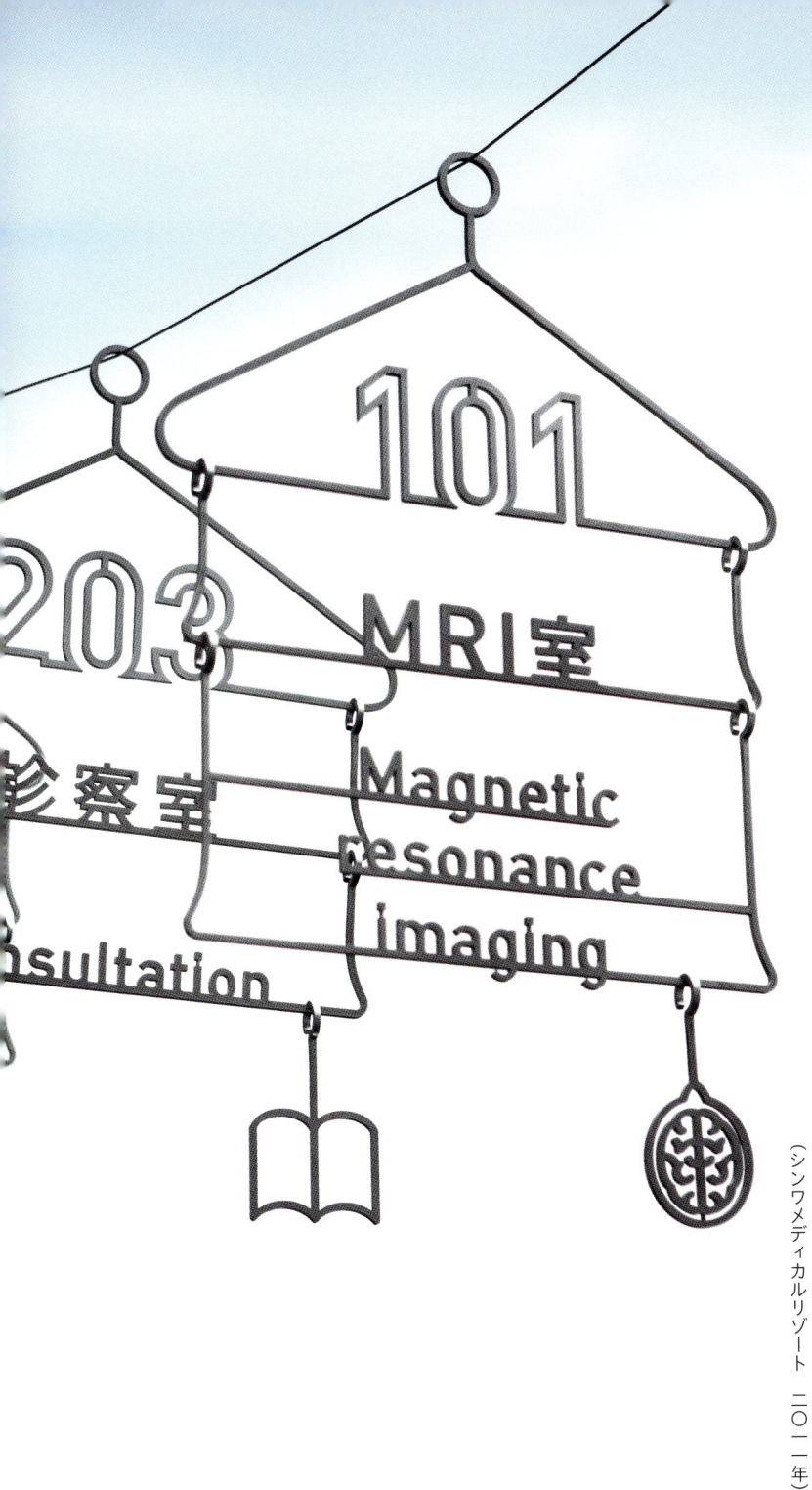

船が航海を終えてドックに入るように、人間もカラダをチェックするために人間ドックを利用するのでまだ病気ではないので利用する人は健康で元気が良い。千葉県に、この人間ドックをさらに進化させた医療リゾート「シンワメディカルリゾート」ができた。検診もするが、スパやフィットネス、割烹料理も楽しめる医療リゾート。

サインデザインはハンガーをモチーフにデザインし、各部屋の特徴を表したアイコンがワンポイントになっている。

（シンワメディカルリゾート　二〇一一年）

アタマと手

研究は、はじめに仮説を考え、それを立証するために実験を繰り返す。一瞬のひらめきを生むアタマと、実際に行動する手が必要なのである。自動車や電化製品に使用されているプラスチックの部品を開発するニフコの新技術開発センターのサインデザインを考えた。技術研究者の手をアイコン化して文字と絡ませ、人間的で楽しいサインができた。
（ニフコ技術開発センター 二〇一三年）

Head and Hands

Each research process begins with identifying and formulating a hypothesis. Following this, a series of experiments must be conducted in order to gather conclusive evidence.
This process requires the brain, the source of the initial inspiration, as well as the hands, which execute the required tasks. We were asked to design a sign for Nifco's Technology Development Center. The center develops plastic components for automobiles and electrical appliances. By combining an icon showing a research developer's hand with lettering, we produced a cheerful and visually enjoyable sign.
(Nifco Technology Development Center, 2013)

157

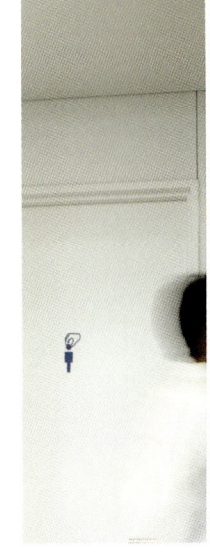

A Water Drop's Thoughts

When I was young, thirsty, after extracurricular activities, I drank water straight from the faucet. I still remember how refreshing it tasted. Concerns about the safety of drinking tap water materialized only after the availability of bottled water. Did you know that worldwide, there are only 15 countries, including Japan, where tap water is safe to drink? Japan has an abundance of water, which has fostered business opportunities for water-related companies. One such business is TOTO. TOTO has grown to provide a range of products, from sanitation hardware to a toilet seat called WASHLET. The WASHLET became popular worldwide in the 1980s.

TOTO's slogan is "Water, Earth, and A Better Tomorrow." To achieve this, TOTO has continued to develop water-related products that interact with us during our daily lives. In 2017, TOTO will mark its 100th anniversary. To commemorate this, the "TOTO MUSEUM" was completed in Kokura, Kitakyushu. Obviously, having a relationship with water, icons resembling drops of water is the prevailing theme. Visitors are welcomed with 1,000 water drops. As one passes the information counter, all signage in the museum is based off of a water drop. Each water drop seems to represent nature and quality of life in Japan.
(TOTO MUSEUM, 2015)

しずくの気持ち

部活のあと、蛇口に口をつけて飲む水の美味しさは格別だった。ボトルで水が売られるようになるまではなんの疑いもなく水道水をゴクゴク飲んでいたのだ。安全に水道水が飲める国は、世界で十五カ国しかないことを知っているだろうか。豊かな水の国日本は、水にまつわる産業がたくさん発達した。

TOTOもそのひとつ。衛生陶器の製造からはじまり、一九八〇年に発売した「ウォシュレット」は今では海外でも使用されている。

「水と地球の、あしたのために。」を環境のスローガンに、まさに生活の「水まわり」を担っている。

二〇一七年、百周年を迎える記念事業として北九州小倉市に「TOTOミュージアム」をオープンした。

水にまつわるミュージアムは、水滴がアイコンになっている。エントランス脇では約一〇〇〇個の水滴が出迎え、案内カウンターから誘導サイン、トイレ表示までしずくがみずみずしく付着している。ひとつひとつのしずくは、日本の自然と生活の豊かさを表しているようだ。

(TOTO MUSEUM 二〇一五年)

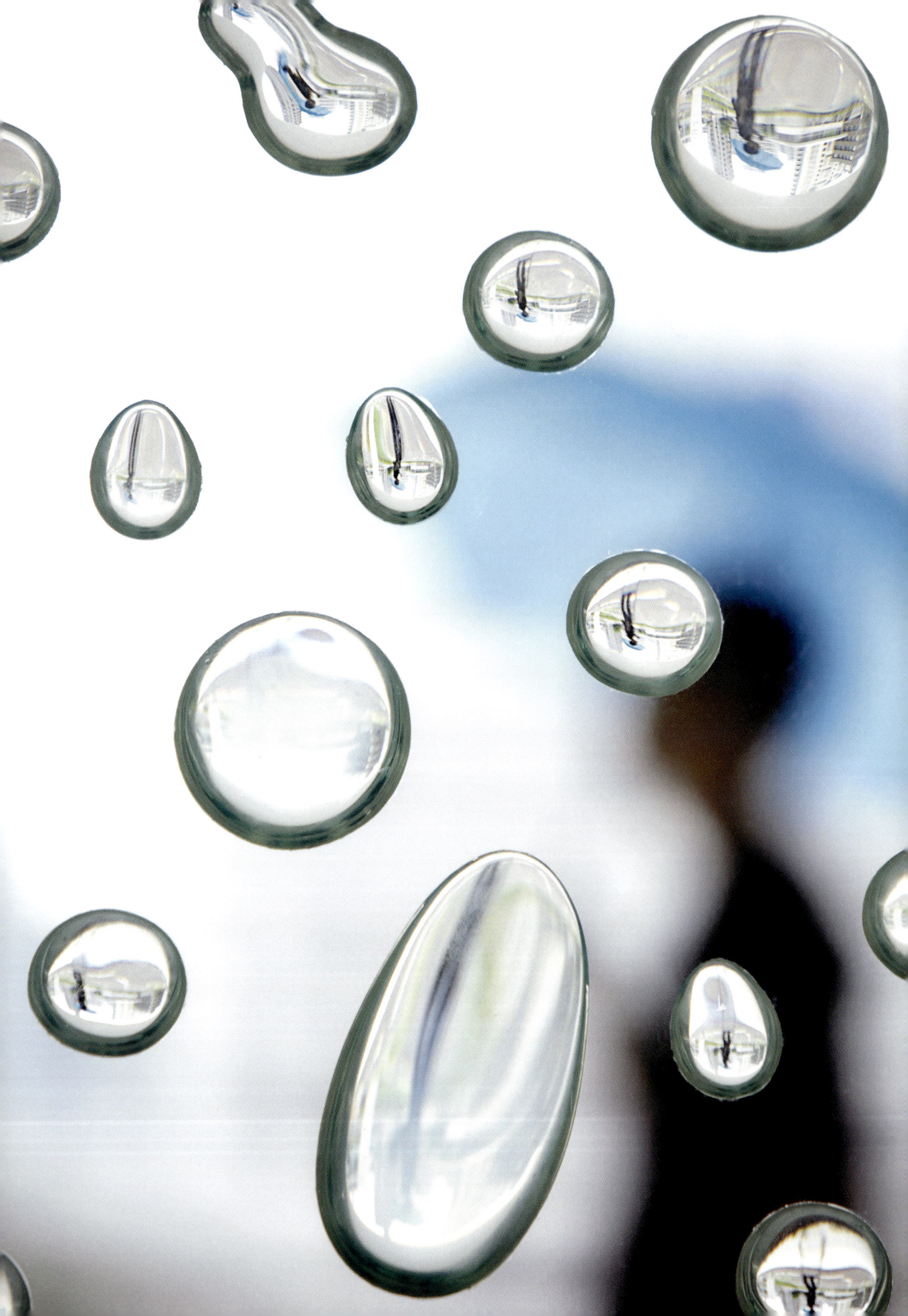

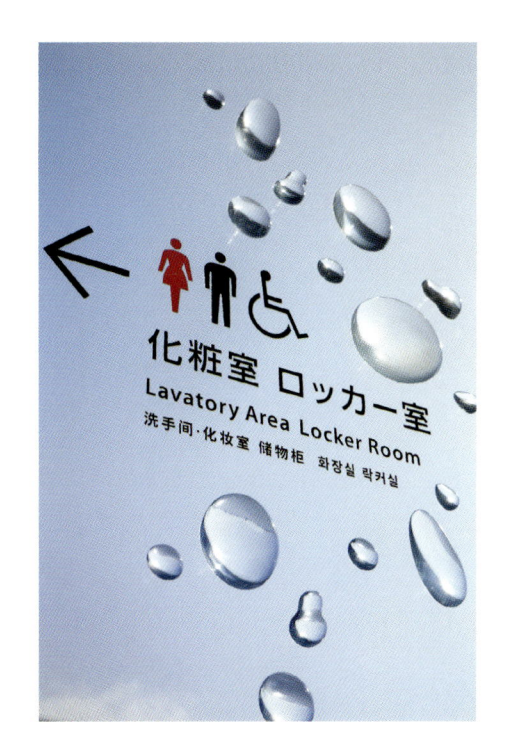

↑2
ミュージアム
MUSEUM
博物馆　박물관

化粧室 ロッカー室
Lavatory Area Locker Room
洗手间·化妆室 储物柜 화장실 락커실

4

TOTO
MUSEUM

あたらしくある。なつかしくある。
すみだの魅力を
国内外に伝える
「商品」「メニュー」を
募集します。

すみだモダン
2015募集中

〈商品部門〉〈飲食店メニュー部門〉
募集期間 2015年8月3日［月］〜8月31日［月］
説 明 会 2015年8月10日［月］
①15時〜16時 ②19時〜20時 ※2回とも同じ内容です。
会場 すみだリバーサイドホール 会議室（墨田区役所1階）
予約不要 直接会場にお越しください。

すみだ地域ブランド推進協議会事務局 墨田区産業観光部産業経済課内
電話 03-5608-6188 ファックス 03-5608-6934
メール BRAND@city.sumida.lg.jp
「すみだ地域ブランド戦略」ホームページ http://sumida-brand.jp

すみだ地域ブランド 検索

すみだモダン

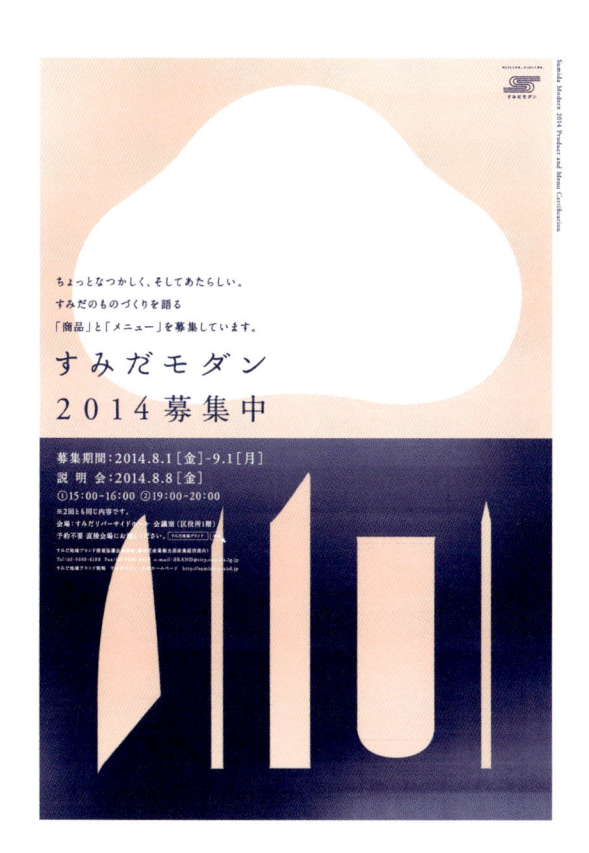

Sumida Modern

Since the TOKYO SKYTREE® was completed, downtown Sumida became very crowded. During the Edo Period (1600-1868), Sumida prospered, and was known for its popular culture. Today, there are a number of companies that play key roles to invigorate the town, ranging from industry to businesses that we use in our day to day lives. One example is modern manufacturing derived from traditional craftsmanship. Another is joint development projects or OEM's with technologically advanced global brands. Cuisine culture should also be discussed, as there is a wide variety of food to be enjoyed. Monjya, food similar to a pancake, is an all-time favorite. Also, B-grade or hole-in-the-wall restaurants are scattered about. Sumida has commissioned the "Sumida Modern" initiative.
This project aims to certify various businesses and products from companies and stores in Sumida, in order for them to be more widely known. The more we know about Sumida, the more we are charmed by its old, yet modern, features.
(Sumida Modern, 2011–)

モダンなすみだ

東京スカイツリー®が建てられてから、下町は騒がしい。墨田区は江戸時代、庶民文化が栄えた中心地。伝統的な職人技を現代に継承したものづくりから、高い技術力で世界的なブランドの共同開発やOEMまで産業から暮らしまで重要な部分を支えている企業がたくさんある。
また食文化も見逃せない。定番のもんじゃから隠れた名店、B級グルメまでバラエティがある。
「すみだモダン」という認証事業が区の主導ではじまった。墨田区の製造事業者や飲食店の商品・メニューを認証して、多くの人に知ってもらう事業である。
知れば知るほど、古くてモダンなすみだは面白い。
(すみだモダン 二〇一一年ー)

Sumida is old and yet also modern, we wondered how to express this through graphic design. There is an abstract feel to Sumida, one can feel tradition and see manufacturing. It has cosmopolitan atmosphere and yet there are discount confectionary stores and small restaurants serving home-style cooking. To capture this, color was an important element. We thought by using contrasting colors, food and products could depict the traditional and the modern. Photographs were shot by zooming in on the subject, in a classic style. The clarity of the focus strongly drew attention to the subject.

古くてモダンなすみだをグラフィックで考えてみる。抽象的でありながら、ものづくりや伝統を感じ、現代的でありながらB級グルメや駄菓子のセンスもある。色彩も重要な要素。対比する二色を使い、伝統とモダン、プロダクトと食品を感じさせるように考えた。写真はなるべくオーソドックスに、ピントを一点に合わせることで見るポイントを明解にする。

あたらしくある。

なつかしくある。

江戸の昔、このまちには隅田川を中心として
縦横に運河がながれていました。

川のまわりには身近な生活品の工房が集まり、
職人たちが腕を競いあっていました。

もっと美しいもの、
もっと洒落たもの、
もっと使いやすいもの。

明治、大正、昭和、ずっとずっとそうでした。

今もすみだには時を超えてあたらしく、
そしてなつかしい、ものづくりがあります。

あなたも感じてください、すみだモダン。

珈琲も味噌汁もおいしく。
本漆し塗り マグカップ

漆は「うるわし」とも呼ばれ、漆塗りは縄文時代から続く、世界に誇る日本の伝統文化だ。安宅さんは歴史ある建造物を手がける漆塗職人。日常の中で、気軽にふだん使いできる本物をつくろうと考えた。手に取るとふわりと軽く、漆の持つ重厚感ある色と艶、やさしい温もりが魅力。

〔認証理由〕文化財の修復を任されている高度な漆職人の技が、日常生活品に活かされている。

① map
安宅漆工店
代表者／安宅信太郎
東京都墨田区向島3-38-10
平蔵門線／都営浅草線押上駅より徒歩5分
電話 03-3622-1582
hozonkai.com/Shintarou_Ataka.html

表具文化の粋に触れる。
趣向裂カード入れ 蓋付

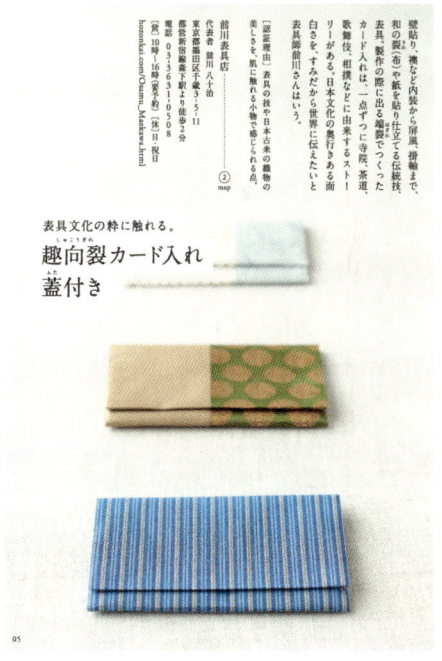

壁貼り、襖から内装まで、和の製作（布）や紙を貼り仕立てる伝統技、表具製作の際に出る端布でつくったカード入れは、一点ずつに寺院・茶道・歌舞伎・相撲などに由来するストーリーがある。相撰さんは、日本文化の奥行きある面白さを、すみだから世界に伝えたいと表具師前川さんらはいう。

〔認証理由〕表具の技や日本古来の織物の美しさを、肌に触れる小物で感じられる6点。

② map
前川表具店
代表者／前川八十治
東京都墨田区千歳3-5-11
都営新宿線馬喰横山駅より徒歩2分
電話 03-3631-0508
〔営〕10時〜16時半頃〔休〕日・祝日
hozonkai.com/Omaru_Maekawa.html

An Eternal Resting Place

It is hard to say what happens after we die. Is there an afterlife? Do we go to a heaven or a hell? Or, do we become ghosts and wander around, like in the film "Ghost?" Nobody who is living really knows. To others, when our lives end, our bodies will become nothing but objects. Some hope that our souls will remain, perhaps because of religious beliefs. The Japanese word "ohaka," a grave, seems to be derived from "hateka" or "hateru." Those words refer to a place of demise, where we go when our lives are finished. I was introduced to Futakama, Director of Futakamiya Corporation. The company located near a cemetery in Tokorozawa, Saitama Prefecture, has provided services related to graves for 80 years. In much detail, Futakami explained about the current state of the Japanese market, to choosing a stone, as well as the depth of tombstone engravings.

His explanations had much depth, similarly is the history of graves and gravestone. After thinking so much about graves, I felt the need to pay my respects to my ancestors. I do not know much about ghosts or spirits. However, I would say that it is a good thing to remember our ancestors from time to time.
(Futakamiya, 2015)

最後の場所

人生が終わった後のことはわからない。あの世があるのか、天国や地獄に行くのか、映画「ゴースト」のように亡霊になってさまようのか、本当にわからない。

シャッターが降りるように一生が終われば肉体はただの物体になってしまう。でも魂は存在しているだろうと願うのは信心の証かもしれない。

お墓は日本語のハテカ、またはハテルが語源らしい。それは終焉の場所という意味で、人生最後に行き着くところという意味なのだ。

そのお墓の仕事を所沢の霊園近くで八〇年続けている「二上家」の二上さんを紹介してもらった。肩書きはお墓ディレクター。「そもそもお墓とは、」からはじまり、日本のお墓市場の現状、石の選択から彫り込む文字の深さまで、歴史の分だけ話も深い。

お墓のことを考えていたら、墓参りがしたくなった。魂とか霊とかのことはわからないけれど、先祖のことを想うひとときがあってもいい。

(二上家　二〇一五年)

8 | Weaving Information

There used to be a program on TV called "The Association Game." Divided into two teams of reds and whites, the contestants would guess the answers to questions through associations based on small clues. The host would begin every show with the words "There are as many associations as there are people. What kind of funny and unique associations are we going to hear from our contestants tonight."

What was fun about this program was seeing how much of a common platform or set of shared assumptions the players had, or didn't have, as was often the case. With different backgrounds and values, it was interesting to see how they tried to come up with a single unified answer from such a small clue. "There are as many associations as there are people"; the assumption being that everyone is different, and that this program was at its most entertaining when demonstrating just how different and idiosyncratic our imaginations can be.

Our associations are very much dependent on qualia, or individual instances of subjective experience. Whether we associate the color blue with the sky, or hangovers with headaches, it is our subjective experiences that link these images together. Vague feelings of "somewhat" and "~like" mesh over one another to form a clear and distinct image in our minds.

Design also depends heavily on association. Whether a mass-produced design or a particular message conveyed via the media, the value of a design is determined by how much it can stretch the imagination of its individual recipients.

Sign design can be said to direct associations of information in an even more specific way. Directing symbolizations, indications, and significations are all part of 'sign design.' From a desire to convey a lot, complex information is woven into a single thread and then transmitted to the public arena.

These woven pieces of information rush through our network of neurons, awakening our memories.

八、情報を編む

昭和のテレビ番組に「連想ゲーム」というのがあった。紅白に分かれて、わずかなヒントから回答を連想するゲームである。

番組は、司会者の「連想は十人十色と申します。今夜はどんなに楽しい、そしてユニークな連想が飛び出してくるのでしょうか」という言葉で始まる。

この番組の楽しさは、出演者同士に共通の土台（プラットホーム）がどれだけあるのかというのがポイント。生まれや育ちが違う、価値観も違う人々が小さなヒントからひとつの回答を探していくプロセスが面白いのだ。

「連想は十人十色」なのだ、人と違っていて当たり前、違った連想が番組を盛り上げる。

連想はクオリア（感覚質）が大きく影響する。青色から空を連想し、二日酔いから頭痛を想像するように、主観的な体験から得られる感覚がイメージをつくる。「何となく」「そんな感じ」といった曖昧な感覚の意識が重なり、はっきりした像を描く。

デザインも連想がとても重要。大量生産のデザインであってもマスメディアに向けたメッセージであっても、受け取る個人の想像をどれだけ広げられるかがデザインの価値になる。

サインデザインはさらに具体的に情報の連想を導くデザインと言える。記号化（サイン）し、指示（サイン）し、印（サイン）に導くのがサインデザインなのだ。伝えたいことはたくさんある。複雑な情報を分かりやすく一本の糸に編み込んで届ける。

編み込まれた情報は、脳のニューロンネットワークを駆け巡り、記憶の感覚が呼び覚まされる。

インフォライン

道のない山や森に入るとき、人は標（しるし）を記しておく。同じ間隔で、途中の曲がり角や休んだところに、迷わぬためにリボンをつけ、枝を折り自分の痕跡を残す。人は空間に法則を探す。同じ印（しるし）や線（ライン）など、何か共通することがないか意識を凝らし、見つけようとする。しるしを残し、しるしを探すのは、人が生きるために本能的に身につけた行動パターン。それを活用したのがサインデザインの始まりである。
（東京工芸大学新三号館　二〇一一年）

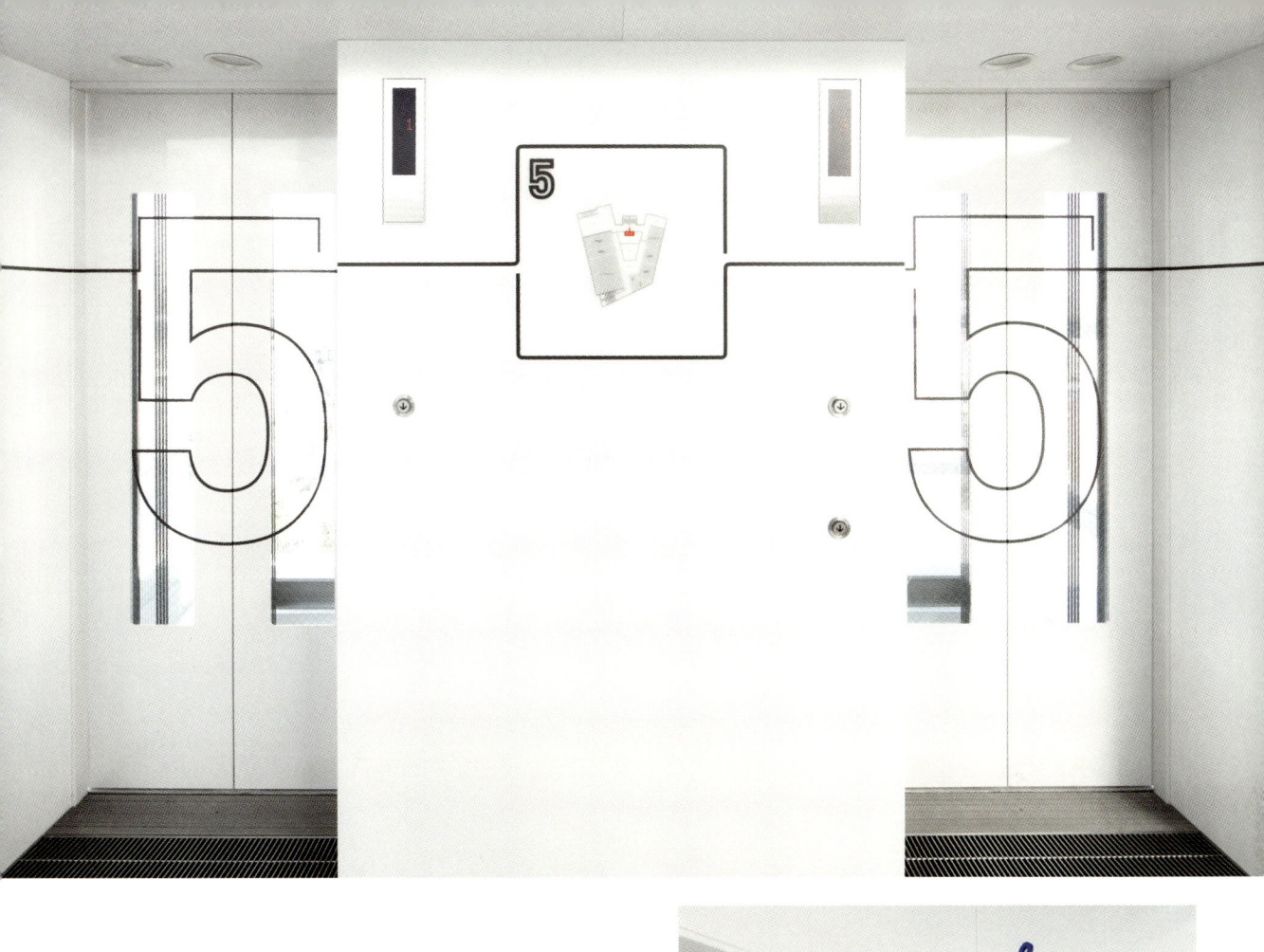

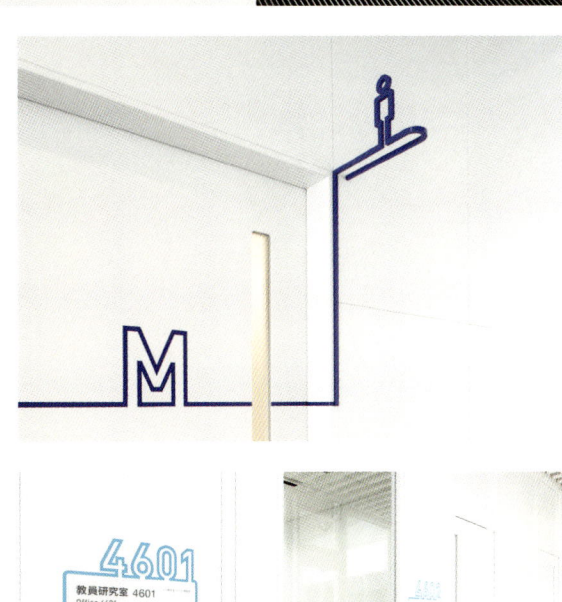

Infoline

When venturing into mountains or forests with no roads, people leave markers to find their way around. In equal intervals, they may tie ribbons or break off branches at various turns or resting spots, leaving traces behind them so as not to get lost on their way back. People naturally look for patterns and laws in the spaces they occupy, trying to fix their awareness on similarities in signs and lines. Leaving signs behind and searching for new ones is an instinctive pattern of behavior in humans. The origin of sign design lies in the application of this fact.
(Tokyo Polytechnic University Nakano Campus, 2011)

シンクロするブルー

小説「若きウェルテルの悩み」や詩劇「ファウスト」などを生んだドイツの文豪ゲーテ。彼が晩年二〇年間を費やして書きあげたのが「色彩論」。ゲーテはその書物の中で「根源的な色は青と黄色、色彩は光と闇の相互作用により生まれる」と論じている。光にいちばん近い黄色、闇の本質を表す青、それらの頂点には燃え上がる赤という三原色の理論である。
二〇一三年、真夏に始まるアートイベント「あいちトリエンナーレ」に関わることになった。テーマは「揺れる大地」。東日本大震災を受け、アートでもこの重いテーマを真摯に考えていこうということだ。直感的にこのアートイベントを色でまとめようと考えた。使う色はブルー、印刷で使うシアン一〇〇％のブルーをメインカラーにした。闇を表し、冷たく澄んでいるブルー。七月の名古屋は暑い。ブルーのフラッグやサインに街は染められ、行き交う人々とシンクロしていた。
（あいちトリエンナーレ2013　二〇一三年）

Synchronized Blue

The German author Goethe, famed for his works such as the novel "The Sorrows of Young Werther" and the play "Faust." Towards the latter part of his literary career, he published "The Theory of Colors", a scientific work 20 years in the making. In it, he claims that "the original colors are blue and yellow, and the variety of colors are born from the mutual interaction between darkness and light." This is a theory of the three primary colors: yellow, which is closest to light, blue, which expresses the essential quality of darkness, and the fiery red, which exists in the peak between them. In 2013, I participated in the Aichi Triennale, an arts festival held in the middle of summer. The theme that year was "the trembling earth." The intent was to reflect on the colossal tragedy of the Great East Japan Earthquake through the medium of art.Instinctively, I felt like I wanted to encapsulate this event with colors. I chose blue, more specifically the 100% cyan used in color printing, as my main color; that cold and clear blue, so expressive of darkness. Nagoya in July is incredibly hot. The city was covered with blue flags and signs, in synch with the crowds of people passing through it.
(Aichi Triennale 2013, 2013)

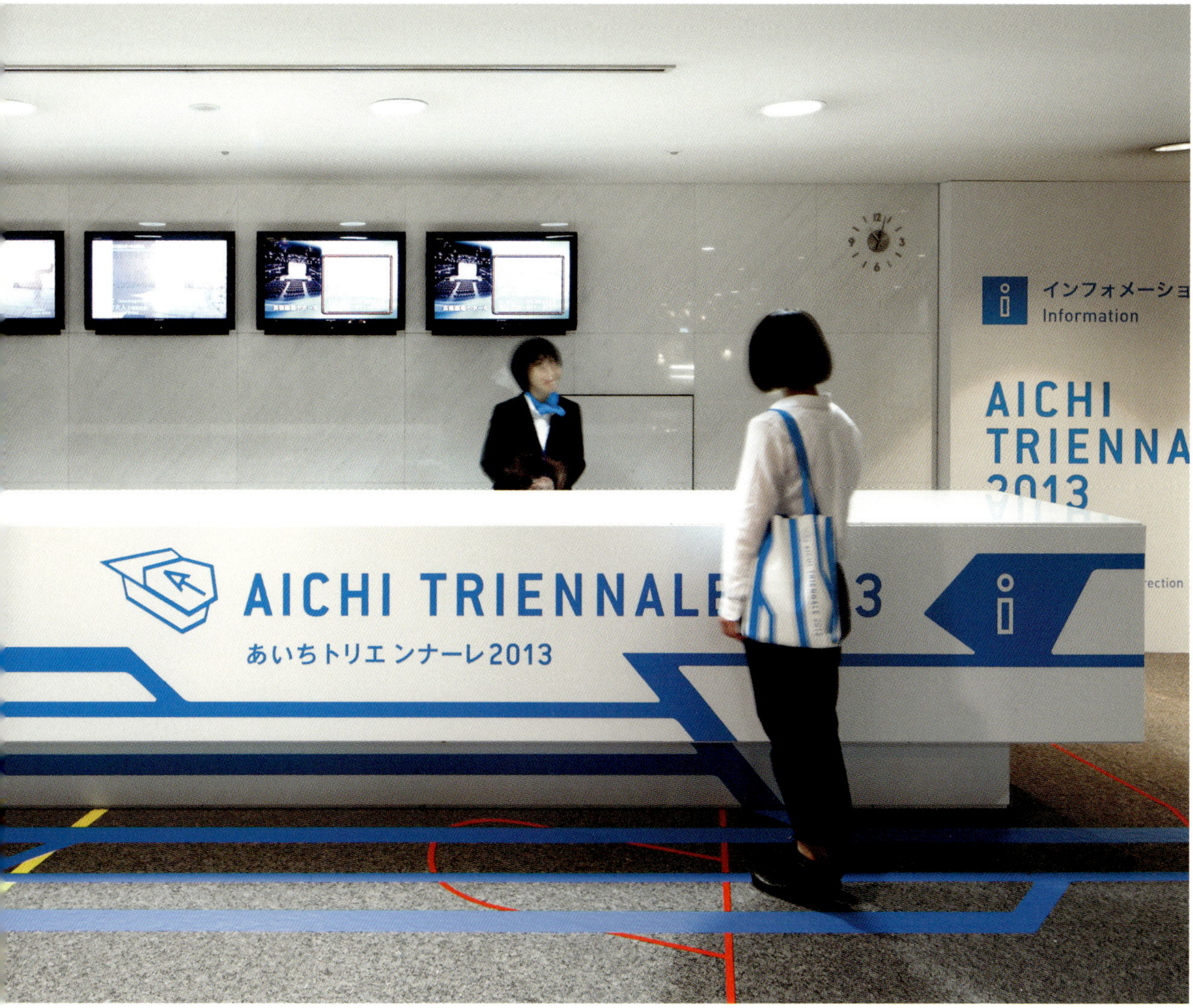
Information
AICHI TRIENNALE
あいちトリエンナーレ2013

174

上段右：ベロタクシー
下段右：告知用３連ポスター
その他：会場風景
Top right: Velotaxi
Bottom right: A series of 3 promotional posters
Other: Scenes from the venue

告知ポスター
Announcement poster

先生と師匠

田中一光は昭和を代表するデザイナー。一九三〇年に奈良で生まれ、京都で学び東京で活躍した。私の師匠である。膨大な作品をつくり、多くの企業と仕事をして、多趣味で、食べることに深いこだわりがあった。社会的な活動に積極的に臨み、多くの成果をあげてたくさん受賞した。世界中に友人がいて贈り物や献本が多く、毎日お礼状を書いていた。田中一光の展覧会が企画され、会場構成を担当することになった。会場は「21_21 DESIGN SIGHT」。単なる作品展ではなく、思考のプロセスを展示しようということになり、保存してあった資料を見直してみた。在籍当時は毎日忙しく、流れるように仕事をこなしていたが、一点一点の密度が恐ろしく濃いことをあらためて認識した。私がアルバイトで手伝いはじめたときから「田中先生」と呼ばれていたのは、学校で先生をしていたからだが、事務所は完全な徒弟制度。入社というよりは弟子入りだと腹をくくった。やはり私には師匠である。

(21_21 DESIGN SIGHT 企画展 田中一光とデザインの前後左右 二〇一二—二〇一三年)

Teacher and Master

Ikko Tanaka is the definitive designer of the Showa Period in Japan. Born in 1930 in Nara Prefecture, he went on to study in Kyoto and work in Tokyo. He was my mentor. He was a prolific artist, collaborated with numerous companies, had many interests, and loved fine dining. Often keen to get involved in social causes, he left behind many achievements and received numerous awards for his work. With friends scattered all over the world, he frequently received books and other gifts, for which he sent out letters of thanks everyday. I had the honor of handling the venue composition for an exhibition dedicated to Ikko Tanaka. The venue was "21_21 DESIGN SIGHT." It was to be not only an exhibition of his works, but also a visual display of his thought processes, and so I had to look over his various archival materials. The time I spent working for him was hectic, and we were never short of work. But looking back on our notes, I was reminded of just how frightfully loaded and meticulously researched each point in those works were. From the days when I started helping him as an intern, everyone called him "Teacher Tanaka" because he used to be a schoolteacher. Joining his office was less like getting a job and more like becoming an apprentice to a strict master craftsman. He was indeed my mentor.

(21_21 DESIGN SIGHT Exhibition Ikko Tanaka and Future / Past / East / West of Design, 2012–2013)

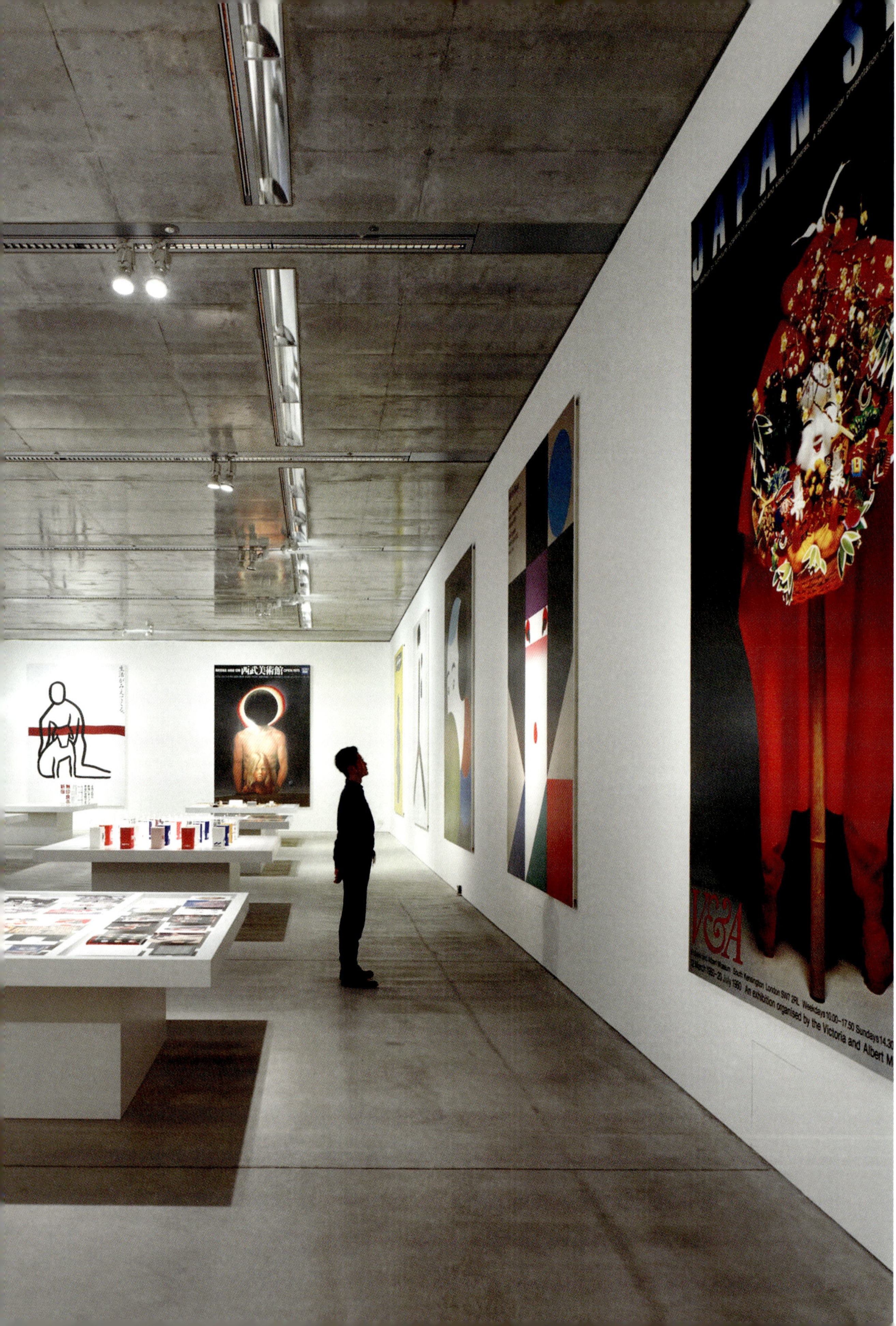
西武美術館
V&A

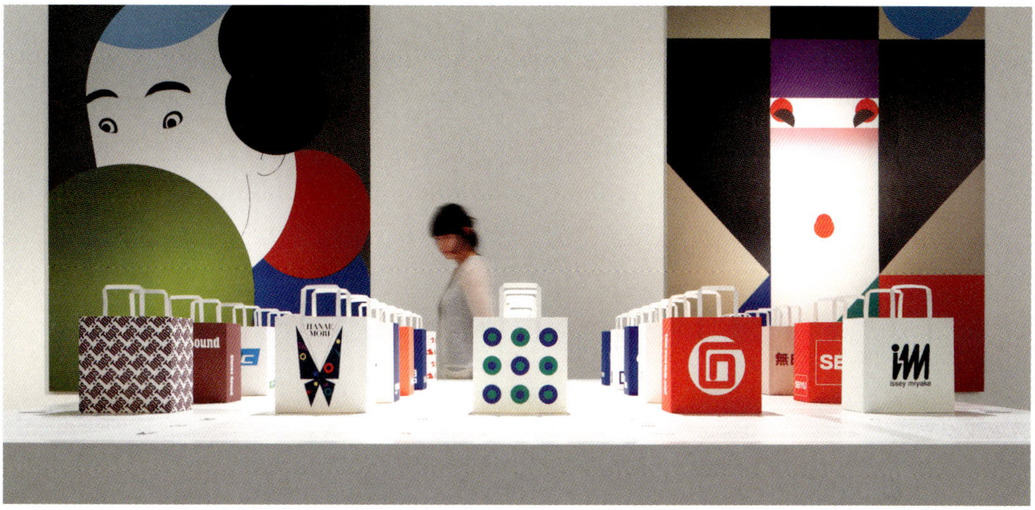
HANAE MORI
issey miyake

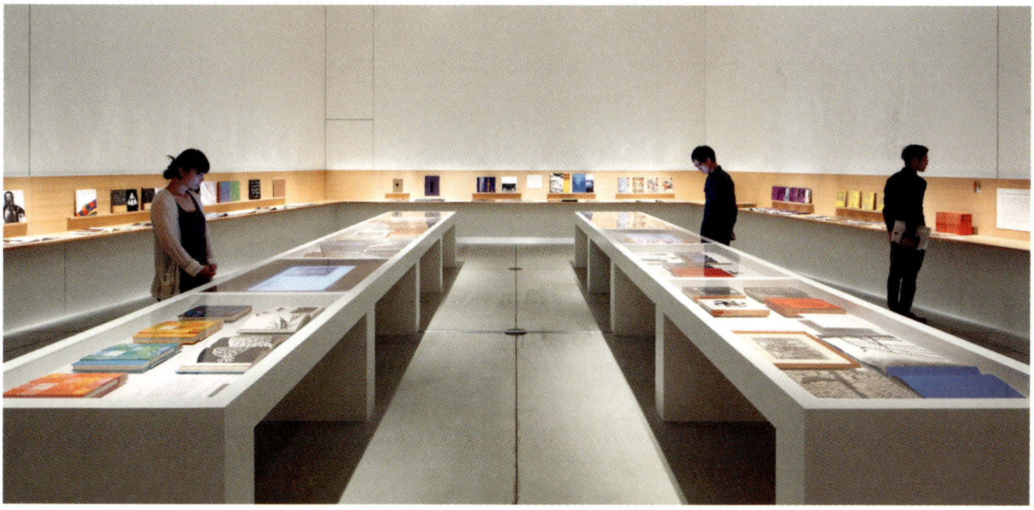

His Colors

Ikko Tanaka oversaw various developments in color schematics. The sheer numbers of the 100-color "CUTTING SHEET®" for Nakagawa Chemicals, or the 150-color "TANT" for Tokushu Tokai Paper Co., Ltd. are probably globally unrivalled in the variety that they offer. We proposed a space combining these two types of materials. The floors were fitted with Cutting Sheet, stretching out of the windows to the exteriors, and with help from paper merchants Takeo, we fixed TANT onto the walls.

(21_21 DESIGN SIGHT Exhibition Ikko Tanaka and Future / Past / East / West of Design, 2012–2013)

ヒズ カラーズ

田中一光は多くの色彩に関する開発を監修していた。なかでも中川ケミカルの「カッティングシート®」一〇〇色、特種東海製紙の「TANT」一五〇色は世界に類をみないほどの多色。その三種類の素材を組み合わせた空間を提案した。床にはカッティングシートを窓から外にまではみ出して配置し、壁にはTANTを、紙の商社、竹尾の協力で設置した。

(21_21 DESIGN SIGHT 企画展 田中一光とデザインの前後左右 二〇一二―二〇一三年)

Musashino no Wa

The Chuo Line linking the stations of Mitaka and Tachikawa has now been reconstructed into an overpass train line. Cutting directly through the area of Musashinodaichi, The Chuo Line was built 100 years ago. This unintentionally divided the area into north and south. To make use of the elevation of the train line, "The Chuo Line Mall Project" was initiated with the aim of redeveloping the underpass areas. 100 years of north-south division runs deep, but considering how such an undertaking might affect the town 100 years on from now makes this a meaningful project indeed. This new underpass development includes small parks, parking areas for cars and bicycles, and rental bicycle facilities. There are also cafes to socialize in, supermarkets, and even doctor's clinics. This sign joins together the Japanese words itsuwa (meaning 'anecdote') and arika (meaning 'whereabouts' or 'locality'), the former signifying that the town of Musashino will be a talking point for all those who congregate there, and the latter suggestive of an old and trusted town center. The name "nonowa" is derived from the phrase Musashino no wa, meaning 'the harmony of Musashino' or 'the circle of Musashino'; a place where the whole community can gather and socialize.
(nonowa, 2014)

むさしののわ

中央線の三鷹から立川駅間が高架になった。
武蔵野台地の真ん中を切り裂くように中央線ができたのは一〇〇年前。
無意識に鉄道が台地を南北に分けてしまった。
線路の高架化をきっかけに高架下の有効利用を考える「中央ラインモールプロジェクト」がはじまった。
一〇〇年間の南北断絶はとても深い。
しかしこれからの一〇〇年を考えればとても意味のあるプロジェクトになる。
小さな公園があり、駐車場や駐輪場、シェアできるレンタル自転車もある。
みんなで集まれるカフェ、スーパーや病院もある。
集まったとき、武蔵野の話ができるように「いつわ」と古くから馴染まれてきた場所「ありか」をサインで繋いだ。
みんなで集まれる「武蔵野の和」で「nonowa」と名前がついた。

(nonowa 二〇一四年)

183

近隣の名所を示した「ありか」と、地域に伝わる「いつわ」を、親しみやすいピクトグラムで表現。
The word arika signifies the local place of interest, and itsuwa its reputation spread by word of mouth, and the two have been expressed in this accessible and friendly pictogram.

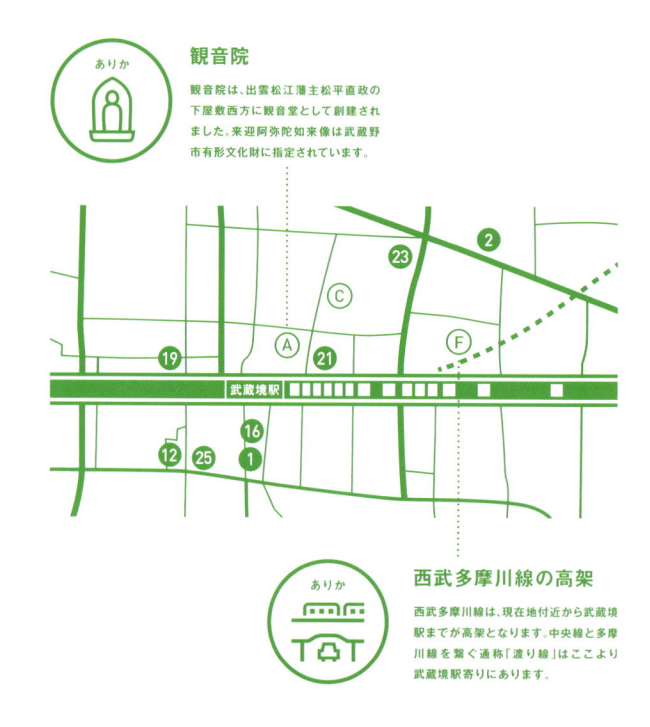

観音院

観音院は、出雲松江藩主松平直政の下屋敷西方に観音堂として創建されました。来迎阿弥陀如来像は武蔵野市有形文化財に指定されています。

西武多摩川線の高架

西武多摩川線は、現在地付近から武蔵境駅までが高架となります。中央線と多摩川線を繋ぐ通称「渡り線」はここより武蔵境駅寄りにあります。

185

9 | Lurking in the Shadows

Color is light. Shadow, also, is light.

Light enters the eye and an image created on the retina is sent to the brain. This is vision. But light also gives birth to shadow. It makes you wonder: Is shadow really necessary in daily life? If we didn't know about shadow in the first place, I feel like we might be perfectly content with a world dominated by light.

But think about shadow for a moment. The darkness created by shadow isn't complete blackness. If you look closely, in that darkness—just outside of the reach of direct light—lies a richness of expression, and we have come to associate a whole plethora of emotions and meaning with this darkness.

Around the time when humankind first invented writing, ancient Sumerians would use a pointed stylus to impress characters onto clay tablets, while in Egypt they were carving hieroglyphs into stone. The origin of Chinese characters can be traced back to oracle bone script, which was engraved onto turtle shells.

One thing that all of these scripts have in common is that they were carved into something. Writing instruments had yet to be developed, so lines were pressed or scratched onto some surface and the shadows created were then read as characters. Characters are grouped together to form words. We came to recognize the shadows formed within indentions under candlelight or in the sun as characters, and developed a sense of respect for these shadows that bestowed upon us the knowledge and information contained within words. Our great sense of attachment and attraction to movable type print is a result of our brains picking up on the oh-so-slight indentations of characters pressed into the paper.

There is light, and so there is shadow. Within the Japanese sense of creativity, one finds clear and concise form combined with deep meaning developed over long periods of time.

九、陰に潜む

色彩は光であり、陰影もまた光である。

光を受け、網膜に結んだ画像が脳に送られるのが視覚。そして光は同時に陰影を生む。日常に陰影は必要なのだろうか？　最初から知らなければ、人は光が照らす世界だけで充分満ち足りるのではないかと考えてしまう。

逆に陰影のことを考えてみる。陰影がつくる暗い闇は漆黒ではない。目を凝らすと直接光が届かない闇には多様な表情があり、人はその暗闇の中に多くの意味や感情を込めてきた。

文字が初めて発明された頃、古代シュメール人は粘土板に尖った筆の先を押して文字を記し、エジプトでは石を刻んでヒエログリフをつくった。漢字の起源は甲骨文字と呼ばれ、亀の甲羅に刻印してある。

いずれの文字にも共通する点は彫ってあるということ。筆記具が発達しておらず、押したり引っ掻いたりした線の陰影を文字として読みとっていたのである。

文字は集まり言葉になる。人はロウソクや日光に照らされてできた窪みの影を文字と認識し、言葉に込められた情報や知識を与えてくれる陰影に敬意を感じてきた。活字で刷られた印刷物に、なんとも言えない愛着と魅力を感じるのは、紙に圧力をかけて押された活字のわずかな窪みを脳が感じとっているからである。

光があって陰影がある。日本の創造性には簡潔で明解な造形と、永い時間に込められた深い意味を読みとることができる。

0301–
0307

OCEAN SUITE

百万ドルの昼影

日本三大夜景のみならず、二〇一二年にモナコ、香港に並び世界三大夜景にまで昇格した長崎。その絶景ポイントの稲佐山中腹にオープンした「ガーデンテラス長崎」。夜景がキレイに見えるこの斜面は、実は昼間はたっぷりと陽の降りそそぐ穏やかな場所でもある。たゆたゆとした陽光は豊かな影を生み、夜だけではなく、真昼も百万ドルの昼影を楽しみながら、ボンヤリと過ごすことができる。

（ガーデンテラス長崎ホテル＆リゾート　二〇〇九年）

Million-dollar Midday Shadows

Not only is Nagasaki one of the top three night views in Japan, but in 2012 it was certified as one of the top three night views in the world, alongside Monaco and Hong Kong. Garden Terrace Nagasaki is located on the side of Mount Inasa, which is a popular observation point for this spectacular night view. While this sloping mountainside offers clear views of the night skyline, it also offers
a peaceful atmosphere showered in sunshine during the daytime as well, allowing one to enjoy a relaxing moment with a million-dollar view of the midday shadows.
(GARDEN TERRACE NAGASAKI HOTEL & RESORTS, 2009)

A Shadow's Texture

The word "hotel" has its origin in the Latin "hospitalia," which can refer to guest chambers as well as the idea of hospitality itself. It was a place for pilgrims, worshippers, or travelers to take refuge for the night. These days, hotels are still ranked according to the level of hospitality offered. This of course includes customer service, but also extends to every detail from the size of the rooms to the type of shampoo found in the bathrooms. A hotel's location can also contribute greatly to making it stand out. A convenient downtown location that offers excellent access can be hard to beat, but a relaxing atmosphere far away from all of the hustle and bustle is also often sought after. Located in Busan, Korea, the PARK HYATT BUSAN occupies the upper floors of a modern skyscraper situated in a beach resort area. Enclosed in walls of glass, the hotel interior is a place to spend quality time while stimulating the senses. The glass walls bathe the interior with sunlight, while perfect climate control maintains a comfortable temperature. The signage designed for this area—both letters and pictographs—has a thickness to it. Long shadows cast as a result of this thickness offer an unconscious reminder of the fulfilling time spent within.
(PARK HYATT BUSAN, 2013)

陰影の質感

ホテルの語源はラテン語の「ホスピタリア」、「無償の接客部屋」とか「手厚いもてなし」という意味で、巡礼者や参拝者、旅人の宿泊所のことであった。
現代のホテルランキングもこの「手厚いもてなし」の差で決まっている。人的なサービスはもとより、部屋の広さからどのようなシャンプーを置いてあるかまで、細かく査定される。
またホテルの立地条件も大きな差別化に繋がる。都市の中心部に位置し、どこに行くにも便利な場所は得点が高いが、人里離れたところでゆっくり過ごすタイプも人気がある。
韓国、釜山にできた「パークハイアット釜山」は、海辺のリゾート地でありながら、近代的なビルの高層階に存在する。ガラスで遮断されたホテルの内部には密度の高い空気と上質な時間が流れる。全面ガラスから陽光がたっぷりと注がれるが、完璧な空調により温度は伝わらない。
この空間にしつらえたサインデザインは厚い。文字もピクトも厚い。サインの厚みは長い影を生み、濃密な時間を無意識に感じさせる。
(パーク ハイアット釜山　二〇一三年)

Hotel signage should be designed so as to blend into
the surroundings as much as possible. We don't want to be
bombarded by unnecessary information when we're trying
to enjoy the moment, but hotels are littered with signs.
At the Park Hyatt Busan, the goal of the design was to
create signage that is only noticed when necessary.
The thick shadows cast by natural or artificial light falling
on the signs serve as a gentle reminder of their presence.

ホテルのサインデザインはなるべく空間に溶け込むのがいい。密度の高い時間を過ごすためには不要な情報は意識したくないものである。しかし、ホテルには大量のサインがある。深い影を生むこのサインは、自然光もしくは照明を受けて落ちる影によってその物体の存在を知らせる。必要なときのみ、ふと気づくようなデザインを目指した。

193

文字の記憶

人類が文字を発明した頃は、引っ掻いたり彫ったりして文字を記録した。そして削られた溝の影を見て文字を知り、文字を読むことを学んできたのである。タイプフォントの「モリサワ」大阪本社は、影をテーマにサインを計画した。壁面に表示された数字や記号は影となって床に伸びている。活字に比べ、オフセット印刷に適し、自由度も高い写真植字はデジタルフォントに移行するまで広く普及した。その経緯を、文字の起源の記憶とともにテーマに込めた。写真植字は光学的に文字を印画紙に焼き付ける手法で、光と影を使い印字するので、活字より早くて文字の大きさも自由である。

（モリサワ新本社ビル　二〇〇九年）

写真植字機用文字盤（写真提供：株式会社モリサワ）
Character plate used in phototypesetting (Photo Credit: Morisawa Inc.)

楔形文字石盤
Slate covered in cuneiform characters

The History of Characters

Around the time that humankind first invented writing, we recorded those characters by scratching or carving them onto some surface. We then studied these characters by observing the shadows created within those grooves and learned to read. I chose shadow as the theme when planning the design of the signage at the Osaka Head Office building of the type foundry, Morisawa. Shadows extend out onto the floor from numbers and symbols placed on the walls. Compared to movable type, phototypesetting was better suited to offset printing and offered a greater degree of freedom, hence its wide use prior to the move toward digital fonts. I incorporated this step in the development of characters—along with a peak into the history of their origin—into my design theme. Phototypesetting uses a photographic process to print characters on photographic paper. Printing via the use of light and shadow was faster than using movable characters and the size of characters could be adjusted freely.
(MORISAWA New Headquarters Office, 2009)

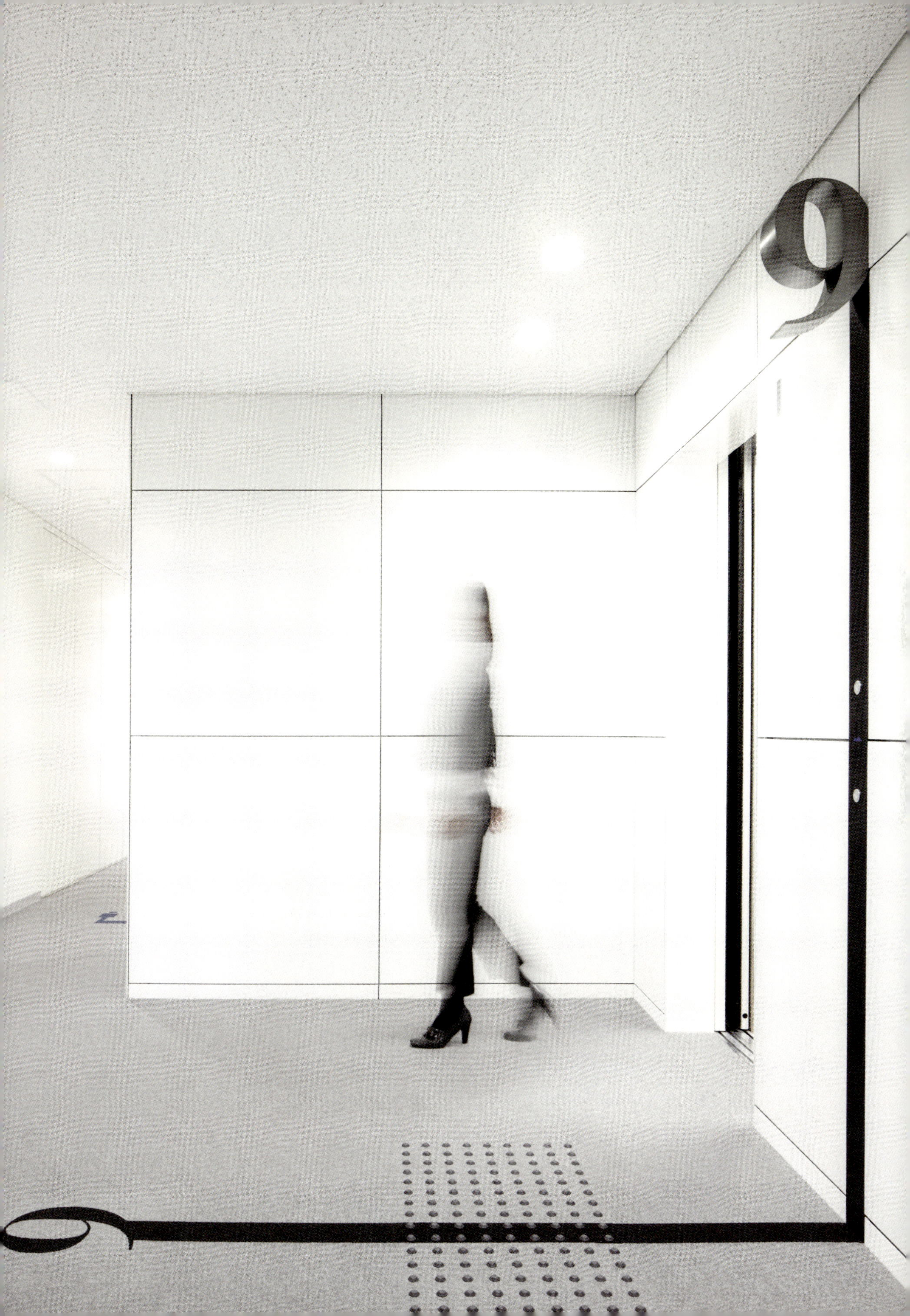
9

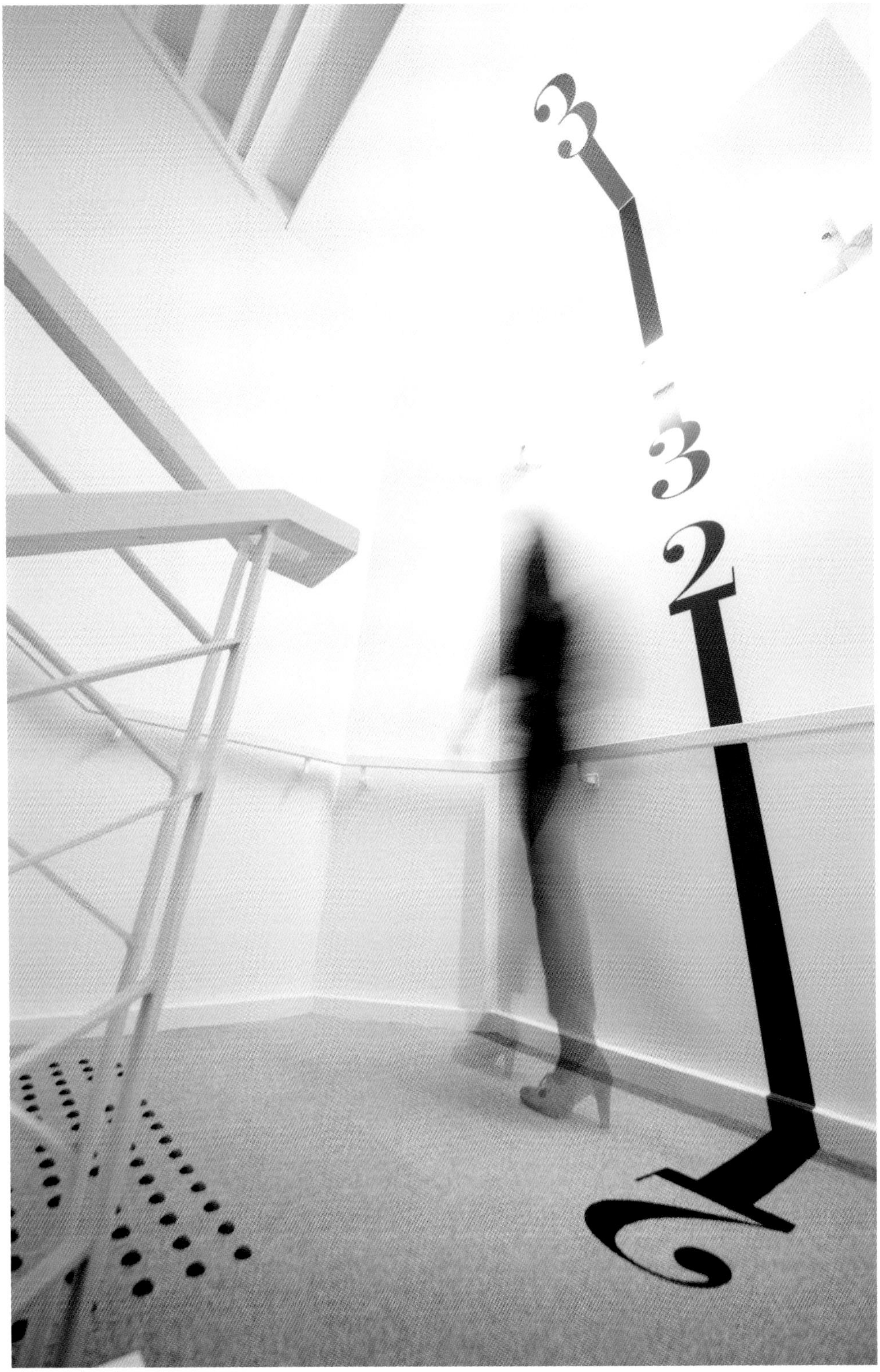
3
3
2
2

壁と床は、光と影。自分の影がいつも一緒のように一対になっている。エレベーターに乗る人のための壁面サイン、降りる人がフロアを確認するための床サイン。トイレのサインは床に伸びたラインが通路まで突き出して利用者を誘導する。

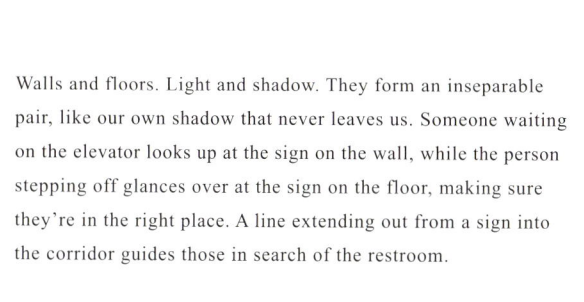

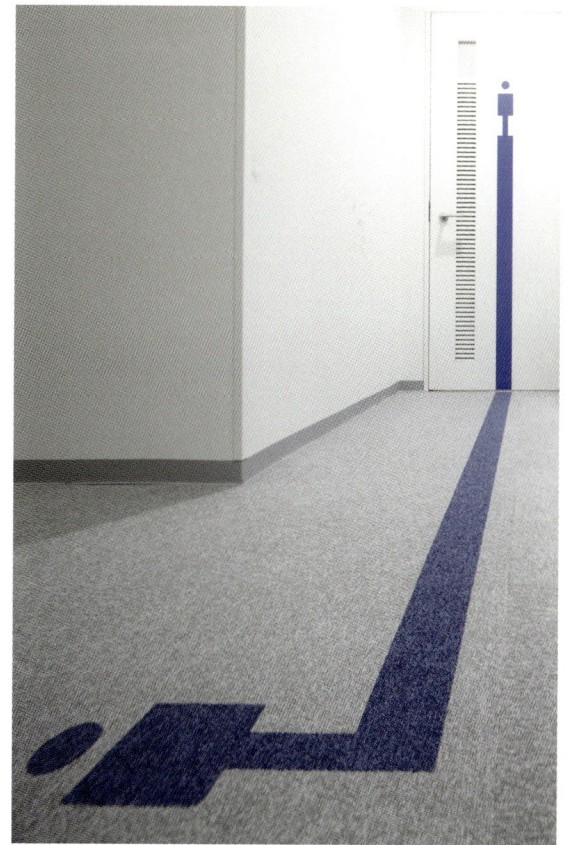

Walls and floors. Light and shadow. They form an inseparable pair, like our own shadow that never leaves us. Someone waiting on the elevator looks up at the sign on the wall, while the person stepping off glances over at the sign on the floor, making sure they're in the right place. A line extending out from a sign into the corridor guides those in search of the restroom.

197

A Single Line

First I draw a single line with my pencil. When I was younger this is how I would always begin, whether drawing a picture or writing a character. Either way, it seems like the result was usually something unrecognizable. When playing outside, I would draw in the sandbox or on the ground with a twig.
At times this would develop into something greater, but for the most part it just ended up as another unrecognizable picture you might mistake for some strange growth on the ground. As I got older, I stopped drawing. I just didn't know what to draw anymore.
For this project, I had the pleasure of working with a clinic in Ginza. Being a clinic exclusively for women, I used fine lines for the logo and designed signs using characters whose shadows extend out as if reaching down toward the ground. For just a moment I was reminded of a younger me with my twig, completely engrossed as I drew in the sandbox at dusk.
(KISHI CLINICA FEMINA, 2014)

一本の線

まず、えんぴつで一本の線を描く。小さな頃からはじまりの合図である。絵を描くときもあれば文字を書くときもある。でもほとんど意味不明の図形だった気がする。
外で遊んでいるときは、小枝で砂場や路面に描く。それが新しい遊びに発展することもあるが、たいがい何かが増殖するような絵でほとんど意味不明だった。
大人になったら描かなくなった。何を描いてよいのかわからないのだ。
今回は銀座のクリニックをお手伝いした。女性専用ということで細い線でロゴタイプをつくり、文字の影が路面に伸びたようなサインをデザインした。
夕暮れの砂場で、無心に小枝で描いていたのを思い出した。
(KISHI CLINICA FEMINA 二〇一四年)

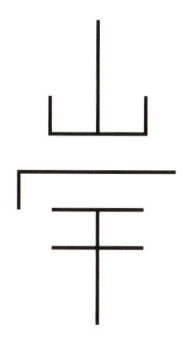

KISHI CLINICA FEMINA

Creating Shadow

I admire lighting designers and other people whose job is to manipulate light. From a graphic design point of view lighting isn't much of a concern, but it becomes of utmost importance when considering how you want a space to be experienced by others.
I had the honor of being involved with a compilation of 25 years of projects by the Lighting Planners Associates (LPA), which was established by Kaoru Mende. According to Mende, it is not adding light, but rather creating darkness, or shadow, wherein the magic lies.
(LPA 1990-2015 Tide of Architectural Lighting Design, 2015)

陰をつくる

ライティングデザイナー、照明設計など、光を操る人に憧れる。グラフィックデザインだけで考えれば光の品質はそれほど気にならないが、空間をどのように体験してほしいかを考える時、光は最も重要な要素になる。面出薫さん率いるLPA（ライティング プランナーズ アソシエーツ）の二五年にわたる仕事の作品集に関わることができた。面出さんは、明るくすることよりも暗さ、陰をつくることが大事だと言う。
（LPA 1990-2015 建築照明 デザインの潮流　二〇一五年）

家族の影

「ライティングオブジェ」というチャリティーイベントに参加している。オリジナル照明をデザインし、オークションを行って活動を支援するもので、二〇一二年の作品は、家族をテーマに制作した。半球の照明器具の頂点に三人の家族を象徴するミニチュアが立っており、点灯すると三方に影が伸びる。災害などでバラバラに分かれてしまった家族が再び出会う感動を照明にした。家の窓からこぼれる灯りは、あたたかい家族の象徴なのだ。

（ライティングオブジェ2012　二〇一二年）

Family's Shadow

I take part in a charity event known as Lighting Objet. Artists design original lighting pieces which are then auctioned off to support the efforts of the host organization. I chose "family" as the theme for my 2012 piece. Three miniature figures representing family stand atop a semi-spherical lighting fixture. When the light is turned on, their shadows extend out in three directions.
The light represents the overwhelming joy experienced by family members reunited after a disaster. Light spilling from the windows of homes at night reminds us of the warm presence that is family.
(Lighting Objet 2012, 2012)

10 | Giving Form to Desire

If necessity is the mother of invention, then I say that desire is the father of design. In other words, almost all design is the materialization—or the embodiment—of people's desires. It includes something beyond simply that which is necessary.

The origins of design can be traced back to the industrial revolution. There was a move toward mass production and mass consumption, and we began to call the act of creating things that people wanted "design," a craft focused not on the advancement of skills or technologies, but rather on giving form to desire.

And then times changed. People no longer want the same things. To act the same. There was a gradual transition from "the masses" to "the individual," which lead to a desire to express that individuality. We now feel an affinity for words like "personal" or "customized" and not "bulk" or "standard."

Design is the act of giving form to desire, and good design is design aligned to the desires of the times. Hence design driven by marketing should be the best design of all, right? But it's not that simple. Sometimes we are drawn to the design born of some personal desire, and not to the design that experience predicts we would be drawn to.

The reality is that we can't rely on theory and experience alone in order to create truly great design. It seems clear to me that the future lies along the path forged by our desires.

十、欲しいをつくる

"必要は発明の母" ならば "欲望はデザインの父" と呼びたい。
デザインのほとんどとは世の中の欲望を可視化、
あるいは具現化することだと解釈してもいい。
そこには必要なだけではない何かが含まれているからだ。

デザインの起源は産業革命に遡る。
大量生産と大量消費がはじまり、人々が望むモノをつくる行為をデザインと呼んだ。
技術を競う工芸ではなく "欲しい" をつくることなのだ。

そして時代は変わる。人々は同じモノや行為に同調しない、
ゆるやかに個々人に分節され "らしさ" を求められる。
マスではなくパーソナル、スタンダードではなくカスタマイズという言葉が喜ばれる。

デザインは欲しいをつくり、時代が欲するデザインが良いデザインである。
ならばマーケティングから生まれるデザインが最良かと問われれば、そうだとは言えない。
経験から予測されたデザインではなく、
個人的な欲望をカタチにしたモノに魅力を感じることがあるからだ。

まだまだ理論や経験だけでは素晴らしいデザインはできないのが現実だが、
人々が望む先に未来があることは事実だろう。

The Little Things

"Big is better!" Echoed by a 1968 commercial, this sentiment basically recapitulated the general feeling in Japan during its post-war economic boom. In the commercial, which was an advertisement for chocolate, a conductor riding in a hot air balloon in front of Mount Fuji is singing enthusiastically. It was a time when people believed in a bright future brought about by mass production and mass consumption. Now over 40 years later, the trend has shifted to greater variety in smaller quantities, with customization being the key word. Kofukuan and Little chef are two new shops at the Seibu Department Store, both of which were developed from a female perspective with the female customer in mind. The focus is on using healthy, quality ingredients, with smaller quantities allowing customers to enjoy a wide variety of tastes.
(Kofukuan, 2014 / Little chef, 2010)

ちいさいこと

「大きいことはいいことだ!」と高度経済成長期の日本を象徴するかのようなコマーシャルが出現したのが一九六八年。
それはチョコレートの広告で、指揮者が富士山をバックに気球の上から大きな口をあけて歌う。
大量生産、大量消費により未来の豊かさを信じた時代だった。
それから四〇年あまり、時代は少量多品種、カスタマイズが合い言葉になった。
西武百貨店に新しい二つの売り場ができた。
「こふくあん」と「リトルシェフ」。
どちらも、女性ならではの視点で女性が中心に開発している。
素材や栄養にこだわり、小ぶりでたくさんの種類を楽しめるのがポイント。

(こふくあん 二〇一四年／Little chef 二〇一〇年)

Little Chef

ZAKKA

雑貨が氾濫している。
本来「こまごました日用品」として大きな領域に属さないモノたちだったが、オモシログッズと呼ばれて売り場の主役に躍り出ている。生活に必要でなくても楽しめるモノ、アイデアとデザインが新しい領域をつくるのである。日本だけではなく「ZAKKA」と世界語にもなっている。
ロフトは一九八〇年代から雑貨を中心に、時代を先取りしたセレクションで全国に広がってきた。新しさが求められる雑貨の領域では、常にチャレンジが行われている。たとえば「SELF&SHELF」は小さいスペースで駅を中心に展開し、明るくカラフルな店舗に文具をメインに学生や女性に合わせた商品を揃えている。
(SELF&SHELF LOFT 二〇一三年)

ZAKKA

Zakka is everywhere. Once just the little daily necessities that didn't really fit into any category, these knickknacks are now thought of as classily kitsch and have found their way into the retail spotlight. Though they may be unnecessary, they bring joy to our lives, and so a merging of the idea and design gave birth to this new category. Even the Japanese word "ZAKKA" has made its way into the global lexicon. LOFT began its spread across Japan in the 1980s, offering a selection of zakka well ahead of its time. In the world of zakka there is a constant demand for the novel, and so the boundaries are always being pushed. Enter SELF&SHELF. These bright and colorful tiny shops—primarily found in train stations—carry a selection of stationery and other goods catering to students and female shoppers.
(SELF&SHELF LOFT, 2013)

notebook marker eraser diary file pencil memo scissors stapler clip calculator ruler blade sketchbook pushpin binder bookmark calendar stamp album wallet postcard envelope tape pen card seal folder bag pouch glue box scissors memo diary file pencil eraser notebook marker pushpin blade calculator clip ruler stapler sketchbook wallet postcard calendar binder stamp bookmark album

SELF &
SHELF

横浜、みなとみらい21の中心的存在のランドマークタワー。日本最古の石造りドックヤードがあった場所に建つ超高層ビルだ。ショッピングゾーンのプロモーションだが、このエリアの魅力を伝えたい。大胆なシルエットのイラストレーションで全国にさわやかな潮風を送ろうと考えた。
(ランドマークプラザ　二〇〇九年-／丸の内商店会　二〇〇六年-)

この秋、ランドマークのファッションがニュースになると思う。

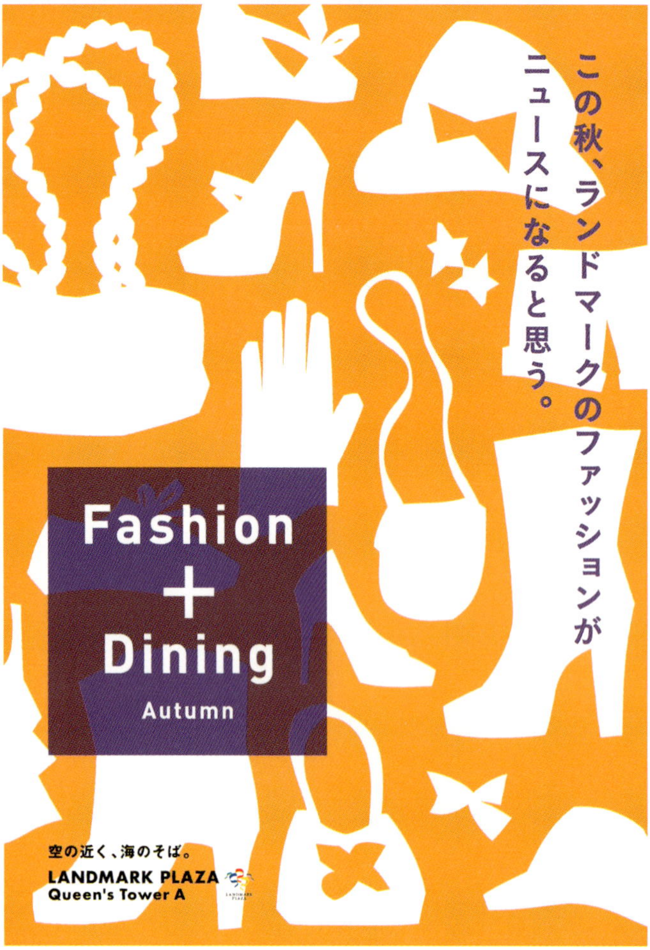

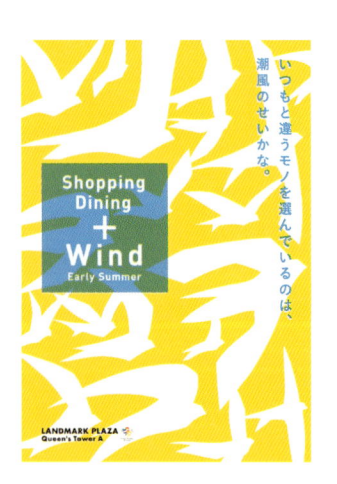

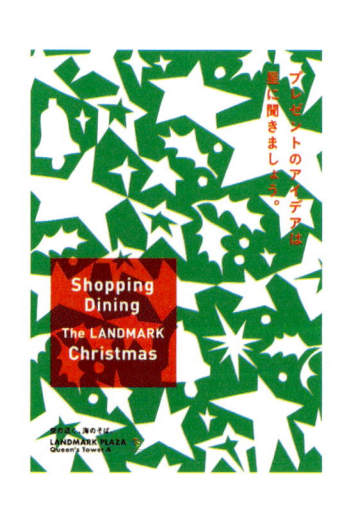

魅力を伝えたい

買い物のためだけではない、その場所に行きたいと思うことがある。その地域、その場が持つ魅力。時間をかけて育てた愛着が人を呼ぶのかもしれない。東京、丸の内。日本を代表するオフィス街にある商店会。モダンな街並みに先端的ファッションのイメージ。実際は樹木が豊かで街路は散策するのが楽しい。それぞれの店は個性的で対応もやさしくて親切。下町のようにあたたかい人達の魅力を表札に込めて伝えた。

Conveying Appeal

Sometimes when we go out shopping somewhere, it's not just to buy things but also because we want to visit the place itself. We are drawn to that place, or to an area. Perhaps it comes from a sense of attachment developed over time. Located in Tokyo, Marunouchi is a shopping area situated in Japan's representative office district. Most people imagine the latest fashion trends and a modern cityscape, but in reality there are trees everywhere and walking the streets is a joy. Shops are full of personality, and shop clerks are kind and helpful. I chose a wooden nameplate to convey the appeal of this sense of warmth that you might expect to find in traditional areas of downtown Tokyo. The centerpiece of Yokohama's Minato Mirai 21 district, the Landmark Tower is a super high-rise building built on what was once Japan's oldest stone-built dockyard. The design was a promotion for the shopping mall here, but I wanted to convey the appeal of the area as well. These bold silhouette illustrations were my attempt to share the refreshing sea breeze with the rest of Japan.

(Landmark Plaza, 2009– / Marunouchi Shotenkai, 2006–)

ここは、丸の内〈ヒトをくすぐる〉商店会。

丸の内の皆さま、こんにちは。近頃はネット社会で、ショッピングもベンリになりました。とはいえ、例えば服を買う時、まずは手に取って触れ、お店の人のアドバイスにも耳を傾け、じっくり鏡の前で見たいと思ったことありませんか？また、グルメ情報などを持ち合わせていなくても、匂いにひかれてフラリと入ったお店がおいしかったことってありませんか？見る、聞く、匂う、味わう、触れる。人間の感覚器官のどこかをくすぐる東京ビル、トキア、新丸ビル、丸の内オアゾ、丸の内ビル、丸の内ブリックスクエアを中心に約五〇〇もの店舗が集っています。ビジネス街の真ん中で〈商店会〉というちょっとノスタルジックな名前がついていますが、そこには私たちが忘れてはいけない何かがあると思っています。

私たちは、丸の内〈ヒトをくすぐる〉商店会です。

丸の内商店会　丸の内オアゾ商店会

The Department Store-seum

Most brands have some kind of mark or logo whose job is to express the personality of that brand and to generate interest. The department store is a place where numerous brands find their beginning. It's practically a logo museum. From small sales corners to huge retail outlets, one after another new ventures spring to life and—if unsuccessful—then proceed to disappear. The department store is a reflection of the times. A collection of all of our desires. Even if the way we approach shopping and consumption goes on to change, I hope that the department store never disappears.
(Logos for shops at the SEIBU IKEBUKURO Department Store, 2008–2014)

百貨展

多くのブランドにはマークやロゴタイプがある。どのように「らしさ」を表して、いかに興味を持ってもらうかが目的。百貨店には新しいブランドがたくさん生まれる。まるでマークやロゴタイプの展覧会のようだ。小さなコーナーから広い売場まで、間断なく企画され、結果が出なければ消えてゆく。時代を映す鏡のような百貨店、欲望のすべてが詰まった百貨店、消費のカタチが変化しても場としての百貨店は生き続けてほしい。

(西武池袋本店 インショップロゴ 二〇〇八ー二〇一四年)

11 | Creating Creation

Creativity of the Japanese is forged in the manufacturing process.

We have created many things to help us live comfortably in narrow spaces. This has resulted in making items with compact designs. Thus, they are light enough to be carried around easily. They are also full of original features that take advantage of the special features of each area. Japanese manufacturing has managed to create new values by reaching back into our ancient history. The Japanese spirit of manufacturing has been ingrained in our way of life, which has helped us grow modern industries and advanced technology.

However, a warning light is now flashing at manufacturing sites, which are the result of a countless number of problems. With a smaller labor pool, material and labor costs on the rise, while international competitiveness has decreased. As time passes, society changes, and with those changes come changing demands.

Japanese manufacturing is characterized by flexibility. At different times, as a solution to adversity, the Japanese have had to seek out new manufacturing techniques. This kind of ingenuity and flexibility under pressure has been the bedrock of Japanese creativity.

If we want our future generations to shine as we have in the past and present, we need to think beyond the conventional categories or accepted practices. Science, ergonomics, psychology, and contemporary art are all areas that should be referenced. If we further grow tactile perception and analytical ability, we will be able to make completely original categories. This new kind of creativity will be borne by "creating creation," while we transfer the DNA of Japanese creativity to those who come after.

十一、つくるをつくる

日本の創造性は、ものづくりの過程から生まれた。
狭い空間でもフレキシブルに生活できるよう、さまざまな工夫をし、軽くて簡単に持ち運べるコンパクトな設計ができた。
また、地域の特性を生かしたオリジナリティに富んでいる。
日本のものづくりは、新しい価値を古来の生活の中から生み出してきた。
永く染み込んだものづくりの精神は現代の産業や先端技術にも生かされてきたのである。

しかし、ものづくりの現場には赤信号が点滅している。
問題はいくつもあるだろう、挙げればきりがない。
後継者の不足、原材料や人件費の高騰、国際的競争力の低下など。
時代が変われば社会も変わり、人々の必要としているモノは環境によって変化している。

ものづくりにおける日本の特徴は柔軟性である。
いつの時代でも、厳しい状況を受け入れつつ、次々と新たな技をくり出す知恵とチカラが問題を解決し、独自の創造性が生まれてきた。
その〝たおやか〟な粘り強さが日本のクリエイティブの根幹には流れている。

そして次の時代でも輝くためには、いままでの領域を越えた知見や国を越えた意見が必要なのだろう。科学や人間工学、心理学や現代美術も面白い。
触角を伸ばし分析力を養えば新しいカテゴリーをつくることにもなる。
日本のDNAを継承しつつ、積極的に「つくるをつくる」ことで新しい創造性が生まれる。

ジャパン クリエイティブ

「一切は清純であり、それ故にまた限りなく美しい」と桂離宮を評したのはブルーノ・タウト。
日本の魅力は何度も外国人により再発見されてきた。
日本の美意識の本質は、簡潔、明解、清純であり、それはものづくりの精神でもある。
日本の美意識はものづくりが育んできた。
そして、その創造性は日本の未来にとって重要な資産だと考えている。
JC（ジャパン クリエイティブ）の活動は、日本の創造性を広く世界に示し、未来に繋げていくことを目的にしている。
伝統工芸から先端技術まで日本のものづくりを技術だけではなく、クリエイティビティという価値観で世界に評価してほしい。

Japan Creative

"All is sheer pure, therefore, it has infinite beauty,"—those were the comments made by Bruno Taut, a German architect, about the Katsura Imperial Villa, Katsura Rikyu. People from overseas repeatedly rediscover the qualities that make Japan charming. The essence of the Japanese aesthetic includes precision, clarity, and purity, which are the core of producing things. This aesthetic consciousness spurred the growth of Japanese manufacturing. I believe that such creativity is an important asset for the future of Japan. JC (Japan Creative) aims to globally bring to light the rich aesthetics of Japan, and extend it to future generations. Though Japan is already renowned for its technology and manufacturing, we hope that the value of the creativity involved in traditional craft making to advanced technology will receive more global recognition.

2012年 ミラノサローネでの出展風景
Exhibition at Milano Salone in 2012

Assisting a Disaster Struck Region

The Great East Japan Earthquake struck shortly after Japan Creative was launched. At that time, we were working on an idea to create new products, made collaboratively by designers from overseas and Japanese manufacturers. Quickly, to contribute to the relief efforts, we searched for manufacturers from the disaster hit north-eastern region. We came across Mizusawa City in Iwate Prefecture, an area with a long history of ironware manufacturing, dating back to the 7th century. A number of Nambu ironware factories remain in operation. We approached Japan Creative's first project, JCO1 (Oigen). Oigen is an iron casting manufacturer, with a strong following of loyal professional chefs. Jasper Morrison was selected as the designer for this project. Morrison produces high quality products, which have received worldwide acclaim. After thoroughly researching Oigen's concept of craftsmanship, where the user is first and foremost, he then went work proposing a modern and universal product series called "Palma."

被災地との出会い

JCが発足して間もなく東日本大震災が起きた。日本のものづくりの現場（マニュファクチュア）と海外のデザイナーをマッチングして新しいプロダクトを世界に問いたいと考えていた折の災害だった。急遽、被災地支援も考えて東北を中心にマニュファクチュアを探した。岩手県奥州市水沢、この地では七世紀頃から鉄器づくりがはじまり、今も南部鉄器の工場が多く存在する。

我々が「JC01」で選んだマニュファクチュアは及源鋳造、プロの料理人たちが厚い信頼を寄せる南部鉄器メーカーである。一方デザイナーは、ジャスパー・モリソン。日常で使うプロダクトを高い完成度でデザインし、世界中から注目されている。モリソンは及源鋳造の「使い手を第一に考えた実直なものづくり」を丁寧にリサーチし、現代的で普遍性の高いプロダクトのシリーズ「Palma」を提案した。

JC 01

及源鋳造 × ジャスパー・モリソン
Oigen in collaboration with Jasper Morrison

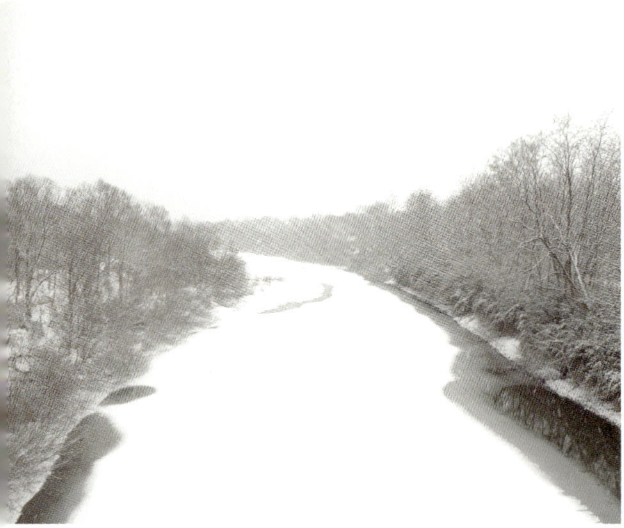
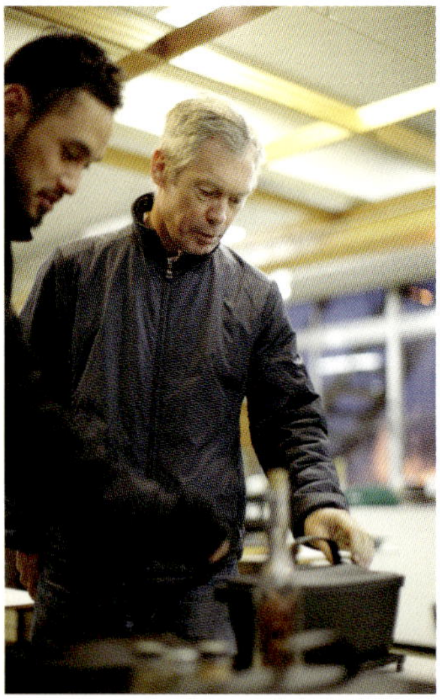
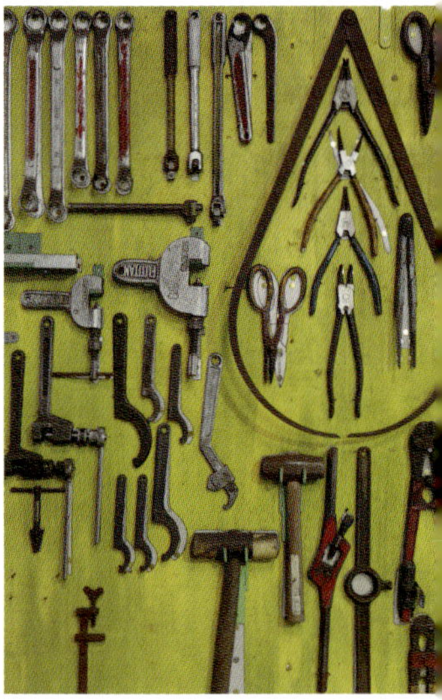
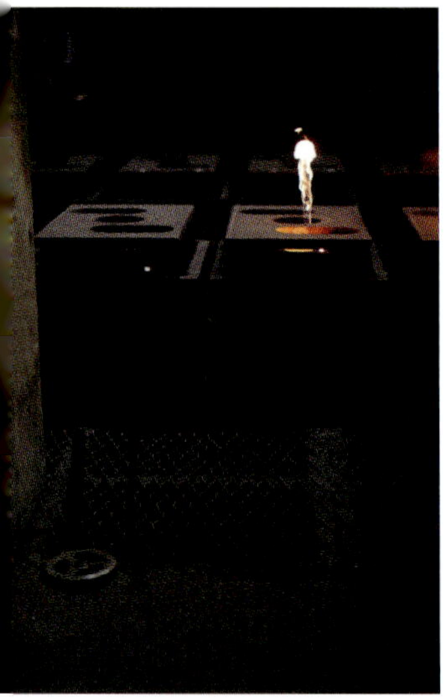
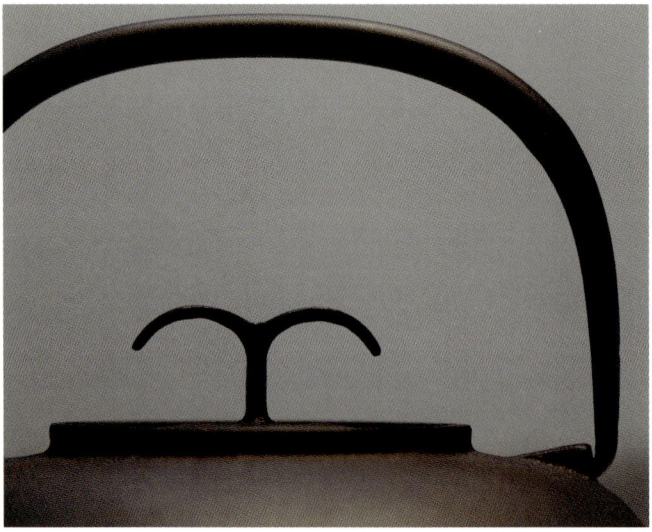
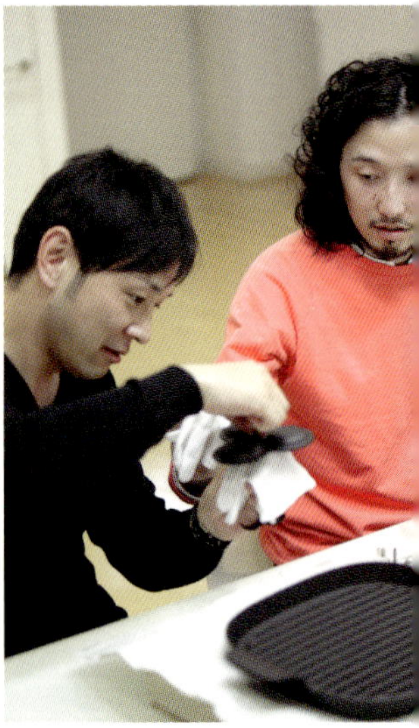

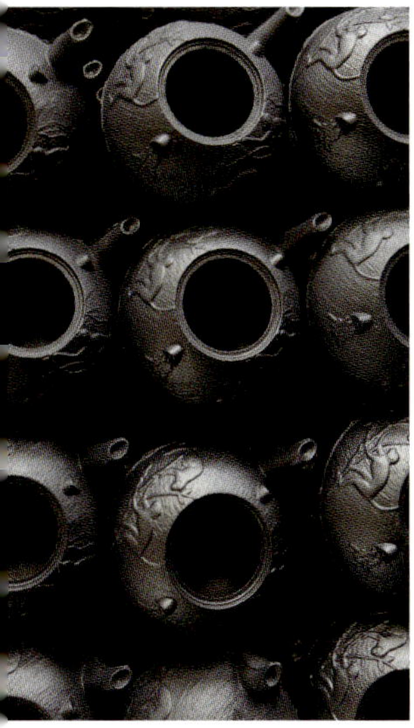
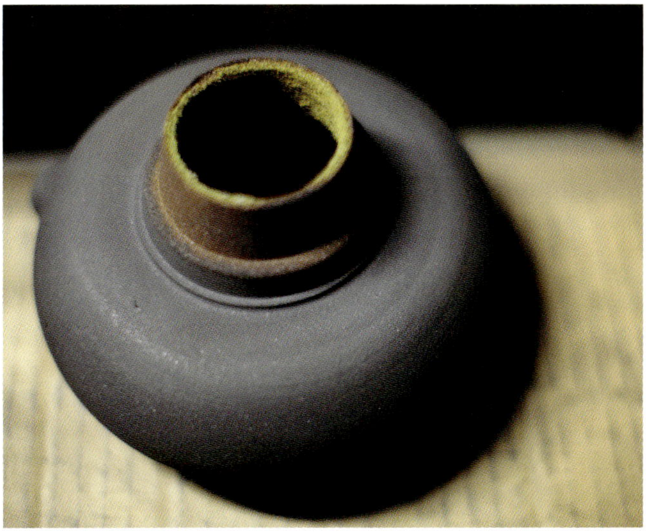
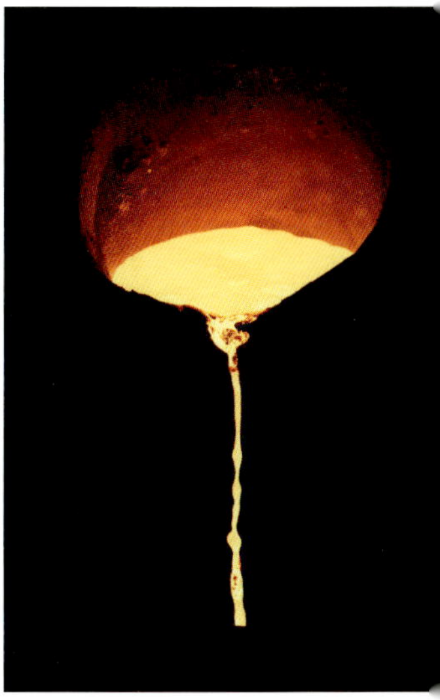
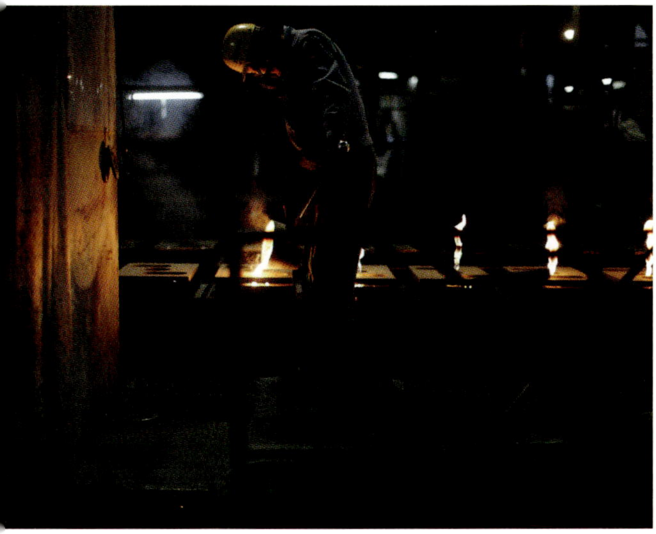
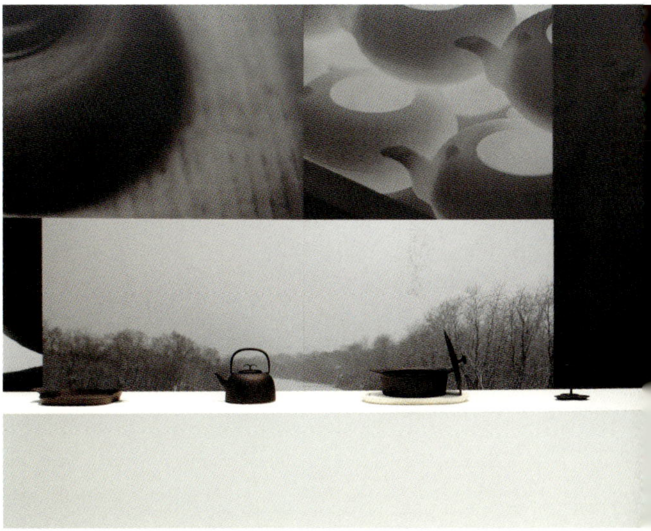

JC 08

柴舟小出 × ポーリーン・デルトゥア
Shibafune Koide in collaboration with Pauline Deltour

Japanese Confectionery

Japanese traditional sweets, "wagashi," are considered delicious in areas that practice the tea ceremony. Along with Kyoto and Matsue in Shimane Prefecture, tea culture had also thrived in Kanazawa in Ishikawa Prefecture. Under the Maeda Clan, Kanazawa was a very prosperous domain, yielding one million koku of rice. The first feudal lord, Maeda Toshiie, is said to have learned the tea ceremony from Sen-no-Rikyu, a great tea master. The practice spread to commoners and gradually resulted in a more refined "wagashi." I was introduced to Koide from Shibafune Koide, a long established confectionery shop, renowned for its ginger rice crackers. Japan Creative would like to introduce Japanese foods to the world, to include "wagashi," which is universally considered aesthetically pleasing. To create a special "wagashi" unlike any before, a collaborative project with Shibafune Koide and Pauline Deltour was launched. Based in Paris, her designs have a distinctively simple and sophisticated form, with elegant curves. She proposed 5 types of "wagashi." Among these a mountain silhouette, overlapped as in an ink painting. This was done by using jelly and "yokan," a red bean jellied paste, producing a "layer" with beautiful clarity. Green tea was used for a mountain in spring, and autumn leaves were beautifully represented using wine.

和菓子を超えた和菓子

茶の湯が栄えたところは必ず和菓子が美味しい。京都や松江と並んで金沢もお茶文化が盛んだった。加賀百万石の歴代藩主は茶の湯を好み、藩祖前田利家は千利休の弟子だったという。そしてそれは庶民にも広まり、自然と和菓子も洗練されてきたのだ。

その金沢で「柴舟」という生姜煎餅で有名な老舗、小出さんを紹介してもらった。

JCでは「食」に挑戦したいと考えていたが、なかでも和菓子は世界でも優れた美しさを備えたお菓子だ。海外のデザイナーと一緒に、和菓子を超えた和菓子を期待してお願いした。

デザイナーは、ポーリーン・デルトゥア。パリで活躍し、シンプルながら優雅な曲線、洗練されたフォルムが特徴的なプロダクトを生む女性だ。ポーリーンは、五つの菓子を提案してくれた。

なかでも山のシルエットが水墨画のように重なる「レイヤー」は、羊羹とゼリーで美しい透明感を醸し出している。春の山は抹茶の緑で、秋の紅葉はワインを使い見事に表現した。

222

223

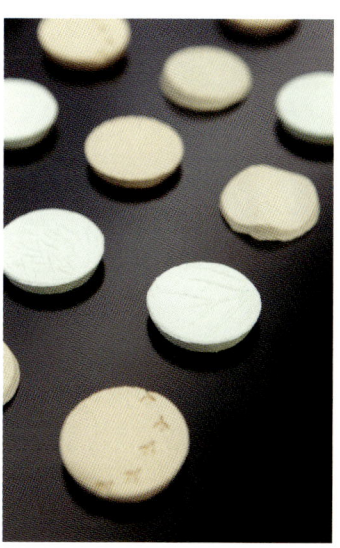

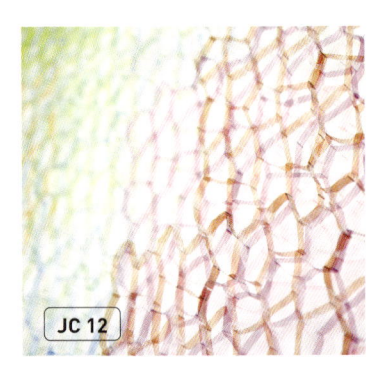

JC 02	ヒノキ工芸 [木工] ×ピーター・マリゴールド Hinoki Kogei in collaboration with Peter Marigold	
JC 03	パイオニア [有機EL] ×ポール・コクセッジ Pioneer in collaboration with Paul Cocksedge	
JC 04	三保谷硝子店 [ガラス] ×ヨンギュウ・ユー Mihoya Glass in collaboration with Yeongkyu Yoo	
JC 05	幸兵衛窯 [陶器] ×インガ・センペ Koubei-gama in collaboration with IngaSempé	
JC 06	東レ・カーボンマジック [カーボンファイバー] ×ナチョ・カーボネル (旧 童夢カーボンマジック) Toray Carbon Magic in collaboration with Nacho Carbonell	
JC 07	藤里木工所 [金属加工・家具製造] ×ロン・ジラッド Fujisato Woodcraft in collaboration with Ron Gilad	
JC 09	Art and Textile Workshop [ホームスパン] ×セシリエ・マンツ Art and Textile in collaboration with Cecilie Manz	
JC 10	昭和飛行機工業 [アルミハニカム] ×川上元美 Showa Aircraft Industry in collaboration with Motomi Kawakami	
JC 11	YAMAHA [TLF スピーカー] ×MAP partner of Barber & Osgerby YAMAHA in collaboration with MAP partner of Barber & Osgerby	
JC 12	三洋 [ソフト PVC(ビニル)] ×エマニュエル・ムホー SANYO in collaboration with Emmanuelle Moureaux	
JC 13	SHINDO [シリコーン] ×ピエール・シャルパン SHINDO in collaboration with Pierre Charpin	
JC 14	竹虎・山岸竹材店 [竹] ×ステファン・ディーツ Taketora in collaboration with Stefan Diez	
JC 15	西海陶器 [磁器] ×バーバー・オズガビー SAIKAI TOKI in collaboration with Barber Osgerby	

JC 06

JC 11

JC 10

JC 15

JC 13

JC 09

JC 03

デザインをデザイン

グッドデザイン賞は、日本とアジアのデザインを約六〇年間応援してきた。「良いデザイン」とはなにか、基準を示すことでデザインの意味を探り、本質を知る。そして次の時代に向けての創造的な座標軸をつくることがその目的である。今までに四万二千件もの受賞があり、今でも時代を越えて生き続けているロングライフデザインがたくさんある。永く愛された日本のデザインや、新しく登場した話題性の高いデザインを集めたショップを、香港につくることになった。PMQという元警察所の官舎を改装したビルの一室にできた「グッドデザインストア」。香港にまたひとつ面白い場所ができた。

（グッドデザインストア　二〇一四年）

Designing Design

GOOD DESIGN AWARD has been supporting the design industry in Japan and Asia for approximately 60 years. "What is good design?" GOOD DESIGN AWARD has criteria that seeks the essential quality of design. This provides a foundation for launching creativity for future generations. With this objective, 42,000 design projects have been awarded. Some include "long-life designs" that continue to play a role in the future. Hong Kong was designated as the location for GOOD DESIGN STORE. Here, we will introduce a collection of products including much-loved Japanese designs and the latest popular design products. The store is located in a unit in PMQ Building, which was previously police residential quarters.
(GOOD DESIGN STORE, 2014)

GOOD DESIGN STORE

上：グッドデザインストア店内　下：ショッパー
Top: Inside of the store　Bottom: Store bags

SHIBUYA DESIGN SITE

コンニチハ、シブヤデザイン。

デザインのシブヤへ

東京の十月はデザインが忙しい。明治神宮外苑をはじめ、六本木の東京ミッドタウン、青山や代官山、目黒など大きなイベントから小さな展覧会まで、すべてを廻ることは不可能なほど多くのデザイン催事が行われる。はて、渋谷はどうだろうか? かつての渋谷は公園通りや文化村を中心に、演劇から現代アートまで文化の震源地であり、ライブハウスやクラブでは最新の音楽が鳴っていた。そんな渋谷をもう一度、という訳ではないが、渋谷でもデザインイベントができないかと「SHIBUYA DESIGN SITE」を提案した。百貨店を中心にファッションからインテリア、食品から雑貨まで新しいデザインの提案と、トークセッションを開催した。渋谷からシブヤへ、デザインのシブヤと呼ばれたい。
(シブヤデザインサイト 二〇一三年―)

2013年 会場風景
Scenes from the venue, 2013

Shibuya, a Design Town

Tokyo is busy with design events in October. The events, ranging from small to large are held in Meiji Jingu Gaein Park, Roppongi's Tokyo Midtown, Aoyama, Daikanyama and Meguro. It is said, there are so many events, it would be impossible to see them all. Why not consider Shibuya? It was once a hub of art and culture, people enjoyed theater, modern art and music on Shibuya Koen-Dori Street and in Bunkamura Cultural Complex. The latest music could be heard performed live or played in clubs. I wondered if it would be possible to hold a design event in Shibuya, though I must add, not with the intention of reestablishing the town's former cultural glory. The event, "SHIBUYA DESIGN SITE" featured a selection of the latest designs in fashion, household goods, food and various other products from department stores. Additionally, there was a discussion session. I would like Shibuya to be known as Shibuya, a design town.
(SHIBUYA DESIGN SITE, 2013–)

12 | Settled in Harmony

When it comes to design, God is truly in the details. I don't know what kind of God might reside in any given design, but what I am certain of is that good design always has wonderful details, from its texture to its delicate curves, and from the choice of a font to its spacing, not to mention the practically endless varieties and permutations of color and composition.

In general, the root of a design is in its idea, but precisely where that idea finally ends is a crucial matter for any professional. A design is dependent on its conditions and aims, and the recipient can only ever judge the final result, rendering any appeal to process a mere excuse. For instance, if the budget of a design is strictly limited, then the attempt to work around that limitation can produce something truly great and new.

And the final "settling" of the design determines its end result and quality. In making repeated choices based on one's ideal wishes and external conditions, the whole picture begins to emerge, and the details start to appear. By "settling", I mean harmony; where the parts of the whole fit perfectly together, as if all the intricacies and details could not but be there. When I come upon a great design, I tremble with delight. And at the same time, I despair. There are those that are totally original, and those that are born from a commonplace and everyday observation, but what they all have in common is superb detail.

十二、おさまりで、納まる

デザインの神は細部に宿る、と信じている。
デザインにどのような神が存在するのか怪しいけれど、
優れたデザインはディテールが素晴らしい。
質感から微妙な曲線、書体の選び方から字間、行間まで。
色感は言うに及ばず、絶妙な構図などきりがない。

一般的に、アイデアがデザインの根幹を決定づけているのは間違いないが、
最終的な着地の精度がどれだけ重要か、
プロフェッショナルは身にしみて感じているはずである。
条件や目的があってのデザインなのだ、
見る者は結果で判断するだけで、プロセスは言い訳になる。
コストが厳しければ工夫することで新しいデザインが生まれる。

そして〝おさまり〟は最終的な質を決定する。
希望と条件で選択を繰り返すうちに全体像が現れ、ディテールが見えてくる。
〝おさまり〟は調和するということ。
部分が、細部のディテールがあたかも必然のように
そこに納まって存在し、定着していることなのだ。
素晴しいデザインに出会うとカラダが震える。そして絶望する。
斬新なモノもあれば、日常の気づきから生まれたモノもある。
みなディテールが素晴しいと感じる。

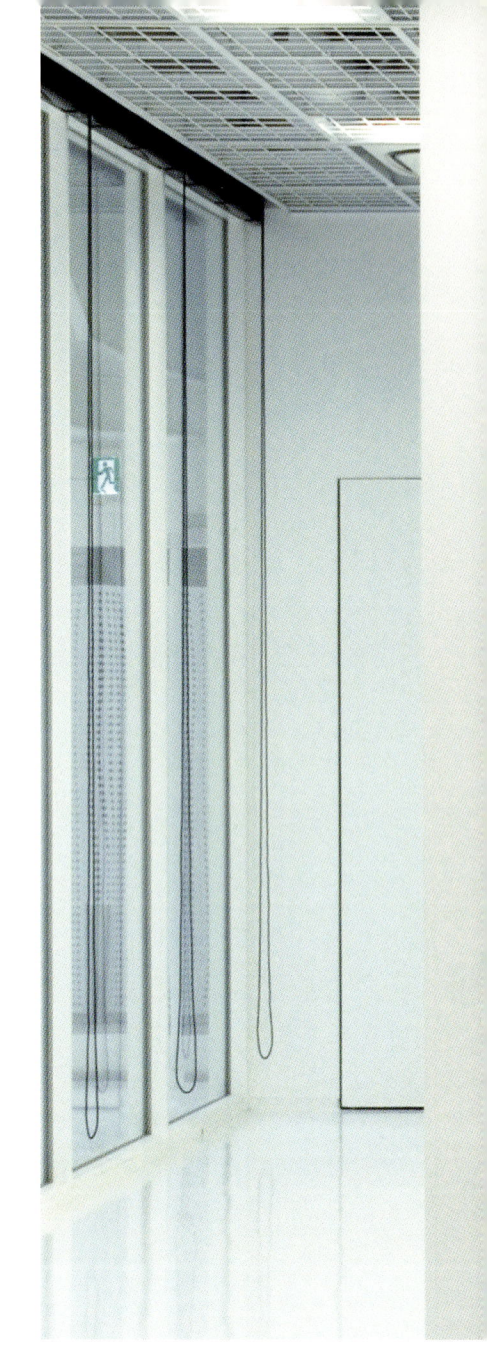

Visual Tricks

Of our five senses, it is said that vision constitutes 80% of what we perceive.
This means that we receive most of our information via the eyes. The brain detects that information and makes hypotheses about it based on past experiences. That it can judge the information precisely, without sense of touch or smell, is in some ways a misinterpretation on the part of the brain, and can lead to instances of the brain tricking itself. Offset printing makes use of just such a visual trick. This printing method makes an image by layering 4-colored halftones. If you look at it closely, it is merely a layer of small dots. Graphic design has evolved greatly as a two-dimensional form of expression, but developments in printing technology and paper-types have made a whole range of visual tricks possible as well. The three posters for Tokyo Polytechnic University feature a design of scattered blue paint depicting the world map. The embossed effect from the students' thumbs is effectively expressed over the top of this bursting mass of ink.

(Tokyo Polytechnic University, 2011)

視覚トリック

人に備わる五感の中で視覚が全体の八〇％を占めるという。ほとんどの情報を視覚から取り入れて判断していることになる。脳は眼球から入る情報を、経験から仮説を立てて認識しており、触ったり、匂いを嗅がなくても判断できるのは脳の思い込みもある。

オフセット印刷はこの視覚のトリックを利用している。四色のアミ点を重ねて画像を再現するのだが、よく見ると点の重なりにすぎない。

グラフィックデザインは、平面のデザインとして進化したが、紙の開発や技術の発達により、さらに眼を欺く視覚トリックが進んでいるのである。

東京工芸大学のポスター三連作は、飛び散ったブルーの塗料で世界を表現している。盛り上がるインクに加え、学生が指で押し出すエンボス加工が効果的に表れている。

（東京工芸大学　二〇一一年）

Symbol of Goods

People are fascinated by gadgets; perhaps men in particular. Whether cars, watches, cameras, audio players, bikes, or models, they are all essentially based on "motion", where a particular mechanism produces visible movement. In preparation for the renovation of the LOFT store in Shibuya, we thought about moving objects to place at the shop entrance. The final display was named "Gearloft", in which the LOFT logo was lodged into a structure made up of 18 cogs of various sizes. As the cogs turn, the logo begins to dismantle, and then return to its original state in 40 seconds. Often referred to as "a [loft] play-area for adults", the store is a giant collection of various household and hobby goods imported from all over the world. Set on a slope, the "Gearloft" piece symbolizes the full and enriching world of hobbies and interests, attracting the attention of the many customers who walk past it.
(Shibuya LOFT main signage, 2012)

雑貨の象徴

特に男性はメカに興味がある。クルマ、時計、カメラ、オーディオ、自転車、模型など多彩で、その本質は「動く」ということ、機械的に動力が伝わり目に見えることが重要なのである。渋谷ロフトのリニューアルにともない入口に動くオブジェを考えた。「ギアロフト」と呼ばれ、大小十九個の歯車にロフトのロゴが入っていて、歯車の回転に合わせてロゴが分解され、四〇秒で元に戻る。

雑貨の集積するロフト、「大人の屋根裏部屋」と呼ばれ、趣味性の高いモノが世界中から集められている。坂の途中にある「ギアロフト」は密度の高い趣味の世界を象徴しており、動き出すたびに道行く人の足を止めている。

(渋谷ロフト シンボルサイン 二〇一二年)

The Joys of Healthy Living

A showroom is a place for companies to present their products and services, and an opportunity to make the best impression possible on prospective buyers. Though the goods on offer are naturally the stars of the show, learning about their origins and the backgrounds to their development can also often be enlightening. The Tokyo Showroom for Omron Healthcare featured a doughnut-shaped table in the middle of the room, which visitors could walk around to view the various products on display. Based on the concepts behind the developments of these products, this spatial design represents a timescale from past to future, and how the joys of healthy living have evolved over time.
(Showroom Omron Healthcare, 2008)

健康という喜び

ショールームは会社の顔として商品やサービスをわかりやすく紹介する場所。商品が主役であることに間違いないが、その商品の成り立ちや開発の背景を知ることで、より理解が深まることもある。オムロンヘルスケアの東京ショールーム。部屋の中心にドーナツ状のテーブルを設置し、廻りながら見てもらう。商品を開発するうえでのコンセプトを軸に、過去から未来へ、時代背景とともに人と生活、健康で暮らす喜びを示している。
(ショールーム オムロンヘルスケア 二〇〇八年)

未来
Future products

現行製品
Current products

過去製品
Past products

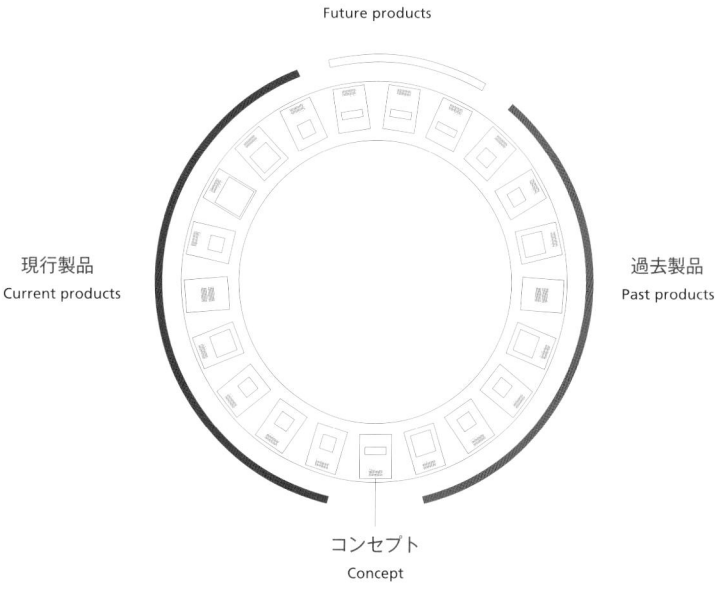

コンセプト
Concept

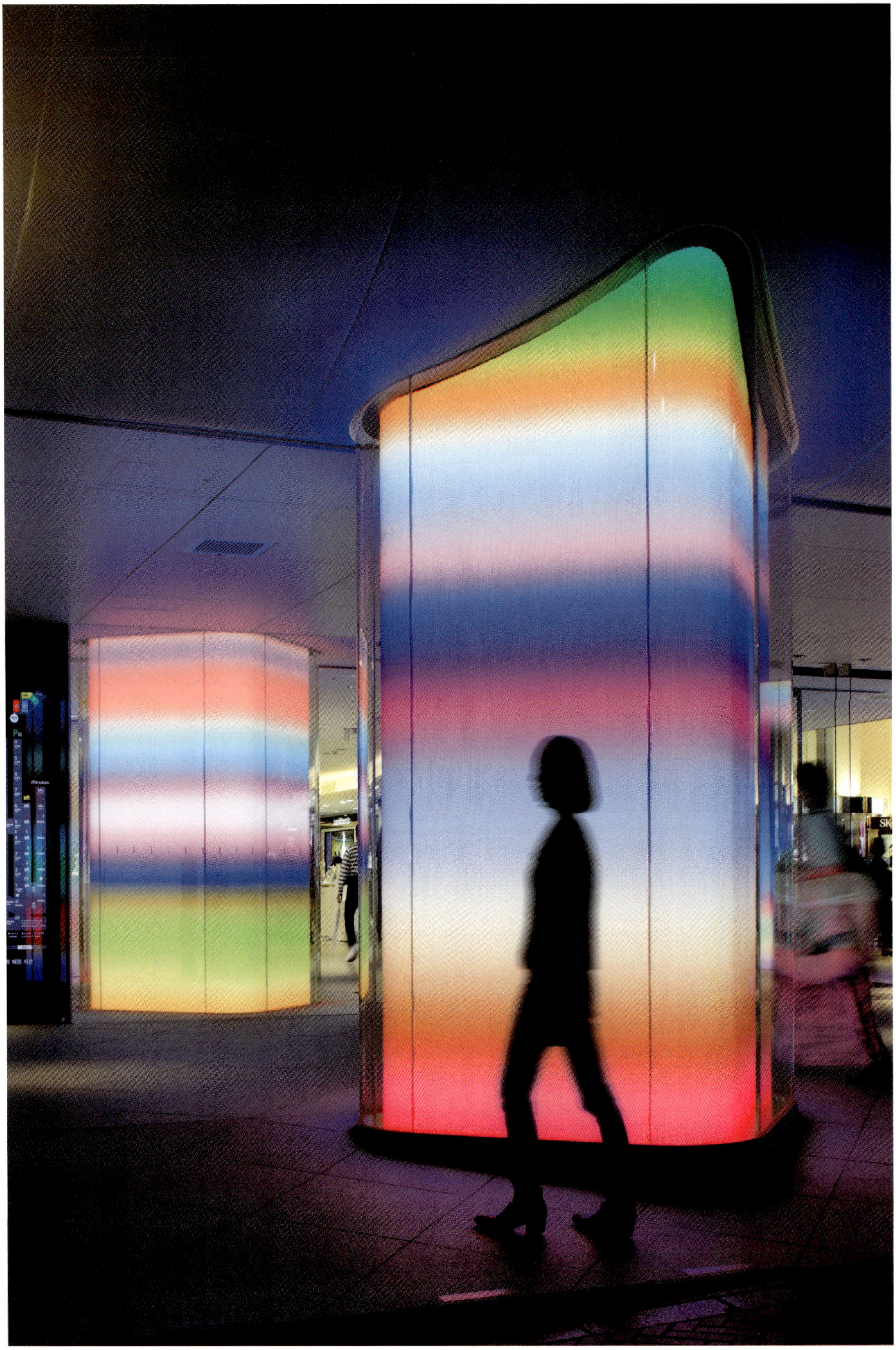

湿潤が生む日本の色彩

色彩の感覚は育った環境によって決まる。日本人が色彩感覚に優れていると言われるのは、日本独自の風土が大きく関係しており、その根底には「うつろい」と「にじみ」という二つの考え方が流れている。

「うつろい」は、四季の移り変わりや人の気持ち、政変や災害によって変化してゆく風景を受け入れようとしている気持ち。「はかなさ」や「期待」を微妙な色彩で表現しようとしてきた。

また「にじみ」は、湿度の高い自然環境での風景のぼかしが独自のグラデーション感覚を育てた。

たとえば朝もやの景色、山並みが墨絵のように霞んで美しい。

西武渋谷店の改装に伴い入口のゲートを提案した。四季の移り変わり、朝から夜にかけて時間の変化、行き交う人々に反応して色彩が変化する柱を計画した。ドイツ人アーティスト、カールステン・ニコライは見事に日本の湿潤的色彩を表現した。

(西武渋谷店 A館エントランス 二〇一五年)

Japanese Colors of Moisture

Your sense of color is dependent on where you grow up. The reason why the Japanese are said to have an acute sense of color has much to do with our distinctive climate and the two underpinning concepts of utsuroi (evanescence) and nijimi (blurring). The word utsuroi also signifies the turning of the seasons and fickleness of human nature, encompassing changes in all kinds of landscapes, from the political to the natural. This concept has been key in creating highly subtle and nuanced colors associated with transience and expectation. The word nijimi has influenced an attuned sense of color gradation, thought to also stem from the humid climate in Japan, and the 'blurring' or 'oozing' effect that this moisture has on our views of the landscape. Take for instance, the beautiful view of a row of mountains in the morning mist, hazy like an ink painting. A new entrance gate was proposed as part of the renovation of the Seibu Department Store in Shibuya. We designed a columnar piece that appears to change color in reaction to the cycle of the four seasons, the changes from morning to night, and the incessant passersby. The German artist Carsten Nicolai did a magnificent job in expressing the colors of moisture so distinctive to Japan.

(SEIBU SHIBUYA entrance, 2015)

The four columns each emit a different color gradation based on their own distinct algorithms. A great Japanophile, Carsten has a deep understanding of the utsuroi of the four seasons and the transience of nijimi. He programed them into this work with great success, ensuring that the combinations of colors would never repeat themselves. Each moment is unique and nonrecurring. The graphic design was also produced around the theme of color gradation. The train posters and flags along the neighboring street all express a different color depending on their location.

四本の柱は独自のアルゴリズムにより別々の色彩グラデーションを流している。日本を愛するドイツ人、カールステンは四季の「うつろい」や、はかない「にじみ」を深く理解しプログラミングしたのだ。色彩は二度と同じ組み合わせにはならない。今の一瞬を大切に、一期一会なのだ。グラフィックデザインも色彩のグラデーションをテーマに制作した。駅貼りのポスターも、公園通りのフラッグも、場所によって異なる表情を見せる。

写真原版
Original Plate

The Allure of Chance

It has been 100 years since the invention of offset printing. Gutenberg invented the technology of mechanical movable type printing in the 15th century, and full-fledged mass color printing finally became possible 5 centuries later.
In the light of this fact, printing technology has developed dramatically over the last 100 years, but the basic 4-color method of offset printing remains unchanged. I participated in an event called "GRAPHIC TRIAL", organized by the printing company Toppan. High-quality printing is now dominated by computer technology. With the advancement of digital photography and illustration, it has become increasingly difficult to work with standardized and consistent color schemes when dealing with proofs. I thought about how we could make the printing process more sensory and instinctive, and so we decided to copy and reproduce the CMYK plate data manually. These hand-drawn plates distort the balance of the originals, creating a strange and alluring effect in the colors they produce. The resultant chance combinations were both surprising and fun to observe.
(GRAPHIC TRIAL, 2008)

偶然の魅力

オフセット印刷が発明されて一〇〇年。グーテンベルグが金属活字を用いた活版印刷技術を発明したのが一五世紀だから、その後五世紀をかけてフルカラーの大量印刷が実現したのだ。
この一〇〇年の間に印刷技術は劇的に進化したが、オフセット印刷が基本四色という条件は変わらない。
凸版印刷が主催する「グラフィック トライアル」に参加した。
精度の高い印刷はコンピュータで制御されている。写真やイラストレーションなどデジタル化が進み、校正などで本来の色調の基準に困ることが多くなった。
そこで印刷表現をもっと感覚的にできないものかと、CMYKに分けられた製版のデータを手描きで模写し、再現した。手描きの版は本来のバランスを崩し不思議な色味が出現する。偶発的なマッチングに面白さを感じた。
(グラフィック トライアル 二〇〇八年)

作品データ

AD	アートディレクション	FD	家具デザイン	PRD	プロダクトデザイン
AR	設計	I	イラストレーション	PH	撮影
AW	アートワーク	ID	インテリアデザイン	PR	プロデュース
C	コピーライティング	L	ランドスケープデザイン	S	担当スタッフ
CD	クリエイティブディレクション	LD	照明デザイン	SD	サウンドデザイン
CL	クライアント	N	ネーミング		
DIR	ディレクション	PD	プリンティングディレクション		

1、いつも、を疑う

008　三保谷硝子店 101年目の試作展
　　　掲載作品　　展示作品、ポスター
　　　所在地　　　東京都港区
　　　開催年　　　2009年
　　　PH（ポスター）　吉田明広
　　　PH（作品）　　平井広行
　　　PH（その他）　ナカサアンドパートナーズ
　　　CL　　　　　三保谷硝子店、
　　　　　　　　　アクシスギャラリー
　　　S　　　　　中尾千絵、丸山智也

012　コープさっぽろ
　　　掲載作品　　VI、パッケージ、冊子
　　　所在地　　　北海道札幌市
　　　制作年　　　2012年−
　　　C　　　　　松木圭三
　　　PH（パッケージ）　伊藤彰浩
　　　PH（畑のレストラン）　松浦靖宏（サファリ・グラフィックス）
　　　CL　　　　　コープさっぽろ、
　　　　　　　　　凸版印刷
　　　S　　　　　阿部航太、関根早弥香

018　福生市庁舎
　　　掲載作品　　サイン計画
　　　所在地　　　東京都福生市
　　　完成年　　　2008年
　　　AR　　　　　山本理顕
　　　FD　　　　　藤森泰司
　　　PH　　　　　大森有起
　　　CL　　　　　福生市
　　　S　　　　　中尾千絵

2、無意識の中の意識

026　Junglin'
　　　掲載作品　　個展
　　　所在地　　　東京都豊島区
　　　開催年　　　2011年
　　　映像撮影　　伊藤彰浩、宇禄、
　　　　　　　　　吉田明広
　　　制作進行　　アマナ
　　　協力　　　　アマナ、そごう・西武、
　　　　　　　　　光和
　　　PH（会場）　　ナカサアンドパートナーズ

036　Junglin' 2
　　　掲載作品　　個展
　　　所在地　　　東京都港区
　　　開催年　　　2014年
　　　映像撮影　　吉田明広
　　　制作進行　　アマナ
　　　協賛　　　　そごう・西武、ロフト
　　　協力　　　　ICE都市環境照明研究所、
　　　　　　　　　アクシスギャラリー、
　　　　　　　　　アクティブ、アマナ、
　　　　　　　　　光和、ジェイアイエヌ、
　　　　　　　　　大日本印刷、デザイン
　　　　　　　　　スタジオエス、特種東海
　　　　　　　　　製紙、ナカムラデザイン
　　　　　　　　　事務所、日本サインデザ
　　　　　　　　　イン協会
　　　PH（会場）　　吉田明広

3、見えないものを見えるように

046　ミヨシファクトリーソープ
　　　掲載作品　　パッケージ
　　　所在地　　　東京都墨田区
　　　完成年　　　2009年
　　　PRD　　　　柴田文江
　　　PH　　　　　伊藤彰浩
　　　CL　　　　　ミヨシ石鹸
　　　S　　　　　大内かよ

050　オムロンヘルスケア
　　　掲載作品　　商品アイコン
　　　所在地　　　京都府向日市
　　　制作年　　　2009年−
　　　PRD　　　　柴田文江
　　　CL　　　　　オムロンヘルスケア
　　　S　　　　　丸山智也、衛藤隆弘

052　TOTO
　　　掲載作品　　ウォシュレット用
　　　　　　　　　ピクトグラム
　　　所在地　　　福岡県北九州市
　　　制作年　　　2013年
　　　CL　　　　　TOTO
　　　S　　　　　衛藤隆弘

054　アクシス「廣村正彰のJunglin'」掲載
　　　掲載年　　　2014年
　　　協力　　　　アクシス
　　　S　　　　　衛藤隆弘

056　東京ステーションギャラリー
　　　掲載作品　　VI、展示作品、グッズ
　　　所在地　　　東京都千代田区
　　　完成年　　　2012年
　　　CD　　　　　柳田芳男、武藤庄八
　　　CD（グッズ）　萩原修
　　　DIR（グッズ製造）　山田明良（福永紙工）
　　　映像撮影、PH（会場）　吉田明広
　　　PH（056頁）　©KENICHI MINORUDA /
　　　　　　　　　SEBUN PHOTO /
　　　　　　　　　amanaimages
　　　PH（ポスター）　山田覚
　　　CL　　　　　東京ステーション
　　　　　　　　　ギャラリー
　　　CL（グッズ）　ジェイアール東日本商事
　　　S　　　　　衛藤隆弘

060　龍谷大学深草キャンパス和顔館
　　　掲載作品　　サイン計画
　　　所在地　　　京都府伏見区
　　　完成年　　　2015年
　　　AR　　　　　飯田善彦
　　　PH　　　　　ナカサアンドパートナーズ
　　　CL　　　　　龍谷大学
　　　S　　　　　藤井北斗、小松裕輔

4、っぽい、感じ

066　すみだ水族館
　　　掲載作品　　VI、サイン計画、ポスター
　　　所在地　　　東京都墨田区
　　　制作年　　　2012年−
　　　N　　　　　三井浩
　　　I　　　　　横山伸省
　　　C　　　　　加藤ジャンプ
　　　LD　　　　　武石正宣
　　　PH　　　　　ナカサアンドパートナーズ
　　　CL　　　　　オリックス不動産
　　　S　　　　　藤井北斗、衛藤隆弘、
　　　　　　　　　小松裕輔

072　有楽町ロフト
　　　掲載作品　　サイン計画
　　　所在地　　　東京都千代田区
　　　完成年　　　2011年
　　　ID　　　　　米谷ひろし、君塚賢
　　　PH　　　　　淺川敏
　　　CL　　　　　ロフト

244

S	藤井北斗、衛藤隆弘	

076 イトーキ東京イノベーションセンター
　　SYNQA
　　掲載作品　サイン計画、VI
　　所在地　　東京都中央区
　　完成年　　2013年
　　CL　　　　イトーキ
　　S　　　　 藤井北斗、本多真実

078 アヤナ リゾート&スパ バリ /
　　リンバ ジンバラン バリ by アヤナ
　　掲載作品　VI、アメニティ
　　所在地　　インドネシア、バリ島
　　完成年　　2009年 / 2013年
　　CL　　　　アヤナ リゾート&スパ バリ
　　S　　　　 大内かよ、中尾千絵、
　　　　　　　阿部航太

080 西武池袋本店 9階屋上
　　食と緑の空中庭園
　　掲載作品　環境、サイン計画、
　　　　　　　グラフィックデザイン
　　所在地　　東京都豊島区
　　完成年　　2015年
　　L　　　　 団塚栄喜、荒木宗一郎
　　店舗デザイン　鈴野浩一、禿真哉
　　　　　　　（トラフ建築設計事務所）
　　LD　　　　東海林弘靖
　　　　　　　LIGHTDESIGN INC.
　　植栽設計・施工・管理　日比谷アメニス
　　C　　　　 松木圭三
　　PH　　　　佐藤振一
　　CL　　　　そごう・西武
　　S　　　　 小松裕輔、衛藤隆弘、
　　　　　　　関根早弥香

082 鉄道博物館
　　掲載作品　VI
　　所在地　　埼玉県さいたま市
　　完成年　　2007年
　　CD　　　　柳田芳男
　　PH　　　　©YOSHIRO TAZAWA /
　　　　　　　SEBUN PHOTO /
　　　　　　　amanaimages
　　CL　　　　東日本鉄道文化財団
　　S　　　　 大内かよ

083 庖丁工房タダフサ
　　掲載作品　VI、パッケージ
　　所在地　　新潟県三条市
　　完成年　　2012年
　　PRD　　　 柴田文江
　　PR　　　　中川淳
　　PH　　　　太田拓実
　　CL　　　　タダフサ
　　S　　　　 阿部航太

084 buchi
　　掲載作品　VI
　　所在地　　長野県塩尻市
　　完成年　　2012年
　　PRD　　　 柴田文江
　　DIR　　　 青木昭夫
　　PH　　　　伊藤彰浩
　　CL　　　　酒井産業
　　S　　　　 衛藤隆弘

085 東北デザインマルシェ
　　掲載作品　VI、展示計画
　　所在地　　東京都港区
　　開催年　　2012年
　　PH　　　　広川智基
　　CL　　　　日本デザイン振興会
　　S　　　　 阿部航太

086 今治市伊東豊雄建築ミュージアム
　　掲載作品　VI、サイン計画
　　所在地　　愛媛県今治市
　　完成年　　2011年
　　AR　　　　伊東豊雄
　　PH　　　　阿野太一
　　CL　　　　NPO これからの建築を
　　　　　　　考える 伊東建築塾
　　S　　　　 丸山智也

087 今治市岩田健母と子のミュージアム
　　掲載作品　VI
　　所在地　　愛媛県今治市
　　完成年　　2011年
　　AR　　　　伊東豊雄
　　CL　　　　NPO これからの建築を
　　　　　　　考える 伊東建築塾
　　S　　　　 丸山智也

087 ヤオコー川越美術館 三栖右嗣記念館
　　掲載作品　VI、サイン計画
　　所在地　　埼玉県川越市
　　完成年　　2009年
　　AR　　　　伊東豊雄
　　CL　　　　ヤオコー
　　S　　　　 阿部航太

5、秩序を誘う

090 9h ナインアワーズ京都 / 成田空港
　　掲載作品　VI、サイン計画
　　所在地　　京都市下京区 /
　　　　　　　千葉県成田市
　　完成年　　2009年 / 2014年
　　CD, PRD　 柴田文江
　　ID　　　　中村隆秋
　　PH（環境）　ナカサアンドパートナーズ
　　PH（アメニティ）吉田明広
　　CL　　　　ナインアワーズ
　　S　　　　 丸山智也、衛藤隆弘

096 ヤマトグループ 羽田クロノゲート
　　掲載作品　サイン計画
　　所在地　　東京都大田区
　　完成年　　2013年
　　AR　　　　日建設計
　　PH　　　　ナカサアンドパートナーズ
　　CL　　　　ヤマトホールディングス
　　S　　　　 丸山智也、阿部航太、
　　　　　　　関根早弥香

100 天津図書館
　　掲載作品　サイン計画
　　所在地　　中国天津市
　　完成年　　2012年
　　AR　　　　山本理顕
　　FD　　　　藤森泰司
　　カーペットデザイン　安東陽子
　　LD　　　　岡安泉
　　CL　　　　天津市
　　S　　　　 阿部航太

102 チャールズ・イームズ写真展
　　100 images × 100 words
　　—偉大なるデザイナーのメッセージ
　　掲載作品　展示計画、ポスター
　　所在地　　東京都港区
　　開催年　　2008年
　　PH　　　　ナカサアンドパートナーズ
　　CL　　　　アクシスギャラリー
　　S　　　　 大内かよ

103 Pam
　　掲載作品　　展示計画
　　所在地　　　静岡県駿東郡
　　完成年　　　2004年
　　AD (共同)　秋田寛
　　PH (103頁上)　高山幸三
　　PH (103頁下)　皆川勇
　　CL　　　　　特種東海製紙
　　S　　　　　 前田豊、阿部航太、
　　　　　　　　関根早弥香

104 シスメックス
　　掲載作品　　パッケージ
　　所在地　　　兵庫県神戸市
　　完成年　　　2011年
　　コンセプト　柴田文江
　　CL　　　　　シスメックス
　　S　　　　　 阿部航太

105 タウパー
　　掲載作品　　パッケージ
　　所在地　　　静岡県島田市
　　完成年　　　2012年
　　PH　　　　　吉田明広
　　CL　　　　　トライフ
　　S　　　　　 黄善佳、阿部航太

6、呼び起こされる記憶

108 立川ロフト
　　掲載作品　　サイン計画
　　所在地　　　東京都立川市
　　完成年　　　2012年
　　ID　　　　　米谷ひろし、君塚賢
　　PH (グラフィック)　アマナ
　　PH (環境)　ナカサアンドパートナーズ
　　CL　　　　　小原清、安永ケンタウロス、
　　　　　　　　宇禄、吉田明広、川上祐樹
　　S　　　　　 黄善佳、藤井北斗

112 あべのハルカス
　　掲載作品　　サイン計画
　　所在地　　　大阪府大阪市
　　完成年　　　2014年
　　CD　　　　　原田哲夫（竹中工務店）
　　AR　　　　　竹中工務店
　　PH　　　　　ナカサアンドパートナーズ
　　CL　　　　　近畿日本鉄道

　　S　　　　　 藤井北斗、衛藤隆弘、
　　　　　　　　竹本新

114 西武渋谷店 モヴィーダ館
　　掲載作品　　サイン計画
　　所在地　　　東京都渋谷区
　　完成年　　　2013年
　　ID　　　　　鈴野浩一、禿真哉
　　　　　　　　（トラフ建築設計事務所）
　　PH　　　　　阿野太一
　　CL　　　　　そごう・西武
　　S　　　　　 藤井北斗

116 臺北文創
　　掲載作品　　サイン計画
　　所在地　　　台湾台北市
　　完成年　　　2014年
　　AR　　　　　伊東豊雄
　　PH　　　　　中村絵
　　CL　　　　　臺北文創
　　S　　　　　 丸山智也、黄善佳、
　　　　　　　　阿部航太

118 乃村工藝社本社ビル
　　掲載作品　　サイン計画
　　所在地　　　東京都港区
　　完成年　　　2007年
　　PH　　　　　中島洋介
　　CL　　　　　乃村工藝社
　　S　　　　　 丸山智也

120 POST 切手 郵便が変わり始めた。
　　切手のデザインはどう変わる。
　　掲載作品　　展示作品、展示計画
　　所在地　　　東京都港区
　　開催年　　　2007年–2008年
　　PH　　　　　淺川敏
　　CL　　　　　日本グラフィック
　　　　　　　　デザイナー協会
　　S　　　　　 黄善佳

122 エアラス・性能と品質
　　掲載作品　　展示計画、VI
　　所在地　　　東京都港区
　　開催年　　　2015年
　　C　　　　　 松木圭三
　　LD　　　　　武石正宣
　　PH (会場)　ナカサアンドパートナーズ
　　PH (100歳の記憶展ポスター)　カルステン・トーマエレン

　　撮影進行　　ライトパブリシティ大阪
　　(100歳の記憶展ポスター)
　　CL　　　　　特種東海製紙
　　共同企画　　コープさっぽろ、
　　　　　　　　凸版印刷
　　S　　　　　 阿部航太、関根早弥香

7、デザインのスピード

150 横須賀美術館
　　掲載作品　　サイン計画
　　所在地　　　神奈川県横須賀市
　　完成年　　　2007年
　　AR　　　　　山本理顕
　　PH　　　　　近藤泰夫
　　CL　　　　　横須賀市
　　S　　　　　 丸山智也

154 シンワメディカルリゾート
　　掲載作品　　サイン計画
　　所在地　　　千葉県八千代市
　　完成年　　　2011年
　　ID　　　　　橋本夕紀夫
　　PH　　　　　ナカサアンドパートナーズ
　　CL　　　　　医療法人社団 心和会
　　S　　　　　 黄善佳

156 ニフコ技術開発センター
　　掲載作品　　サイン計画
　　所在地　　　神奈川県横須賀市
　　完成年　　　2013年
　　AR　　　　　坂倉建築研究所
　　PH　　　　　船来洋志
　　CL　　　　　ニフコ
　　S　　　　　 丸山智也、阿部航太

158 TOTO MUSEUM
　　掲載作品　　VI、サイン計画
　　所在地　　　福岡県北九州市
　　完成年　　　2015年
　　AR　　　　　梓設計
　　L、LD　　　 ソラ・アソシエイツ
　　PH　　　　　ナカサアンドパートナーズ
　　CL　　　　　TOTO
　　S　　　　　 衛藤隆弘

162 すみだモダン
　　掲載作品　　ポスター、冊子
　　所在地　　　東京都墨田区

制作年　　2011年–
C　　　　三井千賀子（2011年–）
PH　　　吉田明広
CL　　　すみだ地域ブランド
　　　　 推進協議会
S　　　　黄善佳、竹本新

166　二上家
　掲載作品　VI、サイン計画
　所在地　　埼玉県所沢市
　完成年　　2015年
　ID　　　　中村隆秋
　PH　　　　ナカサアンドパートナーズ
　CL　　　　二上家
　S　　　　 衛藤隆弘、小松裕輔

8、情報を編む

170　東京工芸大学新3号館
　掲載作品　サイン計画
　所在地　　東京都中野区
　完成年　　2011年
　AR　　　　坂倉建築研究所
　PH　　　　ナカサアンドパートナーズ
　CL　　　　東京工芸大学
　S　　　　 宮本太一

172　あいちトリエンナーレ 2013
　掲載作品　VI、ポスター、サイン計画
　所在地　　愛知県名古屋市、岡崎市
　開催年　　2013年
　PH　　　　ナカサアンドパートナーズ
　CL　　　　あいちトリエンナーレ
　　　　　　実行委員会
　S　　　　 阿部航太、関根早弥香

176　21_21 DESIGN SIGHT 企画展
　　　田中一光とデザインの前後左右
　掲載作品　展示計画、ポスター
　所在地　　東京都港区
　会期　　　2012年9月21日–
　　　　　　2013年1月20日
　展覧会
　ディレクター　小池一子
　設計協力　ナカムラデザイン事務所
　PH　　　　吉村昌也
　協力　　　中川ケミカル「カッティング
　(His Colors)　シート®」、竹尾「タント」

CL　　　　21_21 DESIGN SIGHT、
　　　　　公益財団法人 三宅一生
　　　　　デザイン文化財団
S　　　　衛藤隆弘、本多真実

182　nonowa
　掲載作品　サイン計画
　所在地　　東京都武蔵野市
　完成年　　2014年
　L　　　　 団塚栄喜、荒木宗一郎
　LD　　　　東海林弘靖
　　　　　　LIGHTDESIGN INC.
　PH　　　　ナカサアンドパートナーズ
　CL　　　　JR 中央ラインモール
　S　　　　 阿部航太、関根早弥香

9、陰に潜む

188　ガーデンテラス長崎 ホテル＆リゾート
　掲載作品　サイン計画
　所在地　　長崎県長崎市
　完成年　　2009年
　AR　　　　隈研吾建築都市設計事務所
　PH　　　　ナカサアンドパートナーズ
　CL　　　　メモリード
　S　　　　 中尾千絵

190　パーク ハイアット 釜山
　掲載作品　サイン計画
　所在地　　韓国釜山
　完成年　　2013年
　ID　　　　杉本貴志(スーパーポテト)
　PH　　　　ナカサアンドパートナーズ
　CL　　　　HDC HOTEL IPARK
　S　　　　 黄善佳

194　モリサワ新本社ビル
　掲載作品　サイン計画
　所在地　　大阪府大阪市
　完成年　　2009年
　PR　　　　森澤武士
　AR　　　　東畑建築事務所
　PH　　　　ナカサアンドパートナーズ
　PH (194頁　©TAKASHI KATAHIRA /
　楔形文字石盤)　SEBUN PHOTO /
　　　　　　amanaimages
　CL　　　　モリサワ
　S　　　　 丸山智也

198　KISHI CLINICA FEMINA
　掲載作品　VI、サイン計画
　所在地　　東京都中央区
　完成年　　2014年
　ID　　　　中村隆秋
　PH　　　　ナカサアンドパートナーズ
　CL　　　　KISHI CLINICA FEMINA
　S　　　　 藤井北斗、関根早弥香

200　LPA 1990-2015
　　　建築照明デザインの潮流
　掲載作品　書籍
　完成年　　2015年
　編著者　　面出薫 + LPA
　発行所　　六耀社
　CL　　　　ライティング プラン
　　　　　　ナーズ アソシエーツ
　S　　　　 藤井北斗

201　ライティングオブジェ 2012
　掲載作品　展示作品
　所在地　　東京都千代田区
　開催年　　2012年
　CL　　　　ライティング・オブジェ
　　　　　　制作委員会
　S　　　　 本多真実

10、欲しいをつくる

204　こふくあん
　掲載作品　VI
　所在地　　東京都豊島区
　完成年　　2014年
　N　　　　 蓑田雅之
　CL　　　　そごう・西武
　S　　　　 衛藤隆弘、小松裕輔

205　Little chef
　掲載作品　VI
　所在地　　東京都豊島区
　完成年　　2010年
　CL　　　　そごう・西武
　S　　　　 藤井北斗

206　SELF&SHELF LOFT
　掲載作品　VI、サイン計画
　所在地　　東京都豊島区
　完成年　　2013年
　ID　　　　平綿久晃、渡部智宏

```
         N        蓑田雅之
         PH       ナカサアンドパートナーズ
         CL       ロフト
         S        藤井北斗

208  ランドマークプラザ
         掲載作品   ポスター
         所在地    神奈川県横浜市
         完成年    2009年−
         C        松木圭三
         I        舟橋全二
         CL       三菱地所プロパティ
                  マネジメント
         S        中尾千絵、黄善佳

209  丸の内商店会
         掲載作品   ポスター
         所在地    東京都千代田区
         完成年    2006年−
         C        松木圭三
         PH       伊藤彰浩
         CL       三菱地所プロパティ
                  マネジメント
         S        中尾千絵、黄善佳

210  西武池袋本店 インショップロゴ
         掲載作品   VI
         制作年    2008年−2014年
         CL       そごう・西武
         S        藤井北斗、宮本太一、
                  小松裕輔


     11、つくるをつくる

214  ジャパンクリエイティブ
         掲載作品   クリエイティブディレクション、
                  グラフィックデザイン
         設立年    2000年−
         PH       ナカサアンドパートナーズ
         名誉理事   内藤廣
                  （内藤廣建築設計事務所）
         代表理事   廣村正彰
                  （廣村デザイン事務所）
         理事     イヴ・ブゴン
                  （ハースト婦人画報社）
         理事     川島蓉子
                  （ifs 未来研究所 所長）
         監事     松本隆
                  （そごう・西武）

         R&D      田渕智也
                  （office for creation）
         R&D      倉本仁
                  （JIN KURAMOTO STUDIO）
         R&D      角田陽太
                  （YOTA KAKUDA DESIGN）
         R&D      熊野亘
         CL       ジャパンクリエイティブ
         S        丸山智也、衛藤隆弘、
                  竹本新、小松裕輔

226  グッドデザインストア
         掲載作品   VI
         所在地    香港セントラル地区
         完成年    2014年
         シンボル   亀倉雄策
         マーク
         PH（店舗） Simon J Nicol
         CL       日本デザイン振興会
         S        阿部航太

228  シブヤデザインサイト
         掲載作品   VI、展示計画
         所在地    東京都渋谷区
         完成年    2013年−
         C        松木圭三
         PH       ナカサアンドパートナーズ
         CL       そごう・西武、ロフト
         S        衛藤隆弘、小松裕輔


     12、おさまり、で納まる

232  東京工芸大学
         掲載作品   ポスター
         所在地    東京都中野区
         制作年    2011年
         PH       ナカサアンドパートナーズ
         CL       東京工芸大学
         S        藤井北斗

234  渋谷ロフト シンボルサイン
         掲載作品   シンボルサイン
         所在地    東京都渋谷区
         完成年    2012年
         SD       コーネリアス
         PH       ナカサアンドパートナーズ
         CL       ロフト
         S        藤井北斗

236  ショールーム オムロンヘルスケア
         掲載作品   展示計画
         所在地    東京都品川区
         完成年    2008年
         ID       中村隆秋
         PH       髙山幸三
         CL       オムロンヘルスケア
         S        丸山智也

238  西武渋谷店 A館エントランス
         掲載作品   クリエイティブディレクション、
                  ポスター
         所在地    東京都渋谷区
         完成年    2015年
         AW       カールステン・ニコライ.
                  "クロマ・アクター".2015
         技術協力   金築浩史
         LD       武石正宣
         C        松木圭三
         PH       ナカサアンドパートナーズ
         CL       そごう・西武
         S        竹本新

242  グラフィックトライアル
         掲載作品   ポスター
         所在地    東京都文京区
         完成年    2008年
         PD       尾河由樹
         PH（原版） 近藤泰夫
         CL       凸版印刷
         S        中尾千絵、黄善佳
```

Data of Works

AD	Art Direction	FD	Furniture Design	PRD	Product Design
AR	Architectural Design	I	Illustration	PH	Photography
AW	Art Work	ID	Interior Design	PR	Produce
C	Copywriting	L	Landscape Design	S	Staff
CD	Creative Direction	LD	Lighting Design	SD	Sound Design
CL	Client	N	Naming	SP	Sponsor
CO	Cooperation	PD	Printing Direction	VP	Video Production
DIR	Direction				

1, Question the Ordinary

008 101st Anniversary Works-in-Progress for Mihoya Glass
- Category: Exhibition Piece, Poster
- Place: Minato, Tokyo
- Year: 2009
- PH(Poster): Akihiro Yoshida
- PH(Exhibition Piece): Hiroyuki Hirai
- PH(Others): Nacása & Partners Inc.
- CL: MIHOYA GLASS / AXIS GALLERY
- S: Chie Nakao / Tomoya Maruyama

012 CO-OP Sapporo
- Category: VI / Package Design / Booklet Design
- Place: Sapporo, Hokkaido
- Year: 2012-
- C: Keizo Matsuki
- PH(Package): Akihiro Ito
- PH(Meals in the Fields): Yasuhiro Matsuura (Safari Graphics)
- CL: Consumers Co-op Sapporo / TOPPAN PRINTING CO., LTD.
- S: Kota Abe / Sayaka Sekine

018 Fussa City Hall
- Category: Signage System
- Place: Fussa, Tokyo
- Completion: 2008
- AR: Riken Yamamoto
- FD: Taiji Fujimori
- PH: YUKI OMORI
- CL: Fussa City
- S: Chie Nakao

2, Consciousness in the Unconscious

026 Junglin'
- Category: Exhibition
- Place: Toshima, Tokyo
- Year: 2011
- Movie: Akihiro Ito / Uroku / Akihiro Yoshida
- VP: amana inc.
- CO: amana inc. / Sogo & Seibu Co., Ltd. / KOWA Co., Ltd.
- PH(On Site): Nacása & Partners Inc.

036 Junglin'2
- Category: Exhibition
- Place: Minato, Tokyo
- Year: 2014
- Movie: Akihiro Yoshida
- VP: amana inc.
- SP: Sogo & Seibu Co., Ltd. / THE LOFT CO., LTD.
- CO: Illumination Of City Environment / AXIS inc. / ACTIVE CO., LTD. / amana inc. / KOWA Co., Ltd. / JIN CO., LTD. / Dai Nippon Printing Co., Ltd. / Design Studio S / Tokushu Tokai Paper Co., Ltd. / Nakamura Design Office / Japan Sign Design Association
- PH(On Site): Akihiro Yoshida

3, Making the Invisible Visible

046 MIYOSHI FACTORY SOAP
- Category: Package Design
- Place: Sumida, Tokyo
- Completion: 2009
- PRD: Fumie Shibata
- PH: Akihiro Ito
- CL: MIYOSHI SOAP CORPORATION
- S: Kayo Ouchi

050 Omron Healthcare
- Category: Product Icon
- Place: Muko, Kyoto
- Year: 2009-
- PRD: Fumie Shibata
- CL: OMRON HEALTHCARE Co., Ltd.
- S: Tomoya Maruyama / Takahiro Eto

052 TOTO
- Category: Pictogram for WASHLET
- Place: Kitakyushu, Fukuoka
- Year: 2013
- CL: TOTO LTD.
- S: Takahiro Eto

054 "Junglin' by Masaaki Hiromura", published in AXIS
- Publication: 2014
- CO: AXIS inc.
- S: Takahiro Eto

056 TOKYO STATION GALLERY
- Category: VI / Exhibition Piece / Souvenir Items
- Place: Chiyoda, Tokyo
- Completion: 2012
- CD: Yoshio Yanagita / Syohachi Muto
- CD(Souvenir Items): Shu Hagiwara
- DIR(Souvenir Items): Akiyoshi Yamada (fukunaga-print co., ltd.)
- Movie / PH(On Site): Akihiro Yoshida
- PH(056): ©KENICHI MINORUDA / SEBUN PHOTO / amanaimages
- PH(Poster): Satoru Yamada
- CL: TOKYO STATION GALLERY
- CL(Souvenir Items): EAST JAPAN RAILWAY TRADING CO., LTD.
- S: Takahiro Eto

060 Ryukoku University Fukakusa Campus
- Category: Signage System
- Place: Fushimi, Kyoto
- Completion: 2015
- AR: Yoshihiko Iida
- PH: Nacása & Partners Inc.
- CL: RYUKOKU UNIVERSITY
- S: Hokuto Fujii / Yusuke komatsu

4, That Ish Feeling

066 Sumida Aquarium
- Category: VI / Signage System / Poster
- Place: Sumida, Tokyo
- Year: 2012-
- N: Hiroshi Mitsui
- I: Shinsei Yokoyama
- C: Jump Kato
- LD: Masanobu Takeishi
- PH: Nacása & Partners Inc.
- CL: ORIX Real Estate Corporation
- S: Hokuto Fujii / Takahiro Eto / Yusuke Komatsu

072 Yurakucho LOFT
　　Category　　Signage System / Poster
　　Place　　　 Chiyoda, Tokyo
　　Completion 2011
　　ID　　　　　Hiroshi Yoneya /
　　　　　　　　Ken Kimizuka
　　PH　　　　　Satoshi Asakawa
　　CL　　　　　THE LOFT CO., LTD.
　　S　　　　　 Hokuto Fujii /
　　　　　　　　Takahiro Eto

076 ITOKI Tokyo Innovation Center
　　SYNQA
　　Category　　Signage System / VI
　　Place　　　 Chuo, Tokyo
　　Completion 2013
　　CL　　　　　ITOKI CORPORATION
　　S　　　　　 Hokuto Fujii /
　　　　　　　　Makoto Honda

078 Ayana Resort and Spa BALI /
　　RIMBA Jimbaran Bali by AYANA
　　Category　　VI / Amenity Goods
　　Place　　　 Indonesia, Bali
　　Completion 2009 / 2013
　　CL　　　　　AYANA RESORT AND
　　　　　　　　SPA BALI
　　S　　　　　 Kayo Ouchi / Chie Nakao /
　　　　　　　　Kota Abe

080 SEIBU IKEBUKURO Roof Garden
　　Category　　Total Direction / Signage
　　　　　　　　System / Graphic Design
　　Place　　　 Toshima, Tokyo
　　Completion 2015
　　L　　　　　 Eiki Danzuka /
　　　　　　　　Soichiro Araki
　　Store Design Koichi Suzuno /
　　　　　　　　Shinya Kamuro
　　　　　　　　(TORAFU ARCHITECTS)
　　LD　　　　　Hiroyasu Shoji
　　　　　　　　LIGHTDESIGN INC.
　　Planting　　 HIBIYA AMENIS
　　Design　　　CORPORATION
　　C　　　　　 Keizo Matsuki
　　PH　　　　　Shinichi Sato
　　CL　　　　　Sogo & Seibu Co., Ltd.
　　S　　　　　 Yusuke Komatsu /
　　　　　　　　Takahiro Eto /
　　　　　　　　Sayaka Sekine

082 THE RAILWAY MUSEUM
　　Category　　VI
　　Place　　　 Saitama, Saitama

　　Completion 2007
　　CD　　　　　Yoshio Yanagita
　　PH　　　　　©YOSHIRO TAZAWA /
　　　　　　　　SEBUN PHOTO /
　　　　　　　　amanaimages
　　CL　　　　　East Japan Railway
　　　　　　　　Culture Foundation
　　S　　　　　 Kayo Ouchi

083 TADAFUSA
　　Category　　VI / Package Design
　　Place　　　 Sanjo, Niigata
　　Completion 2012
　　PRD　　　　 Fumie Shibata
　　PR　　　　　Jun Nakagawa
　　PH　　　　　Takumi Ota
　　CL　　　　　TADAFUSA Co., Ltd.
　　S　　　　　 Kota Abe

084 buchi
　　Category　　VI
　　Place　　　 Shiojiri, Nagano
　　Completion 2012
　　PRD　　　　 Fumie Shibata
　　DIR　　　　 Akio Aoki
　　PH　　　　　Akihiro Ito
　　CL　　　　　Sakai Sangyo co., Ltd.
　　S　　　　　 Takahiro Eto

085 TOHOKU DESIGN MARCHE
　　Category　　VI / Exhibition Design
　　Place　　　 Minato, Tokyo
　　Year　　　　2012
　　PH　　　　　Tomoki Hirokawa
　　CL　　　　　Japan Institute
　　　　　　　　of Design Promotion
　　S　　　　　 Kota Abe

086 Toyo Ito Museum of Architecture,
　　Imabari
　　Category　　VI / Signage System
　　Place　　　 Imabari, Ehime
　　Completion 2011
　　AR　　　　　Toyo Ito
　　PH　　　　　Daici Ano
　　CL　　　　　Initiative for Tomorrow's
　　　　　　　　Opportunities in
　　　　　　　　architecture, Ito Juku
　　S　　　　　 Tomoya Maruyama

087 Ken Iwata Mother and Child
　　Museum, Imabari City
　　Category　　VI
　　Place　　　 Imabari, Ehime

　　Completion 2011
　　AR　　　　　Toyo Ito
　　CL　　　　　Initiative for Tomorrow's
　　　　　　　　Opportunities in
　　　　　　　　architecture, Ito Juku
　　S　　　　　 Tomoya Maruyama

087 Yaoko Kawagoe Museum
　　Yuji Misu Memorial Hall
　　Category　　VI / Signage System
　　Place　　　 Kawagoe, Saitama
　　Completion 2009
　　AR　　　　　Toyo Ito
　　CL　　　　　Yaoko Co., Ltd.
　　S　　　　　 Kota Abe

5, Inviting Decorum

090 9h nine hours Kyoto / Narita Airport
　　Category　　VI / Signage System
　　Place　　　 Shimogyo, Kyoto /
　　　　　　　　Narita, Chiba
　　Completion 2009 / 2014
　　CD / PRD　　Fumie Shibata
　　ID　　　　　Takaaki Nakamura
　　PH(On Site)　Nacása & Partners Inc.
　　PH　　　　　Akihiro Yoshida
　　(Amenity Goods)
　　CL　　　　　nine hours Inc.
　　S　　　　　 Tomoya Maruyama /
　　　　　　　　Takahiro Eto

096 Yamato Group's Conventional Logistics
　　Terminals Haneda Chronogate
　　Category　　Signage System
　　Place　　　 Ota, Tokyo
　　Completion 2013
　　AR　　　　　NIKKEN SEKKEI LTD
　　PH　　　　　Nacása & Partners Inc.
　　CL　　　　　YAMATO HOLDINGS
　　　　　　　　CO., LTD.
　　S　　　　　 Tomoya Maruyama /
　　　　　　　　Kota Abe / Sayaka Sekine

100 Tianjin Library
　　Category　　Signage System
　　Place　　　 Tianjin, China
　　Completion 2012
　　AR　　　　　Riken Yamamoto
　　FD　　　　　Taiji Fujimori
　　Carpet Design Yoko Ando
　　LD　　　　　Izumi Okayasu
　　CL　　　　　Tianjin-city
　　S　　　　　 Kota Abe

102 CHARLES EAMES Photo Exhibition
100 images × 100 words
—A Message from a Great Designer
- Category: Exhibition Design
- Place: Minato, Tokyo
- Year: 2008
- PH: Nacása & Partners Inc.
- CL: AXIS GALLERY
- S: Kayo Ouchi

103 Pam
- Category: Exhibition Design
- Place: Sunto, Shizuoka
- Completion: 2004
- AD (Collaboration): Kan Akita
- PH (103 Top): Kozo Takayama
- PH (103 Bottom): Isamu Minagawa
- CL: Tokushu Tokai Paper Co., Ltd.
- S: Yutaka Maeda / Kota Abe / Sayaka Sekine

104 Sysmex
- Category: Package Design
- Place: Kobe, Hyogo
- Completion: 2011
- Concept: Fumie Shibata
- CL: SYSMEX CORPORATION
- S: Kota Abe

105 Towper
- Category: Package Design
- Place: Shimada, Shizuoka
- Completion: 2012
- PH: Akihiro Yoshida
- CL: TRY-FU CO., LTD.
- S: Fang Songa / Kota Abe

6, Awakened Memories

108 Tachikawa LOFT
- Category: Signage System
- Place: Tachikawa, Tokyo
- Completion: 2012
- ID: Hiroshi Yoneya / Ken Kimizuka
- PH (Graphic): Kiyoshi Obara / Kentauros Yasunaga / Uroku / Akihiro Yoshida / Yuki Kawakami
- PH (On Site): Nacása & Partners Inc.
- CL: THE LOFT CO., LTD.
- S: Fang Songa / Hokuto Fujii

112 ABENO HARUKAS
- Category: Signage System
- Place: Osaka, Osaka
- Completion: 2014
- CD: Tetsuo Harada (Takenaka Corporation)
- AR: Takenaka Corporation
- PH: Nacása & Partners Inc.
- CL: KINTETSU REAL ESTATE Co., Ltd.
- S: Hokuto Fujii / Takahiro Eto / Arata Takemoto

114 SEIBU SHIBUYA-MOVIDA Bld.
- Category: Signage System
- Place: Shibuya, Tokyo
- Completion: 2013
- ID: Koichi Suzuno / Shinya Kamuro (TORAFU ARCHITECTS)
- PH: Daici Ano
- CL: Sogo & Seibu Co., Ltd.
- S: Hokuto Fujii

116 Taipei New Horizon
- Category: Signage System
- Place: Taipei, Taiwan
- Completion: 2014
- AR: Toyo Ito
- PH: Kai Nakamura
- CL: Taipei New Horizon
- S: Tomoya Maruyama / Fang Songa / Kota Abe

118 NOMURA Headquarters Building
- Category: Signage System
- Place: Minato, Tokyo
- Completion: 2007
- PH: Yosuke Nakajima
- CL: NOMURA Co., Ltd.
- S: Tomoya Maruyama

120 Post Stamps: The Japanese postal service has begun to change. But how will postage stamps evolve?
- Category: Exhibition Piece / Exhibition Design
- Place: Minato, Tokyo
- Year: 2007 - 2008
- PH: Satoshi Asakawa
- CL: Japan Graphic Designers Association Inc.
- S: Fang Songa

122 airus—mechanism and quality
- Category: Exhibition Design, VI
- Place: Minato, Tokyo
- Year: 2015
- C: Keizo Matsuki
- LD: Masanobu Takeishi
- PH (On Site): Nacása & Partners Inc.
- PH (Portrait): Karsten Thormaehlen
- Coordination (Poster for Happy at Hundred for airus): Light Publicity Co., Ltd.
- CL: Tokushu Tokai Paper Co., Ltd.
- Cooperative Planning: Consumers Co-op Sapporo / TOPPAN PRINTING CO., LTD.
- S: Kota Abe / Sayaka Sekine

7, Speed of Design

150 Yokosuka Museum of Art
- Category: Signage System
- Place: Yokosuka, Kanagawa
- Completion: 2007
- AR: Riken Yamamoto
- PH: Yasuo Kondo
- CL: Yokosuka City
- S: Tomoya Maruyama

154 Shinwa medical resort
- Category: Signage System
- Place: Yachiyo, Chiba
- Completion: 2011
- ID: Yukio Hashimoto
- PH: Nacása & Partners Inc.
- CL: Healthcare Corporation Shinwakai
- S: Fang Songa

156 Nifco Technology Development Center
- Category: Signage System
- Place: Yokosuka, Kanagawa
- Completion: 2013
- AR: Sakakura Associates architects and engineers
- PH: Hiroshi Funaki
- CL: Nifco Inc.
- S: Tomoya Maruyama / Kota Abe

158 TOTO MUSEUM
- Category: VI / Signage System
- Place: Kitakyushu, Fukuoka
- Completion: 2015
- AR: AZUSA SEKKEI
- L / LD: sola associates

	PH	Nacása & Partners Inc.	Period	2012/9/21-2013/1/20		AR	TOHATA ARCHITECTS & ENGINEERS
	CL	TOTO LTD.	Exihibition Director	Kazuko Koike			
	S	Takahiro Eto				PH	Nacása & Partners Inc.
			CO	Nakamura Design Office		PH (p.194) Slate covered in cuneiform characters	©TAKASHI KATAHIRA / SEBUN PHOTO / amanaimages
162	Sumida Modern		PH	Masaya Yoshimura			
	Category	Poster / Booklet Design	CO (His Colors)	Nakagawa Chemical Inc. (CUTTING SHEET®) / TAKEO Co., Ltd.(TANT)			
	Place	Sumida, Tokyo				CL	Morisawa Inc.
	Year	2011-				S	Tomoya Maruyama
	C	Chikako Mitsui(2011-)	CL	21_21 DESIGN SIGHT / THE MIYAKE ISSEY FOUNDATION			
	PH	Akihiro Yoshida			198	KISHI CLINICA FEMINA	
	CL	Sumida Local Brand Promoting Conference				Category	VI / Signage System
			S	Takahiro Eto / Makoto Honda		Place	Chuo, Tokyo
	S	Fang Songa / Arata Takemoto				Completion	2014
			182	nonowa		ID	Takaaki Nakamura
166	Futakamiya		Category	Signage System		PH	Nacása & Partners Inc.
	Category	VI / Signage System	Place	Musashino, Tokyo		CL	KISHI CLINICA FEMINA
	Place	Tokorozawa, Saitama	Completion	2014		S	Hokuto Fujii / Sayaka Sekine
	Completion	2015	L	Eiki Danzuka / Soichiro Araki			
	ID	Takaaki Nakamura			200	LPA 1990-2015 Tide of Architectural Lighting Design	
	PH	Nacása & Partners Inc.	LD	Hiroyasu Shoji LIGHTDESIGN INC.			
	CL	Futakamiya Corporation				Category	Book Design
	S	Takahiro Eto / Yusuke Komatsu	PH	Nacása & Partners Inc.		Completion	2015
			CL	JR Chuo Line Mall Co., Ltd.		Author	Kaoru Mende + LPA (Lighting Planners Associates)
			S	Kota Abe / Sayaka Sekine			
8, Weaving Information						Publishing House	Rikuyosha Co., Ltd.
			9, Lurking in the Shadows				
170	Tokyo Polytechnic University Nakano Campus					CL	Lighting Planners Associates
			188	GARDEN TERRACE NAGASAKI HOTEL & RESORTS		S	Hokuto Fujii
	Category	Signage System			201	Lighting Objet 2012	
	Place	Nakano, Tokyo	Category	Signage System		Category	Exhibition Piece
	Completion	2011	Place	Nagasaki, Nagasaki		Place	Chiyoda, Tokyo
	AR	Sakakura Associates architects and engineers	Completion	2009		Year	2012
			AR	Kengo Kuma & Associates		CL	LIGHTING OBJET PRODUCTION COMMITTEE
	PH	Nacása & Partners Inc.	PH	Nacása & Partners Inc.			
	CL	TOKYO POLYTECHNIC UNIVERSITY	CL	Memolead Group		S	Makoto Honda
			S	Chie Nakao			
	S	Taichi Miyamoto			10, Giving Form to Desire		
			190	PARK HYATT BUSAN			
172	Aichi Triennale 2013		Category	Signage System	204	Kofukuan	
	Category	VI / Poster / Signage System	Place	Busan, South Korea		Category	VI
			Completion	2013		Place	Toshima, Tokyo
	Place	Nagoya and Okazaki, Aichi	ID	Takashi Sugimoto (SUPER POTATO CO., LTD.)		Completion	2014
	Year	2013				N	Masayuki Minoda
	PH	Nacása & Partners Inc.	PH	Nacása & Partners Inc.		CL	Sogo & Seibu Co., Ltd.
	CL	The Aichi Triennale Organizing Committee	CL	HDC HOTEL IPARK		S	Takahiro Eto / Yusuke Komatsu
			S	Fang Songa			
	S	Kota Abe / Sayaka Sekine	194	MORISAWA New Headquarters Office	205	Little chef	
176	21_21 DESIGN SIGHT Exhibition Ikko Tanaka and Future / Past / East / West of Design					Category	VI
			Category	Signage System		Place	Toshima, Tokyo
			Place	Osaka, Osaka		Completion	2010
	Category	Exhibition Design, Poster	Completion	2009		CL	Sogo & Seibu Co., Ltd.
	Place	Minato, Tokyo	PR	Takeshi Morisawa			

　　　　S　　　　　　Hokuto Fujii

206 SELF&SHELF LOFT
　　　　Category　　VI / Signage System
　　　　Place　　　　Toshima, Tokyo
　　　　Completion 2013
　　　　ID　　　　　Hisaaki Hirawata /
　　　　　　　　　　Tomohiro Watabe
　　　　N　　　　　Masayuki Minoda
　　　　PH　　　　Nacása & Partners Inc.
　　　　CL　　　　THE LOFT CO., LTD.
　　　　S　　　　　Hokuto Fujii

208 Landmark Plaza
　　　　Category　　Poster
　　　　Place　　　　Yokohama, Kanagawa
　　　　Completion 2009-
　　　　C　　　　　Keizo Matsuki
　　　　I　　　　　 Zenji Funabashi
　　　　CL　　　　Mitsubishi Jisho Property
　　　　　　　　　　Management Co., Ltd.
　　　　S　　　　　Chie Nakao / Fang Songa

209 Marunouchi Shotenkai
　　　　Category　　Poster
　　　　Place　　　　Chiyoda, Tokyo
　　　　Completion 2006-
　　　　C　　　　　Keizo Matsuki
　　　　PH　　　　Akihiro Ito
　　　　CL　　　　Mitsubishi Jisho Property
　　　　　　　　　　Management Co., Ltd.
　　　　S　　　　　Chie Nakao / Fang Songa

210 Logos for shops at the SEIBU IKEBUKURO
　　　　Department Store
　　　　Category　　VI
　　　　Year　　　　2008-2014
　　　　CL　　　　Sogo & Seibu Co., Ltd.
　　　　S　　　　　Hokuto Fujii /
　　　　　　　　　　Taichi Miyamoto /
　　　　　　　　　　Yusuke Komatsu

11, Creating Creation

214 Japan Creative
　　　　Category　　Creative Direction/
　　　　　　　　　　Graphic Design
　　　　Year　　　　2011-
　　　　PH　　　　Nacása & Partners Inc.
　　　　Honorary　Hiroshi Naito
　　　　Director
　　　　　　　　　　(Naito Architect & Associates)
　　　　Representative Masaaki Hiromura
　　　　Director
　　　　　　　　　　(Hiromura Design Office)

　　　　Director　　Yves Bougon
　　　　　　　　　　(Hearst Fujingaho Co., Ltd.)
　　　　Director　　Yoko Kawashima
　　　　　　　　　　(Itochu Fashion System Co., Ltd.)
　　　　Director　　Ryu Matsumoto
　　　　　　　　　　(Sogo & Seibu Co., Ltd.)
　　　　R&D　　　Tomoya Tabuchi
　　　　　　　　　　(office for creation)
　　　　R&D　　　Jin Kuramoto
　　　　　　　　　　(JIN KURAMOTO STUDIO)
　　　　R&D　　　Yota Kakuda
　　　　　　　　　　(YOTA KAKUDA DESIGN)
　　　　R&D　　　Wataru Kumano
　　　　CL　　　　General Incorporated
　　　　　　　　　　Association
　　　　　　　　　　JAPAN CREATIVE
　　　　S　　　　　Tomoya Maruyama /
　　　　　　　　　　Takahiro Eto /
　　　　　　　　　　Arata Takemoto /
　　　　　　　　　　Yusuke Komatsu

226 GOOD DESIGN STORE
　　　　Category　　VI
　　　　Place　　　　Central, Hong Kong
　　　　Completion 2014
　　　　Logo　　　　Yusaku Kamekura
　　　　PH　　　　Simon J Nicol
　　　　CL　　　　Japan Institute of
　　　　　　　　　　Design Promotion
　　　　S　　　　　Kota Abe

228 SHIBUYA DESIGN SITE
　　　　Category　　VI / Exhibition Design
　　　　Place　　　　Shibuya, Tokyo
　　　　Completion 2013-
　　　　C　　　　　Keizo Matsuki
　　　　PH　　　　Nacása & Partners Inc.
　　　　CL　　　　Sogo & Seibu Co., Ltd. /
　　　　　　　　　　THE LOFT CO., LTD.
　　　　S　　　　　Takahiro Eto /
　　　　　　　　　　Yusuke Komatsu

12, Settled in Harmony

232 Tokyo Polytechnic University
　　　　Category　　Poster
　　　　Place　　　　Nakano, Tokyo
　　　　Completion 2011
　　　　PH　　　　Nacása & Partners Inc.
　　　　CL　　　　TOKYO POLYTECHNIC
　　　　　　　　　　UNIVERSITY
　　　　S　　　　　Hokuto Fujii

234 Shibuya LOFT main signage
　　　　Category　　Main Signage
　　　　Place　　　　Shibuya, Tokyo
　　　　Completion 2012
　　　　SD　　　　CORNELIUS
　　　　PH　　　　Nacása & Partners Inc.
　　　　CL　　　　THE LOFT CO., LTD.
　　　　S　　　　　Hokuto Fujii

236 Showroom Omron Healthcare
　　　　Category　　Exhibition Design
　　　　Place　　　　Shinagawa, Tokyo
　　　　Completion 2008
　　　　ID　　　　　Takaaki Nakamura
　　　　PH　　　　Kozo Takayama
　　　　CL　　　　OMRON HEALTHCARE
　　　　　　　　　　Co., Ltd.
　　　　S　　　　　Tomoya Maruyama

238 SEIBU SHIBUYA entrance
　　　　Category　　Creative Direction /
　　　　　　　　　　Poster
　　　　Place　　　　Shibuya, Tokyo
　　　　Completion 2015
　　　　AW　　　　Carsten Nicolai. "chroma
　　　　　　　　　　actor". 2015
　　　　Technical　Hiroshi kanechiku
　　　　Support
　　　　LD　　　　Masanobu Takeishi
　　　　C　　　　　Keizo Matsuki
　　　　PH　　　　Nacása & Partners Inc.
　　　　CL　　　　Sogo & Seibu Co., Ltd.
　　　　S　　　　　Arata Takemoto

242 GRAPHIC TRIAL
　　　　Category　　Poster
　　　　Place　　　　Bunkyo, Tokyo
　　　　Completion 2008
　　　　PD　　　　Yuki Ogawa
　　　　Original　　Yasuo Kondo
　　　　Art Work
　　　　CL　　　　TOPPAN PRINTING CO., LTD.
　　　　S　　　　　Chie Nakao / Fang Songa

廣村正彰 略歴

1954年	愛知県生まれ
1977年	武蔵野美術短期大学商業デザイン専攻科卒業｜田中一光デザイン室 入社
1988年	廣村デザイン事務所設立
2008年–	東京工芸大学芸術学部教授

主な仕事・展覧会

1989年	イッセイミヤケ im VI 計画｜無印良品 AD
1990年	株式会社ヴィーヴル CI 計画｜KIDS PARK VI 計画
1991年	西武渋谷店食品館 COO(クー) VI 計画｜ICLA'91(第 13 回国際比較文学会) AD
1992年	JAGDA 年鑑 AD｜パルコ劇場 The Woman in Black AD
1993年	東京ガス「リビングアートコンペティション」AD｜駒ケ根高原美術館 サイン計画
1994年	亀老山展望公園 サイン計画｜東京ガス OZONE「リビングデザインギャラリー」AD
1995年	八代広域消防本部 サイン計画｜日吉ダムビジターセンター サイン計画
1996年	岩出山中学校 サイン計画｜小田原市立総合文化体育館 サイン計画
1998年	国民宿舎足摺テルメ CI、サイン計画｜大方あかつき館 CI、サイン計画
1999年	埼玉県立大学 サイン計画、AD｜公立函館みらい大学 UI 計画
2000年	東京証券取引所 サイン計画｜竹尾見本帖本店 総合プロデュース
2001年	日本科学未来館 CI、サイン計画｜東京ウエルズ CI、サイン計画
2002年	六本木一丁目泉ガーデン CI、サイン計画｜愛知県名城大学 サイン計画
	デザインギャラリー 1953 にて『空間のグラフィズム』展開催
2003年	CODAN 東雲 VI 計画、サイン計画｜東海村総合交流会館 CI、サイン計画
2004年	北千住丸井 サイン計画｜丸善丸の内本店 サイン計画｜北京健外 SOHO サイン計画
2005年	大阪関電ビル サイン計画｜丸ビル 年間宣伝計画｜ホテル JAL CITY サイン計画
2006年	日産自動車デザインセンター サイン計画｜奈良平城遷都 1300 年記念事業マーク
	竹尾湾岸物流センター サイン計画｜丸ビル 年間宣伝計画
2007年	横須賀美術館 VI 計画｜鉄道博物館 ロゴマーク｜丸ビル 年間宣伝計画
	ギンザ・グラフィック・ギャラリーにて『2D → 3D』展開催
2008年	乃村工藝社本社ビル サイン計画｜ショールーム オムロンヘルスケア サイン、展示計画｜福生市庁舎 サイン計画｜タカラレーベン CI 計画
2009年	アヤナ リゾート＆スパ バリ CI 計画｜9h ナインアワーズ 京都 AD、サイン計画｜モリサワ新本社ビル サイン計画
	六本木アートナイト ロゴマーク｜DNP アートコミュニケーションズ ロゴマーク
2010年	西武池袋本店リニューアル 総合 AD｜イトーヨーカドー「タノシア」VI 計画
	COREDO 室町 サイン計画｜東京工芸大学中野キャンパス サイン計画
2011年	今治市伊東豊雄建築ミュージアム CI、サイン計画｜新静岡セノバ VI 計画｜公益財団法人日本デザイン振興会（JDP）VI 計画
	有楽町ロフト 総合 AD｜シンワメディカルリゾート サイン計画｜西武ギャラリーにて『Junglin' 意識が動く瞬間』展開催
2012年	ミラノ・サローネ Japan Creative エキシビション 総合 AD｜すみだ水族館 VI、サイン計画｜渋谷ロフト 総合 AD
	立川ロフト 総合 AD｜21_21 DESIGN SIGHT 企画展 田中一光とデザインの前後左右 AD
	東京ステーションギャラリー VI 計画｜天津図書館 サイン計画｜庖丁工房タダフサ VI 計画
2013年	メゾン・エ・オブジェ Japan Creative エキシビション 総合 AD｜パーク ハイアット釜山 サイン計画
	ニフコ技術開発センター サイン計画｜ヤマトグループ 羽田クロノゲート サイン計画｜西武渋谷店モヴィーダ館リニューアル 総合 AD
	堂島リバービエンナーレ AD｜シブヤデザインサイト AD｜リンバ ジンバラン バリ by アヤナ VI 計画｜あいちトリエンナーレ 2013 総合 AD
2014年	アンビエンテ Japan Creative エキシビション 総合 AD｜あべのハルカス サイン計画｜GOOD DESIGN STORE VI 計画
	9h ナインアワーズ 成田空港 AD、サイン計画｜AXIS ギャラリーにて『Junglin'2 無意識の中の意識』展開催
2015年	安城市民ギャラリーにて『廣村正彰 デザインからデザインまで』展開催
	ストックホルムファニチャー＆ライトフェア Japan Creative エキシビション 総合 AD
	龍谷大学深草キャンパス和顔館 サイン計画｜虎ノ門ヒルズにて『エアラス・性能と品質』展開催｜西武渋谷店リニューアル 総合 AD

Masaaki Hiromura

1954	Born in Aichi prefecture
1977	Graduated from Commercial Design Course, Musashino Art University / Entered Tanaka Ikko Design Office
1988	Established Hiromura Masaaki Design Office
2008-	Professor at Tokyo Polytechnic University Faculty of Arts

Selected works

1989	VI, Issey Miyake im / AD, Muji.
1990	CI, Vivre International Inc / VI, Kids Park.
1991	VI, Food Shop COO, SEIBU SHIBUYA Department Store / AD, 13th Conference of the International Comparative
1992	AD, JAGDA Annual Book / AD, "The Woman in Black", ParcoTheater
1993	AD, Living Art Competition, Tokyo Gas / Signage System, the Komagane Kogen Art Museum
1994	Signage System, Kirosan Panoramic Park / AD, Ozone Living Design Gallery, Tokyo Gas
1995	Signage System, the Yatsushiro Greater Area Fire Department / Signage System, the Hiyoshi Dam Visitor Center
1996	Signage System, Iwadeyama Junior High School / Signage System, Odawara Arena
1998	CI+Signage System, the Ashizuri Thermae hotel / CI+Signage System, the Ogata Akatsuki Cultural Center
1999	Signage System, Saitama Prefectural University / UI, Future University Hakodate
2000	Signage System, Tokyo Stock Exchange / Direction, Takeo Mihoncho Head Store
2001	CI+Signage System, the National Museum of Emerging Science and Innovation / CI+Signage System, Tokyo Weld
2002	CI+Signage System, Izumi Garden Tower / Signage System, Meijo University, Aichi
	Exhibition "SPACE GRAPHYSM" at design gallery 1953
2003	VI+Signage System, CODAN Shinonome / CI+Signage System, the Tokai Village General Exchange Center
2004	Signage System, Marui Kitasenju Store / Signage System, Maruzen Marunouchi Store / Signage System, Jianwai SOHO, Beijing
2005	Signage System, Osaka Kanden Building / Annual advertisement, Marunouchi Building / Signage System, the Hotel JAL City
2006	Signage System, Nissan Motor Design Center
	Logo, 1300th Year Anniversary Program of the Relocation of the Capital to Heijokyo
	Signage System, Takeo Bayside Logistic Center / Annual advertisement, Marunouchi Shopping District
2007	VI, Yokosuka Museum of Art / Logo, THE RAILWAY MUSEUM / Annual advertisement, Marunouchi Building
	Solo Exhibition "2D-3D" at Ginza Graphic Gallery
2008	Signage System, NOMURA Headquarters Building / Signage System+display, Showroom Omron Healthcare
	Signage System, Fussa City Hall / CI, Takara Leben
2009	CI, Ayana Resort and Spa BALI / AD, Signage System, 9h nine hours Kyoto
	Signage System, MORISAWA New Headquarters Office / Logo, ROPPONGI ART NIGHT / Logo, DNP Art Communications
2010	VI, SEIBU IKEBUKURO Flagship Store Renewal Open / VI, tanosia Ito-yokado
	Signage System, COREDO Muromachi / Signage System, Tokyo Polytechnic University Nakano Campus
2011	Signage System+CI, Toyo Ito Museum of Architecture, Imabari / VI, Shinsizuoka cenova / VI, Japan Institute of Design Promotion
	AD, Yurakucho LOFT / Signage System, Shinwa medical resort / Solo Exhibition "Junglin'" at SEIBU GALLERY
2012	AD, Japan Creative Exhibition at Milano Salone / VI+Signage System, Sumida Aquarium / AD, Shibuya LOFT
	AD, Tachikawa LOFT / AD, 21_21 DESIGN SIGHT Exhibition Ikko Tanaka and Future / Past / East / West of Design
	VI, TOKYO STATION GALLERY / Signage System, Tianjin Library / VI, TADAFUSA
2013	AD, Japan Creative Exhibition at Maison & Objet / Signage System, PARK HYATT BUSAN
	Signage System, Nifco Technology Development Center
	Signage System, Yamato Group's Conventional Logistics Terminals Haneda Chronogate / AD, SEIBU SHIBUYA-MOVIDA Bld.
	AD, Dojima River Biennale 2013 / AD, SHIBUYA DESIGN SITE / AD, RIMBA Jimbaran Bali by AYANA / AD, Aichi Triennale 2013
2014	AD, Japan Creative Exhibition at Ambiente / Signage System, ABENO HARUKAS / VI, GOOD DESIGN STORE
	AD, Signage System, 9h nine hours Narita Airport / Solo Exhibition "Junglin' 2" at AXIS GALLERY
2015	Exhibition "From Design To Design" at Anjo Civic Art Gallery / AD, Japan Creative Exhibition at Stockholm Funiture & Light Fair
	Signage System, Ryukoku University Fukakusa Campus / Exhibition "airus—mechanism and quality" at TORANOMON HILLS
	AD, SEIBU SHIBUYA

デザインからデザインまで

発行日	2015年11月19日 初版第1刷
著者	廣村正彰
編集・構成	飯田彩
翻訳	冨永真奈美
ブックデザイン	廣村正彰 衛藤隆弘・関根早弥香・長田淳美
プリンティング ディレクション	熊倉桂三 (株式会社山田写真製版所)
発行者	久保田啓子
発行	株式会社 ADP ｜ Art Design Publishing 〒165-0024 東京都中野区松が丘 2-14-12 tel 03-5942-6011　fax 03-5942-6015 http://www.ad-publish.com
振替	00160-2-355359
印刷・製本	株式会社山田写真製版所
協力	特種東海製紙株式会社 (本文・ジャケット用紙：エアラス ホワイト 見返し用紙：里紙 すみ) 株式会社モリサワ (タイトル・本文書体(和文)：リュウミン Pro R-KL)

From Design To Design

Date of Publication	First Printing / November 19, 2015
Author	Masaaki Hiromura
Editing & Framing	Aya Iida
Translation	Manami Tominaga
Book Design	Masaaki Hiromura Takahiro Eto / Sayaka Sekine / Atsumi Osada
Printing Direction	Katsumi Kumakura (Yamada Photo Process Co., Ltd.)
Publisher	Keiko Kubota
Publishing House	ADP Company (Art Design Publishing Company) 2-14-12 Matsugaoka, Nakano-ku, Tokyo 165-0024 Japan Phone 81-3-5942-6011 Fax 81-3-5942-6015 http://www.ad-publish.com
Printing & Binding	Yamada Photo Process Co., Ltd.
Support	Tokushu Tokai Paper Co., Ltd. (Interior Paper & Jacket : airus white End Paper: Satogami sumi) Morisawa Inc. (Typeface(JP): Ryumin Pro R-KL)

©Masaaki Hiromura 2015
Printed in Japan
ISBN978-4-903348-47-6 C0072

本書の収録内容の無断転載・複写（コピー）・引用は、著作権法上での例外を除き、禁じられています。
乱丁本・落丁本は、ご購入書店を明記のうえ、小社までお送りください。送料小社負担にてお取り替え致します。
All right reserved. No part of this publication may be reproduced or transmitted in any form means,
electric or mechanical, including photocopy, or any other information storage and retrieval system,
without prior permission in writing from the ADP Company.